BEST-SELLING
COUNTRY & FARMHOUSE
HOME PLANS

CREATIVE HOMEOWNER®, Upper Saddle River, New Jersey

Home Plans Editor: Kenneth D. Stuts, CPBD

Design and Layout: iiCREATiVE (David Kroha, Cindy DiPierdomenico, Judith Kroha); Kathy Wityk, Larissa Stuts

Cover Design: David Geer

Vice President and Publisher: Timothy O. Bakke
Production Coordinator: Sara M. Markowitz

Current Printing (last digit)
10 9 8 7 6 5 4 3 2 1

Manufactured in the United States of America

Best-Selling Country & Farmhouse Home Plans
Library of Congress Control Number: 2010921120
ISBN-10: 1-58011-504-7
ISBN-13: 978-1-58011-504-9

CREATIVE HOMEOWNER®
A Division of Federal Marketing Corp.
24 Park Way
Upper Saddle River, NJ 07458
www.creativehomeowner.com

Note: The homes as shown in the photographs and renderings in this book may differ from the actual blueprints. When studying the house of your choice, please check the floor plans carefully.

Contents

Getting Started

Maybe you can't wait to bang the first nail. Or you may be just as happy leaving town until the windows are cleaned. The extent of your involvement with the construction phase is up to you. Your time, interests, and abilities can help you decide how to get the project from lines on paper to reality. But building a house requires more than putting pieces together. Whoever is in charge of the process must competently manage people as well as supplies, materials, and construction. He or she will have to

- Make a project schedule to plan the orderly progress of the work. This can be a bar chart that shows the time period of activity by each trade.
- Establish a budget for each category of work, such as foundation, framing, and finish carpentry.
- Arrange for a source of construction financing.
- Get a building permit and post it conspicuously at the construction site.
- Line up supply sources and order materials.
- Find subcontractors and negotiate their contracts.
- Coordinate the work so that it progresses smoothly with the fewest conflicts.
- Notify inspectors at the appropriate milestones.
- Make payments to suppliers and subcontractors.

You as the Builder

You'll have to take care of every logistical detail yourself if you decide to act as your own builder or general contractor. But along with the responsibilities of managing the project, you gain the flexibility to do as much of your own work as you want and subcontract out the rest. Before taking this path, however, be sure you have the time and capabilities. Do you also have the time and ability to schedule the work, hire and coordinate subs, order materials, and keep ahead of the accounting required to manage the project successfully? If you do, you stand to save the amount that a general contractor would charge to take on these responsibilities, normally 15 to 30 percent of the construction cost. If you take this responsibility on but mismanage the project, the potential savings will erode and may even cost you more than if you had hired a builder in the first place. A subcontractor might charge extra for hav-

Acting as the builder, above, requires the ability to hire and manage subcontractors.

Building a home, opposite, includes the need to schedule building inspections at the appropriate milestones.

ing to return to the site to complete work that was originally scheduled for an earlier date. Or perhaps because you didn't order the windows at the beginning, you now have to pay for a recent cost increase. (If you had hired a builder in the first place, he or she would absorb the increase.)

Hiring a Builder to Handle Construction

A builder or general contractor will manage every aspect of the construction process. Your role after signing the construction contract will be to make regular progress payments and ensure that the work for which you are paying has been completed. You will also consult with the builder and agree to any changes that may have to be made along the way.

Leads for finding builders might come from friends or neighbors who have had contractors build, remodel, or add to their homes. Real-estate agents and bankers may have some names handy but are more likely familiar with the builder's ability to complete projects on time and budget than the quality of the work itself.

The next step is to narrow your list of candidates to three or four who you think can do a quality job and work harmoniously with you. Phone each builder to see whether he or she is interested in being considered for your project. If so, invite the builder to an interview at your home. The meeting will serve two purposes. You'll be able to ask the candidate about his or her experience, and you'll be able to see whether or not your personalities are compatible. Go over the plans with the builder to make certain that he or she understands the scope of the project. Ask if they have constructed similar houses. Get references, and check the builder's standing with the Better Business Bureau. Develop a short list of builders, say three, and ask them to submit bids for the project.

Contracts

Lump-Sum Contracts

A lump-sum, or fixed-fee, contract lets you know from the beginning just what the project will cost, barring any changes made because of your requests or unforeseen conditions. This form works well for projects that promise few surprises and are well defined from the outset by a complete set of contract documents. You can enter into a fixed-price contract by negotiating with a single builder on your short list or by obtaining bids from three or four builders. If you go the latter route, give each bidder a set of documents and allow at least two weeks for them to submit their bids. When you get the bids, decide who you want and call the others to thank them for their efforts. You don't have to accept the lowest bid, but it probably makes sense to do so since you have already honed the list to builders you trust. Inform this builder of your intentions to finalize a contract.

Cost-Plus-Fee Contracts

Under a cost-plus-fee contract, you agree to pay the builder for the costs of labor and materials, as verified by receipts, plus a fee that represents the builder's overhead and profit. This arrangement is sometimes referred to as "time and materials." The fee can range between 15 and 30 percent of the incurred costs. Because you ultimately pick up the tab—whatever the costs—the contractor is never at risk, as he is with a lump-sum contract. You won't know the final total cost of a cost-plus-fee contract until the project is built and paid for. If you can live with that uncertainty, there are offsetting advantages. First, this form allows you to accommodate unknown conditions much more easily than does a lump-sum contract. And rather than being tied down by the project documents, you will be free to make changes at any point along the way. This can be a trap, though. Watching the project take shape will spark the desire to add something or do something differently. Each change costs more, and the accumulation can easily exceed your budget. Because of the uncertainty of the final tab and the built-in advantage to the contractor, you should think twice before entering into this form of contract.

Contract Content

The conditions of your agreement should be spelled out thoroughly in writing and signed by both parties, whatever contractual arrangement you make with your builder. Your contract should include provisions for the following:

- The names and addresses of the owner and builder.
- A description of the work to be included ("As described in the plans and specifications dated . . .").
- The date that the work will be completed if time is of the essence.
- The contract price for lump-sum contracts and the builder's allowed profit and overhead costs for changes.
- The builder's fee for cost-plus-fee contracts and the method of accounting and requesting payment.
- The criteria for progress payments (monthly, by project milestones) and the conditions of final payment.
- A list of each drawing and specification section that is to be included as part of the contract.
- Requirements for guarantees. (One year is the standard period for which contractors guarantee the entire project, but you may require specific guarantees on

When submitting bids, all of the builders should base their estimates on the same specifications. Once the work begins, communicate with your builder to keep the work proceeding smoothly.

Inspect your newly built home, if possible, before the builder closes it up and finishes it.

certain parts of the project, such as a 20-year guarantee on the roofing.)
- Provisions for insurance.
- A description of how changes in the work orders will be handled.

The builder may have a standard contract that you can tailor to the specifics of your project. These contain complete specific conditions with blanks that you can fill in to fit your project and a set of "general conditions" that cover a host of issues from insurance to termination provisions. It's always a good idea to have an attorney review the draft of your completed contract before signing it.

Working with Your Builder

The construction phase officially begins when you have a signed copy of the contract and copies of any insurance required from the builder. It's not unheard of for a builder to request an initial payment of 10 to 20 percent of the total cost to cover mobilization costs, those costs associated with obtaining permits and getting set up to begin the actual construction. If you agree to this, keep a careful eye on the progress of the work to ensure that the total paid out at any one time doesn't get too far out of sync with the actual work completed.

What about changes? From here on, it's up to you and your builder to proceed in good faith and to keep the channels of communication open. Even so, changes of one sort or another beset every project, and they usually add to its cost.

Light at the End of the Tunnel.

The builder's request for a final inspection marks the end of the construction phase—almost. At the final inspection meeting, you and the builder will inspect the work, noting any defects or incomplete items on a "punch list." When the builder tidies up the punch list items, you should reinspect. Sometimes, builders go on to another job and take forever to clean up the last few details, so only after all items on the list have been completed satisfactorily should you release the final payment, which often accounts for the builder's profit.

Some Final Words

Having a positive attitude is important when undertaking a project as large as building a home. A positive attitude can help you ride out the rigors and stress of the construction process.

Stay Flexible. Expect problems, because they certainly will occur. Weather can upset the schedule you have established for subcontractors. A supplier may get behind on deliveries, which also affects the schedule. An unexpected pipe may surprise you during excavation. Just as certain, every problem that comes along has a solution if you are open to it.

Be Patient. The extra days it may take to resolve a construction problem will be forgotten once the project is completed.

Express Yourself. If what you see isn't exactly what you thought you were getting, don't be afraid to look into changing it. Or you may spot an unforeseen opportunity for an improvement. Changes usually cost more money, though, so don't make frivolous decisions.

Finally, watching your home go up is exciting, so stay upbeat. Get away from your project from time to time. Dine out. Take time to relax. A positive attitude will make for smoother relations with your builder. An optimistic outlook will yield better-quality work if you are doing your own construction. And though the project might seem endless while it is under way, keep in mind that all the planning and construction will fade to a faint memory at some time in the future, and you will be getting a lifetime of pleasure from a home that is just right for you.

Ten Steps You Should Do Before Submitting Your Plans For a Permit

1. Check Your Plans to Make Sure That You Received What You Ordered

You should immediately check your plans to make sure that you received exactly what you ordered. All plans are checked for content prior to shipping, but mistakes can happen. If you find an error in your plans call 1-800-523-6789. All plans are drawn on a particular type of foundation and all details of the plan will illustrate that particular foundation. If you ordered an alternate foundation type, it should be included immediately after the original foundation. Tell your builder which foundation you wish to use and disregard the other foundation.

2. Check to Make Sure You Have Purchased the Proper Plan License

If you purchased prints, your plan will have a round red stamp stating, "If this stamp is not red it is an illegal set of plans." This license grants the purchaser the right to build one home using these construction drawings. It is illegal to make copies, doing so is punishable up to $150,000 per offense plus attorney fees. If you need more prints, call 1-800-523-6789. The House Plans Market Association monitors the home building industry for illegal prints.

It is also illegal to modify or redraw the plan if you purchased a print. If you purchased prints and need to modify the plan, you can upgrade to the reproducible master, PDF files, or CAD files — call 1-800-523-6789. If you purchased a reproducible master, PDF files, or CAD file you have the right to modify the plan and make up to 10 copies. A reproducible master, PDF files, or CAD files comes with a license that you must surrender to the printer or architect making your changes.

3. Complete the "Owner Selection" Portion of the Building Process

The working drawings are very complete, but there are items that you must decide upon. For example, the plans show a toilet in the bathroom, but there are hundreds of models from which to choose. Your individual selection should be made based upon the color, style, and price you wish to pay. This same thing is true for all of the plumbing fixtures, light fixtures, appliances, and interior finishes (for the floors, walls, and ceilings) and exterior finishes. The selection of these items is required in order to obtain accurate competitive bids for the construction of your home.

4. Complete Your Permit Package by Adding Other Documents That May Be Required

Your permit department, lender, and builder will need other drawings or documents that must be obtained locally. These items are explained in the next three items.

5. Obtain a Heating & Cooling Calculation and Layout

The heating and cooling system must be calculated and designed for your exact home and your location. Even the orientation of your home can affect the system size. This service is normally provided free of charge by the mechanical company that is supplying the equipment and installation. However, to get an unbiased calculation and equipment recommendation, we suggest employing the services of a mechanical engineer.

6. Obtain a Site Plan

A site plan is a document that shows the relationship of your home to your property. It may be as simple as the document your surveyor provides, or it can be a complex collection of drawings such as those prepared by a landscape architect. Typically, the document prepared by a surveyor will only show the property boundaries and the footprint of the home. Landscape architects can provide planning and drawings for all site amenities, such as driveways and walkways, outdoor structures such as pools, planting plans, irrigation plans, and outdoor lighting.

7. Obtain Earthquake or Hurricane Engineering if You Are Planning to Build in an Earthquake or Hurricane Zone

If you are building in an earthquake or hurricane zone, your permit department will most likely require you to submit calculations and drawings to illustrate the ability of your home to withstand those forces. This information is never included with pre-drawn plans because it would penalize the vast majority of plan purchasers who do not build in those zones. A structural engineer licensed by the state where you are building usually provides this information.

8. Review Your Plan to See Whether Modifications Are Needed

These plans have been designed to assumed conditions and do not address the individual site where you are building. Conditions can vary greatly, including soil conditions, wind and snow loads, and temperature, and any one of these conditions may require some modifications of your plan. For example, if you live in an area that receives snow, structural changes may be necessary. We suggest:

(i) Have your soil tested by a soil-testing laboratory so that subsurface conditions can be determined at your specific building site. The findings of the soil-testing laboratory should be reviewed by a structural engineer to determine if the existing plan foundation is suitable or if modifications are needed.

(ii) Have your entire plan reviewed by your builder or a structural engineer to determine if other design elements, such as load bearing beams, are sized appropriately for the conditions that exist at your site.

Now that you have the complete plan, you may discover items that you wish to modify to suit your own personal taste or decor. To change the drawings, you must have the reproducible masters, PDF files, or CAD files (see item 2). We can make the changes for you. For complete information regarding modifications, including our fees, go to www.ultimateplans.com and click the "resources" button on the home page; then click on "our custom services."

9. Record Your Blueprint License Number

Record your blueprint license number for easy reference. If you or your builder should need technical support, the license number is required.

10. Keep One Set of Plans as Long as You Own the Home

Be sure to file one copy of your home plan away for safe keeping. You may need a copy in the future if you remodel or sell the home. By filing a copy away for safe keeping, you can avoid the cost of having to purchase plans later.

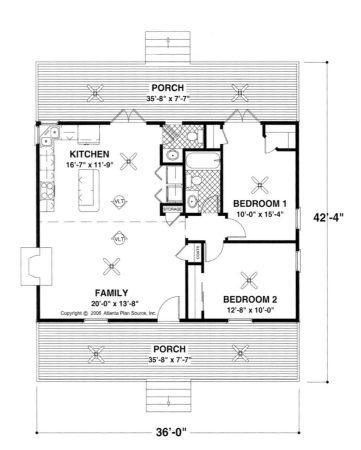

Images provided by designer/architect.

Plan #101147

Dimensions: 36' W x 42'4" D
Levels: 1
Heated Square Footage: 953
Bedrooms: 2
Bathrooms: 1½
Foundation: Crawl space
Materials List Available: No
Price Category: B

Relax on the rocking chair porches of this home.

Features:

- **Porches:** A front and rear porch are wonderful for entertaining with friends or family.

- **Family Room:** This family room shares a vaulted ceiling with the kitchen, which has a sunny corner double sink, and a center island/snack bar.

- **Laundry Center:** Conveiently located off the kitchen, this laundry area will ensure you won't have to run around with loads of clothes while doing other chores.

- **Bedrooms:** Two bedrooms share a full bath. Bedroom 1 opens out to the rear porch for added convenience.

PORCH
35'-8" x 7'-7"

KITCHEN
16'-7" x 11'-9"

STORAGE

BEDROOM 1
10'-0" x 15'-4"

42'-4"

COATS

FAMILY
20'-0" x 13'-8"

BEDROOM 2
12'-8" x 10'-0"

Copyright © 2006 Atlanta Plan Source, Inc.

PORCH
35'-8" x 7'-7"

36'-0"

Copyright by designer/architect.

Images provided by designer/architect.

CAD FILE AVAILABLE

26'-0"

22'-0"

L

W

Sitting/Sleeping
12-9x15-4

Kit/Din
11-4x9-10

R

Covered Porch
26-0x6-0

Copyright by designer/architect.

Plan #631036

Dimensions: 26' W x 22' D

Levels: 1

Heated Square Footage: 416

Bedrooms: 1

Bathrooms: 1

Foundation: Slab

Materials List Available: Yes

Price Category: A

Plan #341146

Dimensions: 40' W x 29'4" D

Levels: 1

Heated Square Footage: 960

Bedrooms: 3

Bathrooms: 2

Foundation: Crawl space, slab, basement, or walkout

Materials List Available: No

Price Category: A

Images provided by designer/architect.

CAD FILE AVAILABLE

STOOP

DINING

D
W

BATH

W.H.

LIN.

KITCHEN
15'-0"x11'-4"

R

BATH

BEDROOM
9'-4" X 9'-0"

COATS
CLOSET

CLOSET

BEDROOM
12'-0"X11'-4"

CLOS.

LIVING ROOM
14'-6" X 11'-4"

BEDROOM
9'-4" X 9'-0"

PORCH

40'-0"

29'-4"

Copyright by designer/architect.

Main Level Floor Plan

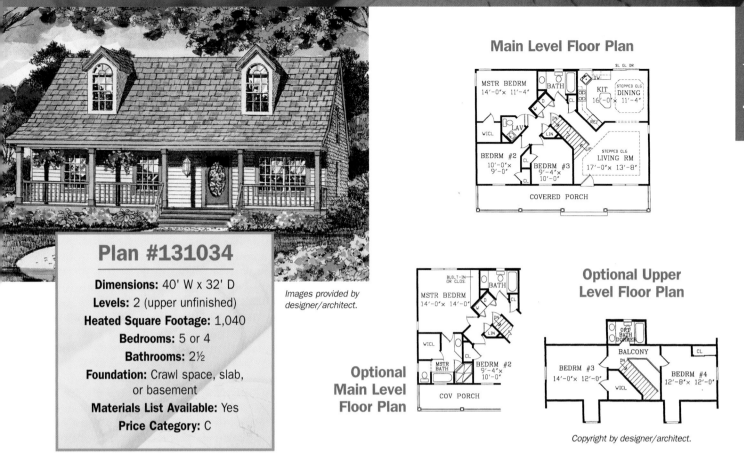

Images provided by designer/architect.

Plan #131034

Dimensions: 40' W x 32' D
Levels: 2 (upper unfinished)
Heated Square Footage: 1,040
Bedrooms: 5 or 4
Bathrooms: 2½
Foundation: Crawl space, slab, or basement
Materials List Available: Yes
Price Category: C

Optional Main Level Floor Plan

Optional Upper Level Floor Plan

Copyright by designer/architect.

Plan #401047

Dimensions: 38' W x 34' D
Levels: 1
Heated Square Footage: 1,064
Bedrooms: 2
Bathrooms: 1
Foundation: Crawl space or basement
Materials List Available: Yes
Price Category: B

Images provided by designer/architect.

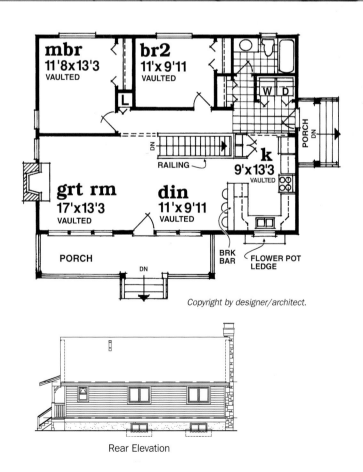

Copyright by designer/architect.

Rear Elevation

Plan #181345

Dimensions: 34' W x 34' D
Levels: 1
Heated Square Footage: 1,079
Bedrooms: 2
Bathrooms: 1
Foundation: Basement; crawl space or slab for fee
Materials List Available: Yes
Price Category: B

Images provided by designer/architect.

CAD FILE AVAILABLE

13'-4"x 12'-0"
4,00 x 3,60

19'-0"x 12'-0"
5,70 x 3,60

12'-0"x 16'-0"
3,60 x 4,80

11'-0"x 10'-0"
3,30 x 3,00

34'-0"
10,2 m

34'-0"
10,2 m

Rear View

Copyright by designer/architect.

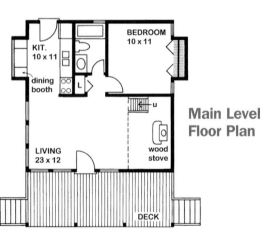

Plan #381066

Dimensions: 29' W x 24' D
Levels: 2
Heated Square Footage: 1,100
Main Level Sq. Ft.: 825
Upper Level Sq. Ft.: 275
Bedrooms: 2
Bathrooms: 1
Foundation: Crawl space
Materials List Available: Yes
Price Category: B

Images provided by designer/architect.

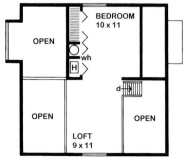

KIT.
10 x 11

dining booth

BEDROOM
10 x 11

LIVING
23 x 12

wood stove

DECK

Main Level Floor Plan

OPEN

OPEN

BEDROOM
10 x 11

wh

OPEN

OPEN

LOFT
9 x 11

Upper Level Floor Plan

Copyright by designer/architect.

Plan #181021

Dimensions: 37' W x 44' D

Levels: 1

Heated Square Footage: 1,124

Bedrooms: 2

Bathrooms: 1

Foundation: Basement

Materials List Available: Yes

Price Category: B

Images provided by designer/architect.

CAD FILE AVAILABLE — CAD

10'-0" X 14'-8" — 3,00 X 4,40

13'-0" X 12'-0" — 3,90 X 3,60

12'-4" X 12'-4" — 3,70 X 3,70

12'-4" X 10'-0" — 3,70 X 3,00

44'-0" — 13,2 m

12'-0" X 15'-0" — 3,60 X 4,50

12'-0" X 20'-0" — 3,60 X 6,00

37'-0" — 11,1 m

Copyright by designer/architect.

Plan #491004

Dimensions: 36' W x 42'6" D

Levels: 2

Heated Square Footage: 1,154

Main Level Sq. Ft.: 672

Upper Level Sq. Ft.: 482

Bedrooms: 2

Bathrooms: 2

Foundation: Crawl space

Material List Available: Yes

Price Category: B

Images provided by designer/architect.

36'-0"

42'-6"

WINDOW SEAT — 13' VAULTED CLG.

LIV./DIN. 23' x 9'4" & 14'6"

WOOD STOVE

8'10" x 8'

GUEST 10'8" x 9'

Main Level Floor Plan

Copyright by designer/architect.

Upper Level Floor Plan

STUDIO 15'4" x 11'8" — 13' VAULTED CLG.

OPEN

BED RM. 15' x 9' — 10' VAULTED CLG.

Front View

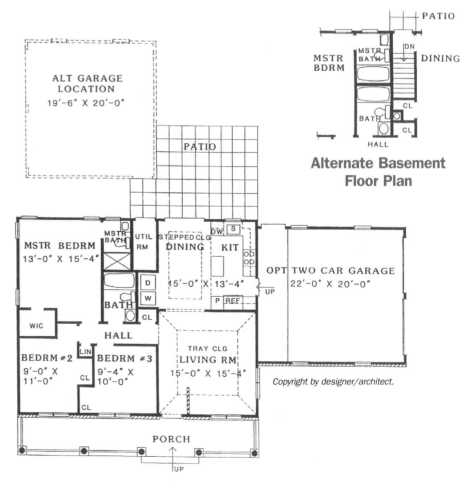

Plan #131004

Dimensions: 59'4" W x 35'8" D

Levels: 1

Heated Square Footage: 1,097

Bedrooms: 3

Bathrooms: 2

Foundation: Crawl space, slab, or basement

Materials List Available: Yes

Price Category: C

This home, as shown in the photograph, may differ from the actual blueprints. For more detailed information, please check the floor plans carefully.

You'll love the extra features you'll find in this charming but easy-to-build ranch home.

Features:

- Porch: This full-width porch is graced with impressive round columns, decorative railings, and ornamental moldings.

- Living Room: Just beyond the front door, the living room entrance has a railing that creates the illusion of a hallway. The 10-ft. tray ceiling makes this room feel spacious.

- Dining Room: Flowing from the living room, this room has a 9-ft.-high stepped ceiling and leads to sliding glass doors that open to the large rear patio.

- Kitchen: This kitchen is adjacent to the dining room for convenience and has a large island for efficient work patterns.

- Master Suite: Enjoy the privacy in this bedroom with its private bathroom.

Alternate Basement Floor Plan

Images provided by designer/architect.

Plan #121012

Dimensions: 40' W x 48'8" D

Levels: 1

Heated Square Footage: 1,195

Bedrooms: 3

Bathrooms: 2

Foundation: Basement

Materials List Available: Yes

Price Category: B

This home, as shown in the photograph, may differ from the actual blueprints. For more detailed information, please check the floor plans carefully.

CAD FILE AVAILABLE

This compact one-level home uses an open plan to make the most of its square footage.

Features:

• Ceiling Height: 8 ft.

• Covered Porch: This delightful area, located off the kitchen, provides a private spot to enjoy some fresh air.

• Open Plan: The family room, dining area and kitchen share a big open space to provide a sense of spaciousness. Moving so easily between these interrelated areas provides the convenience demanded by a busy lifestyle.

• Master Suite: An open plan is convenient, but it is still important for everyone to have their private space. The master suite enjoys its own bath and walk-in closet. The secondary bedrooms share a nearby bath.

• Garage: Here you will find parking for two cars and plenty of extra storage space as well.

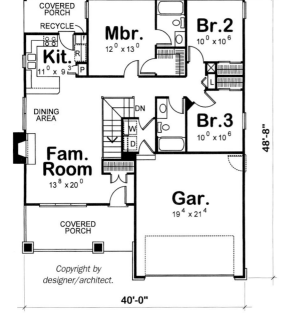

Copyright by designer/architect.

Rendering reflects floor plan

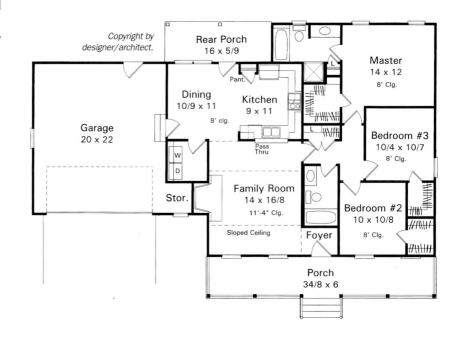

Plan #251001

Dimensions: 61'3" W x 40'6" D

Levels: 1

Heated Square Footage: 1,253

Bedrooms: 3

Bathrooms: 2

Foundation: Crawl space or slab

Materials List Available: Yes

Price Category: B

This charming country home has a classic full front porch for enjoying summertime breezes.

Features:

• Ceiling Height: 8 ft.

• Foyer: Guests will walk through the front porch into this foyer, which opens to the family room.

• Screened Porch: A second porch is screened and is located at the rear of the home off the dining room, so your guests can step out for a bit of fresh air after dinner.

• Family Room: Family and friends will be drawn to this large open space, with its handsome fireplace and sloped ceiling.

• Kitchen: This open and airy kitchen is a pleasure in which to work. It has ample counter space and a pantry.

• Master Bedroom: This master bedroom features a large walk-in closet. It has its own master bath with a single vanity, a tub, and a walk-in shower.

• Garage: This attached garage provides plenty of extra storage space, as well as parking for two cars.

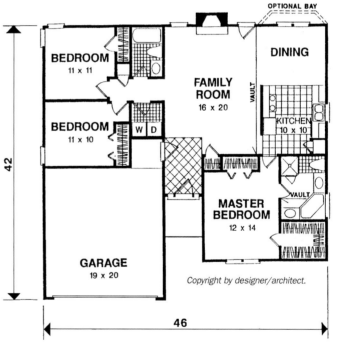

Images provided by designer/architect.

Plan #101002

Dimensions: 46' W x 42' D
Levels: 1
Heated Square Footage: 1,296
Bedrooms: 3
Bathrooms: 2
Foundation: Crawl space, slab, or basement
Materials List Available: No
Price Category: C

This affordable compact home is also strikingly attractive.

Features:

- Ceiling Height: 8 ft.

- Foyer: Beveled glass front provides a luxurious entry.

- Family Room: This spacious 16-ft. x 20-ft. room has a vaulted ceiling.

- Laundry Room: There is ample space to fold clothes.

- Master Bedroom Suite: Split from other bedrooms, this suite has many his and her features.

- Kitchen: This galley kitchen offers open traffic patterns with ample counter space.

- Breakfast Eating Area: A growing family will find additional seating space that leads to a covered porch providing a pleasant retreat.

OPTIONAL BAY

BEDROOM
11 x 11

DINING

FAMILY ROOM
16 x 20

KITCHEN
10 x 10

BEDROOM
11 x 10

W D

42

MASTER BEDROOM
12 x 14

GARAGE
19 x 20

46

Copyright by designer/architect.

SMARTtip

Preparing Walls for Paint

Poor surface preparation is the number-one cause of paint failure. Preparing surfaces properly—including removing loose paint and thoroughly sanding—may be tedious, but it's important for a good-looking and long-lasting finish.

Main Level Floor Plan

Nook

Kitchen

Family
13⁸ · 13⁰

Utility

Bath

Master Bedroom
14⁰ · 11⁰

storage

Foyer

Entry

Images provided by designer/architect.

CAD FILE AVAILABLE

Upper Level Floor Plan

Closet

Bedroom 3
10⁰ · 10²

Bath

Bedroom 2
10⁰ · 11⁰

Copyright by designer/architect.

Garage Floor Plan

1 Car Garage

Opt. 2 Car Garage

Plan #661024

Dimensions: 29'4" W x 33' D
Levels: 2
Heated Square Footage: 1,170
Main Level Sq. Ft.: 820
Upper Level Sq. Ft.: 350
Bedrooms: 3
Bathrooms: 2
Foundation: Slab
Materials List Available: No
Price Category: B

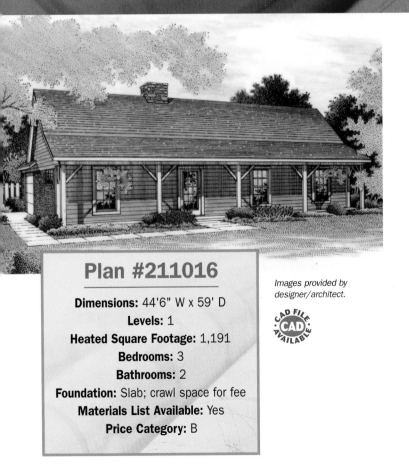

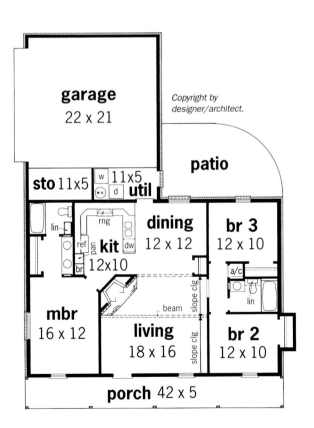

garage
22 x 21

patio

Copyright by designer/architect.

sto 11x5

util

W 11x5
d

dining
12 x 12

br 3
12 x 10

kit
12x10

ref
pan
rng
dw

a/c

lin

mbr
16 x 12

living
18 x 16

br 2
12 x 10

beam

slope clg

porch 42 x 5

Images provided by designer/architect.

CAD FILE AVAILABLE

Plan #211016

Dimensions: 44'6" W x 59' D
Levels: 1
Heated Square Footage: 1,191
Bedrooms: 3
Bathrooms: 2
Foundation: Slab; crawl space for fee
Materials List Available: Yes
Price Category: B

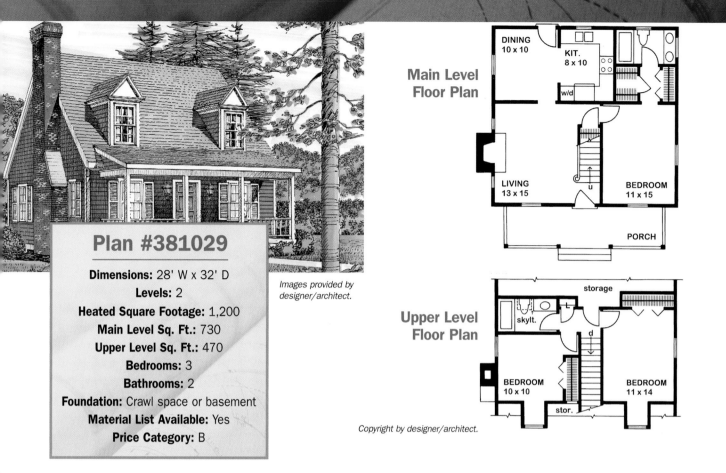

Main Level Floor Plan

DINING 10 x 10

KIT. 8 x 10

w/d

LIVING 13 x 15

BEDROOM 11 x 15

PORCH

Images provided by designer/architect.

Upper Level Floor Plan

storage

skylt.

d

BEDROOM 10 x 10

stor.

BEDROOM 11 x 14

Copyright by designer/architect.

Plan #381029

Dimensions: 28' W x 32' D

Levels: 2

Heated Square Footage: 1,200

Main Level Sq. Ft.: 730

Upper Level Sq. Ft.: 470

Bedrooms: 3

Bathrooms: 2

Foundation: Crawl space or basement

Material List Available: Yes

Price Category: B

Main Level Floor Plan

12'-0" X 12'-0"
3,60 X 3,60

12'-2" X 14'-4"
3,65 X 4,30

12'-6" X 15'-0"
3,75 X 4,50

32'-0"
9,6 m

26'-0"
7,8 m

Upper Level Floor Plan

14'-8" X 12'-0"
4,40 X 3,60

11'-0" X 11'-0"
3,30 X 3,30

Copyright by designer/architect.

Plan #181262

Dimensions: 26' W x 32' D

Levels: 2

Heated Square Footage: 1,226

Main Level Sq. Ft.: 443

Upper Level Sq. Ft.: 783

Bedrooms: 2

Bathrooms: 2

Foundation: Basement

Materials List Available: Yes

Price Category: B

Images provided by designer/architect.

CAD FILE AVAILABLE

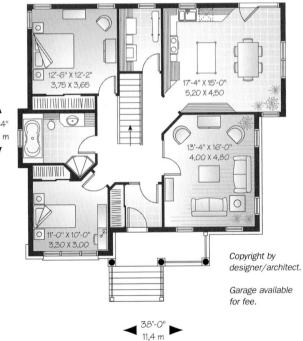

Plan #641006

Dimensions: 66' W x 32' D

Levels: 1

Heated Square Footage: 1,232

Bedrooms: 2

Bathrooms: 2

Foundation: Basement; crawl space slab or walkout for fee

Materials List Available: No

Price Category: B

Images provided by designer/architect.

Kitchen

Front View

Plan #181714

Dimensions: 38' W x 36'4" D

Levels: 1

Heated Square Footage: 1,244

Bedrooms: 2

Bathrooms: 1

Foundation: Basement; crawl space or slab for fee

Materials List Available: Yes

Price Category: B

Images provided by designer/architect.

Copyright by designer/architect.

Garage available for fee.

Plan #181227

Dimensions: 24' W x 29' D

Levels: 2

Heated Square Footage: 1,248

Main Level Sq. Ft.: 624

Upper Level Sq. Ft.: 624

Bedrooms: 3

Bathrooms: 1½

Foundation: Basement; crawl space or slab for fee

Materials List Available: Yes

Price Category: B

Images provided by designer/architect.

CAD FILE AVAILABLE

Main Level Floor Plan

11'-0" X 10'-0" 3,30 X 3,00

11'-8" X 9'-0" 3,50 X 2,70

11'-8" X 13'-8" 3,50 X 4,10

29'-0" 8,7 m

24'-0" 7,2 m

Upper Level Floor Plan

11'-0" X 9'-0" 3,30 X 2,70

11'-8" X 12'-0" 3,50 X 3,60

9'-0" X 12'-0" 2,70 X 3,60

Copyright by designer/architect.

Plan #371005

Dimensions: 52'6" W x 45'8" D

Levels: 1.5

Heated Square Footage: 1,250

Bedrooms: 2

Bathrooms: 2

Foundation: Crawl space, slab or basement

Materials List Available: No

Price Category: B

Images provided by designer/architect.

CAD FILE AVAILABLE

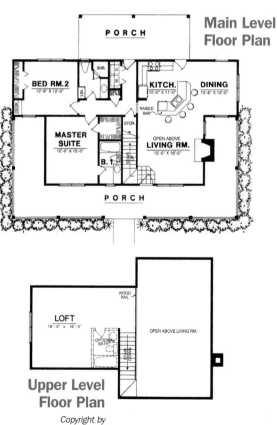

Main Level Floor Plan

PORCH

BED RM.2 12'-6" X 12'-0"

KITCH. 12'-0" X 11'-0"

DINING 10'-6" X 12'-0"

RAISED BAR

MASTER SUITE 12'-0" X 15'-0"

STOR.

OPEN ABOVE LIVING RM. 15'-0" X 16'-0"

B. 1

PORCH

LOFT 18'-0" X 16'-0"

WOOD RAIL

OPEN ABOVE LIVING RM.

OPTIONAL BATH

Upper Level Floor Plan

Copyright by designer/architect.

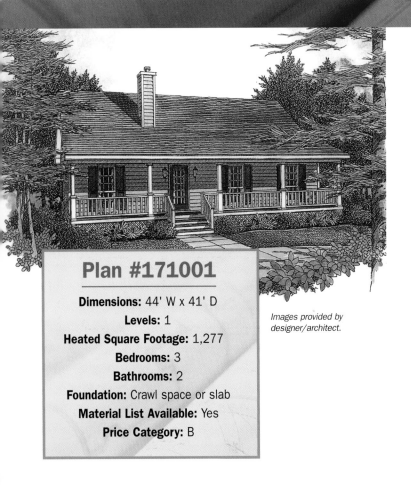

Plan #401031

Dimensions: 42' W x 52' D

Levels: 1

Heated Square Footage: 1,260

Bedrooms: 3

Bathrooms: 2

Foundation: Basement

Materials List Available: Yes

Price Category: B

Images provided by designer/architect.

CAD FILE AVAILABLE

Copyright by designer/architect.

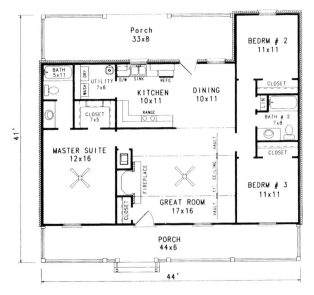

Plan #171001

Dimensions: 44' W x 41' D

Levels: 1

Heated Square Footage: 1,277

Bedrooms: 3

Bathrooms: 2

Foundation: Crawl space or slab

Material List Available: Yes

Price Category: B

Images provided by designer/architect.

Copyright by designer/architect.

Main Level Floor Plan

30'-0"
9,0 m

24'-0"
7,2 m

12'-8" 8'-0"
3,80 x 2,40

10'-0" 11'-0"
3,00 x 3,30

12'-0" 14'-0"
3,60 x 4,20

Upper Level Floor Plan

Copyright by designer/architect.

10'-0" 11'-0"
3,00 x 3,30

9'-0" 10'-0"
2,70 x 3,00

12'-0" 14'-0"
3,60 x 4,20

Images provided by designer/architect.

Plan #181067

Dimensions: 24' W x 30' D
Levels: 2
Heated Square Footage: 1,286
Main Level Sq. Ft.: 643
Upper Level Sq. Ft.: 643
Bedrooms: 3
Bathrooms: 1½
Foundation: Basement
Material List Available: Yes
Price Category: B

CAD FILE AVAILABLE

8'-0"
40'-8"
30'-0"

STORAGE
8'-0" X 6'-0"

BA 1

BEDROOM 1
14'-0"X13'-0"

BEDROOM 2
10'-7"X13'-0"

BA 2

REF

WH

KITCHEN
12'-6"X8'-0"

CLOS CLOS

CLOS

PORCH

DINING ROOM
9'-6"X11'-7"

HALF WALL W/ COLUMN

CLOS

LIVING ROOM
15'-6"X11'-7"

BEDROOM 3
11'-7"X11'-7"

COATS

PORCH

Copyright by designer/architect.

Plan #341297

Dimensions: 48'8" W x 30' D
Levels: 1
Heated Square Footage: 1,291
Bedrooms: 3
Bathrooms: 2
Foundation: Crawl space; slab or basement for fee
Material List Available: Yes
Price Category: B

Images provided by designer/architect.

CAD FILE AVAILABLE

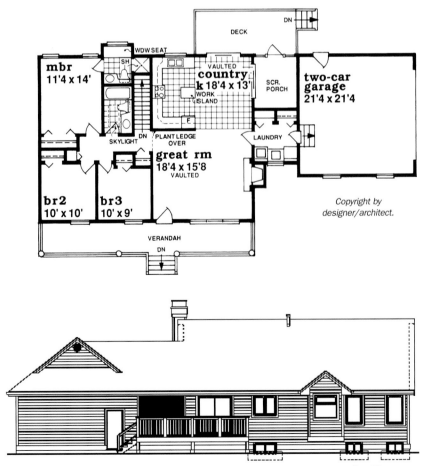

Plan #401024

Dimensions: 70' W x 36' D

Levels: 1

Heated Square Footage: 1,298

Bedrooms: 3

Bathrooms: 2

Foundation: Basement

Materials List Available: Yes

Price Category: B

A front verandah, cedar lattice, and solid-stone chimney enhance the appeal of this one-story country-style home.

Features:

- Porches: At the front of the home is a beautiful verandah, wonderful for greeting guests. A screened-in porch and deck are located at the back of the home, perfect for entertaining or enjoying a meal outside.

- Great Room: This great room includes a fireplace. The wall between the kitchen and great room features a distinctive plant ledge.

- Kitchen: This U-shaped kitchen provides an island work counter and sliding glass doors to the rear deck and a screened porch.

- Master Suite: You'll love this master suite, which is complete with a walk-in closet and a private bath that contains a window seat.

Copyright by designer/architect.

Rear View

Plan #121121

Dimensions: 47'4" W x 45'8"D
Levels: 1
Heated Square Footage: 1,341
Bedrooms: 3
Bathrooms: 2
Foundation: Basement; crawl space or slab for fee
Materials List Available: Yes
Price Category: C

This traditional home is charming and bound to make your life simpler with all its amenities.

Features:

• Great Room: Already equipped with an entertainment center, bookcase and a fireplace by which you can enjoy those books, this room has endless possibilities. This is a room that will bring the whole family together.

• Kitchen: This design includes everything you need and everything you want: a pantry waiting to be filled with your favorite foods, plenty of workspace, and a snack bar that acts as a useful transition between kitchen and breakfast room.

• Breakfast Room: An extension of the kitchen, this room will fill with the aroma of coffee and a simmering breakfast, so you'll be immersed in your relaxing morning. With peaceful daylight streaming in through a window-lined wall, this will easily become the best part of your day.

• Master Suite: Plenty of breathing room for both of you, there will be no fighting for sink or closet space in this bedroom. The full master bath includes dual sinks, and the walk-in closet will hold everything you both need. Another perk of this bathroom is the whirlpool bathtub.

• Garage: This two-car garage opens directly into the home, so there is no reason to get out of your warm, dry car and into unpleasant weather.

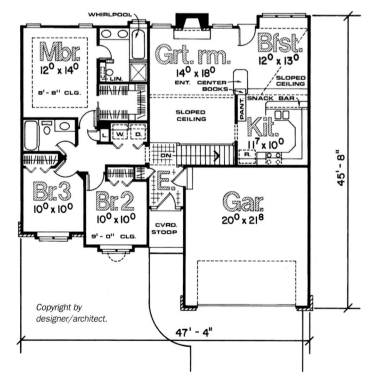

Upper Level Floor Plan

Copyright by designer/architect.

12'-8" x 13'-0"
3,80 x 3,90

10'-0" x 13'-0"
3,00 x 3,90

12'-4" x 11'-0"
3,70 x 3,30

10'-8" x 8'-8"
3,20 x 2,60

6'-0"
7,8 m

15'-0" x 13'-8"
4,50 x 4,10

10'-0" x 9'-8"
3,00 x 2,90

Main Level Floor Plan

30'-0"
9,0 m

Plan #181219

Dimensions: 30' W x 26' D

Levels: 2

Heated Square Footage: 1,311

Main Level Sq. Ft.: 791

Upper Level Sq. Ft.: 520

Bedrooms: 2

Bathrooms: 1½

Foundation: Basement; crawl space or slab for fee

Materials List Available: Yes

Price Category: B

Images provided by designer/architect.

CAD FILE AVAILABLE

Plan #161162

Dimensions: 56'10" W x 43'7" D

Levels: 1

Heated Square Footage: 1,321

Bedrooms: 3

Bathrooms: 2

Foundation: Walkout; crawl space, slab or basement for fee

Material List Available: Yes

Price Category: B

Images provided by designer/architect.

CAD FILE AVAILABLE

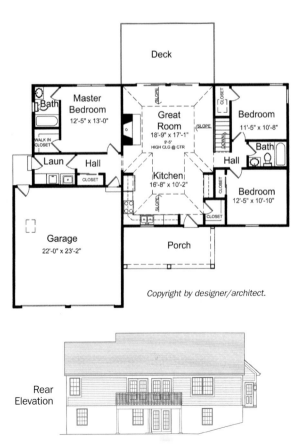

Deck

Bath

Master Bedroom
12'-5" x 13'-0"

Great Room
18'-9" x 17'-1"
9'-5" HIGH CLG @ CTR

Bedroom
11'-5" x 10'-8"

WALK IN CLOSET

Bath

Laun

Hall

Kitchen
16'-8" x 10'-2"

Hall

Bedroom
12'-5" x 10'-10"

Garage
22'-0" x 23'-2"

Porch

Copyright by designer/architect.

Rear Elevation

Main Level Floor Plan

34'-4"

35'-6"

Kit/Dining
14-11x12-0

R D W F

W

Family
14-11x15-6
Vaulted Clg

MBr
12-8x14-1

Up

Covered Porch
32-0x7-0

Images provided by designer/architect.

CAD FILE AVAILABLE

Rear View

Upper Level Floor Plan

Copyright by designer/architect.

Loft/Br 3
10-7x11-11

Dn

Open To Below

Br 2
12-8x10-0

Plan #631025

Dimensions: 34'4" W x 35'6" D
Levels: 2
Heated Square Footage: 1,339
Main Level Sq. Ft.: 924
Upper Level Sq. Ft.: 415
Bedrooms: 2
Bathrooms: 2½
Foundation: Crawl space
Materials List Available: Yes
Price Category: B

Plan #341054

Dimensions: 47' W x 53'8" D
Levels: 1.5
Heated Square Footage: 1,370
Main Level Sq. Ft.: 1,370
Bonus Room Sq. Ft.: 261
Bedrooms: 3
Bathrooms: 2
Foundation: Crawl space; slab or basement for fee
Materials List Available: Yes
Price Category: B

Images provided by designer/architect.

CAD FILE AVAILABLE

47'-0"

53'-8"

PORCH

CLOSET

BEDROOM 3
11'-4" X 10'-0"

PREFAB GAS LOG FIREPLACE

BEDROOM 1
13'-9" X 12'-0"

BATH 2

FAMILY ROOM
15'-0" X 15'-4"

CLOSET

BATH 1

LIN

60" X 40"
GARDEN TUB
& SHOWER

BEDROOM 2
11'-0" X 11'-0"

UP TO UNFIN. REC ROOM

WASH/DRY

FOLDING COUNTER

FOYER

COATS

REF.

RANGE

SINK

CLOSET

UTILITIES

KITCH./DINING
13'-9" X 15'-3"

DW

PANTRY

PORCH

GARAGE
21'-3" X 21'-7"

UNFINISHED RECREATION ROOM
11'-4" X 21'-7"

Copyright by designer/architect.

Bonus Area Floor Plan

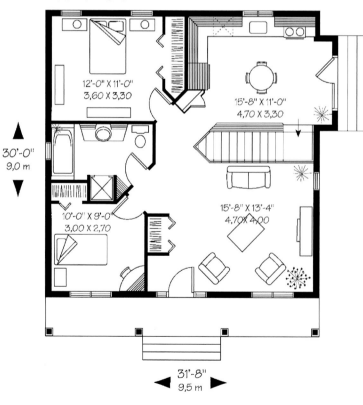

Images provided by designer/architect.

Plan #181216

Dimensions: 31'8" W x 30' D

Levels: 1

Heated Square Footage: 910

Bedrooms: 2

Bathrooms: 1

Foundation: Basement

Materials List Available: Yes

Price Category: A

CAD FILE AVAILABLE

Copyright by designer/architect.

A lot of creativity goes into creating this comfortable home. It begins with a Creole-style covered front porch that lines up across the entire front of the house, beckoning folks to laze awhile in the cool summer shade.

Features:

- Front Door: This entry door has something special—transom and sidelight windows to brighten the interior with natural light.

- Family Room: This large and open room eases to other important rooms—including the great-sized kitchen.

- Kitchen: This large eat-in kitchen has hearty cabinet and counter space.

- Bedrooms: A roomy full bathroom pampers two full-sized bedrooms, which are enhanced by unusual windows and excellent closet space.

30'-0"
9,0 m

12'-0" X 11'-0"
3,60 X 3,30

15'-8" X 11'-0"
4,70 X 3,30

10'-0" X 9'-0"
3,00 X 2,70

15'-8" X 13'-4"
4,70 X 4,00

31'-8"
9,5 m

Plan #251003

Dimensions: 42' W x 42' D

Levels: 1

Heated Square Footage: 1,393

Bedrooms: 3

Bathrooms: 2

Foundation: Crawl space or slab

Materials List Available: Yes

Price Category: B

Images provided by designer/architect.

Come home to this three-bedroom home with its front porch and unattached garage.

Features:

- **Porch:** Located at the front of the home, this beautiful covered porch is wonderful for greeting guests or relaxing with a book.

- **Family Room:** This room feels large and warm with its high ceiling and cozy fireplace.

- **Kitchen:** This island kitchen with dining area has plenty of cabinet space.

- **Master Suite:** This large master bedroom features a walk-in closet and a view of the back yard. The master bath features a soaking tub and a separate shower.

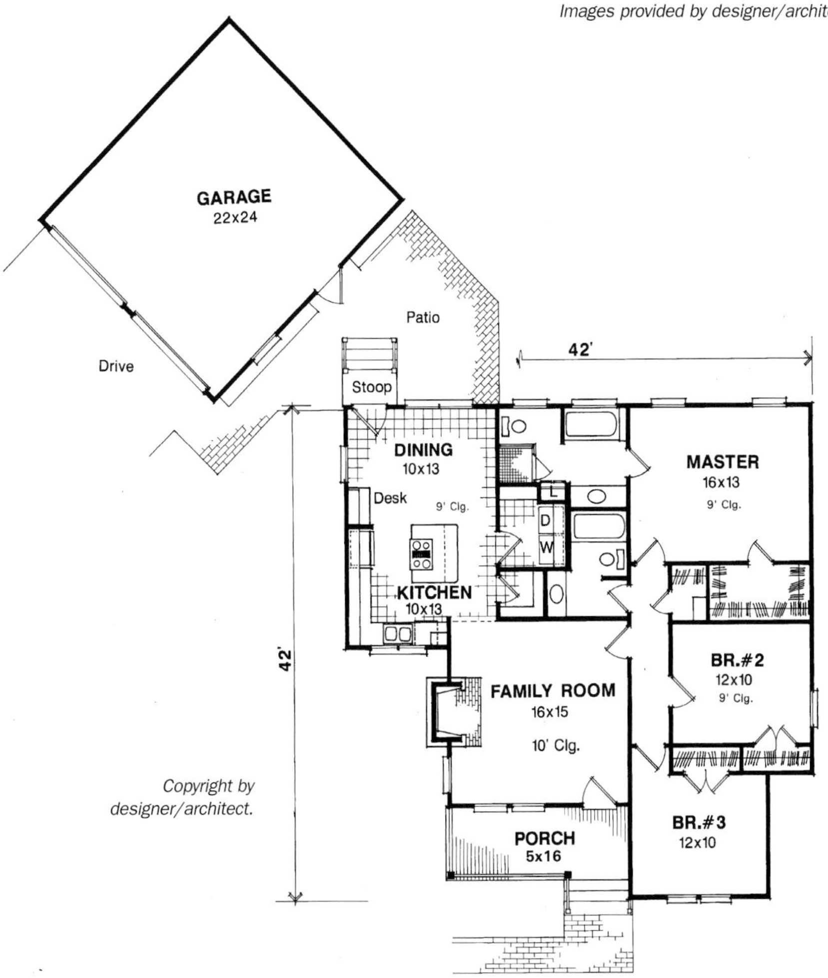

GARAGE
22x24

Drive

Patio

Stoop

DINING
10x13

Desk

9' Clg.

KITCHEN
10x13

MASTER
16x13

9' Clg.

BR.#2
12x10

9' Clg.

FAMILY ROOM
16x15

10' Clg.

42'

42'

Copyright by designer/architect.

PORCH
5x16

BR.#3
12x10

Plan #151413

Dimensions: 32' W x 42' D
Levels: 1.5
Heated Square Footage: 1,400
Main Level Sq. Ft.: 948
Upper Level Sq. Ft.: 452
Bedrooms: 2
Bathrooms: 2
Foundation: Crawl space or slab
CompleteCost List Available: Yes
Price Category: B

Images provided by designer/architect.

Relax on the front porch of this lovely little cottage. It's a great starter home or a weekend getaway.

Features:

• Great Room: Enter from the front porch into this large room, with its vaulted ceiling and stone fireplace.

• Kitchen: This large kitchen has plenty of cabinets and counter space; there is even a raised bar.

• Grilling Porch: Just off the kitchen is this porch. Bedroom 1 has access to this area as well.

• Upper Level: Located on this level are a loft area, a full bathroom, and a bedroom.

Main Level Floor Plan

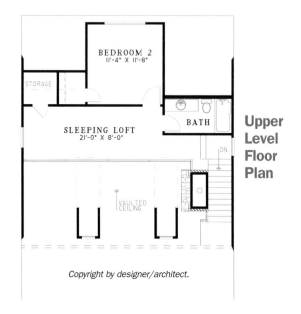

Upper Level Floor Plan

Copyright by designer/architect.

Plan #341064

Dimensions: 58'6" W x 36'9" D

Levels: 1

Heated Square Footage: 1,418

Bedrooms: 3

Bathrooms: 2

Foundation: Crawl space; slab or basement for fee

Materials List Available: Yes

Price Category: B

Images provided by designer/architect.

This sweet starter home has many of the amenities of a larger home.

Features:

• Family Room: Already equipped with gas fireplace, all this room needs is some entertainment options and comfy furniture to welcome guests into the warmth of your home and out of the cold.

• Dining Room: This versatile space can be used for formal dinners or for barbecues that have been cooked on the deck.

• Kitchen: This efficiently designed space features a large pantry and an elevated bar for informal meals on the run. Or use the bar as a serving or buffet area for hosting dinner parties.

• Master Suite: A cozy retreat, this main bedroom features two walk-in closets and a full master bath with a garden tub.

Copyright by designer/architect.

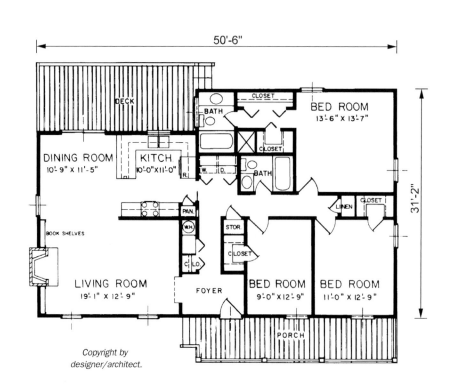

Plan #341096

Dimensions: 50'6" W x 31'2"D
Levels: 1
Heated Square Footage: 1,447
Bedrooms: 3
Bathrooms: 2
Foundation: Crawl space; slab or basement for fee
Material List Available: No
Price Category: B

The perfect-size plan and a pretty facade add up to a great home for your family.

Features:

• Family Room: This casual gathering area boasts a corner fireplace and a vaulted ceiling. The open layout allows friends and family to flow among the family room, kitchen, and breakfast nook.

• Dining Room: Located off of the entry, this formal dining area features a serving counter with cabinets above.

• Office: This large home office will make working at home feel easy. Its private entrance will allow clients to come and go without disturbing the family.

• Master Suite: You'll be close to your family, but in a world of your own, in this master suite.

Plan #121035

Dimensions: 45'4" W x 38' D
Levels: 2
Heated Square Footage: 1,463
Main Level Sq. Ft.: 716
Upper Level Sq. Ft.: 747
Bedrooms: 3
Bathrooms: 2½
Foundation: Basement
Materials List Available: Yes
Price Category: B

Images provided by designer/architect.

This convenient and elegant home is designed to expand as the family does.

Features:

- Ceiling Height: 8 ft. unless otherwise noted.

- Family Room: An open staircase to the second level visually expands this room where a built-in entertainment center maximizes the floor space. The whole family will be drawn to the warmth from the handsome fireplace.

- Kitchen: Cooking will be a pleasure in this

bright and efficient kitchen that features a corner pantry. A snack bar offers a convenient spot for informal family meals.

- Dining Area: This lovely bayed area adjoins the kitchen.

- Room to Expand: Upstairs is 258 sq. ft. of unfinished area offering plenty of space for expansion as the family grows.

- Garage: This two-bay garage offers plenty of storage space in addition to parking for cars.

Main Level Floor Plan

Upper Level Floor Plan

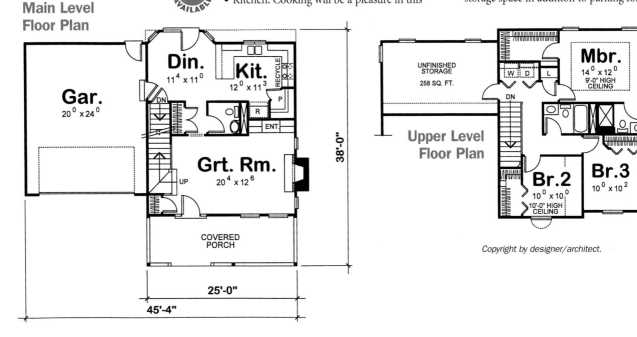

Copyright by designer/architect.

Main Level Floor Plan

Images provided by designer/architect.

CAD FILE AVAILABLE

Upper Level Floor Plan

Copyright by designer/architect.

Plan #151412

Dimensions: 40'4" W x 41'6" D

Levels: 1.5

Heated Square Footage: 1,374

Main Level Sq. Ft.: 1,070

Upper Level Sq. Ft.: 304

Bedrooms: 3

Bathrooms: 2

Foundation: Crawl space or slab

CompleteCost List Available: Yes

Price Category: B

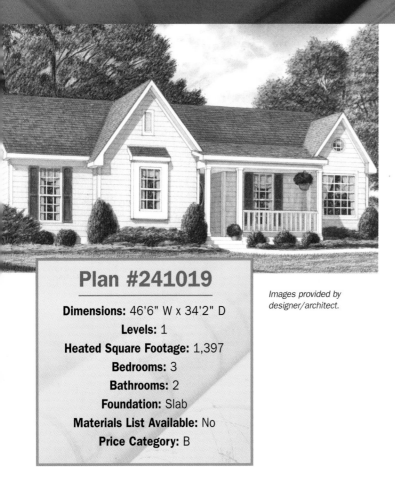

Images provided by designer/architect.

Copyright by designer/architect.

Plan #241019

Dimensions: 46'6" W x 34'2" D

Levels: 1

Heated Square Footage: 1,397

Bedrooms: 3

Bathrooms: 2

Foundation: Slab

Materials List Available: No

Price Category: B

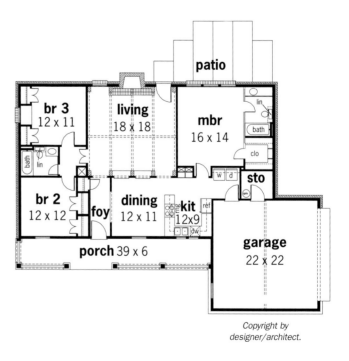

Plan #371001

Dimensions: 52' W x 45' D

Levels: 1

Heated Square Footage: 1,418

Bedrooms: 3

Bathrooms: 2

Foundation: Slab

Materials List Available: No

Price Category: B

Images provided by designer/architect.

Copyright by designer/architect.

Plan #211024

Dimensions: 61' W x 44' D

Levels: 1

Heated Square Footage: 1,418

Bedrooms: 3

Bathrooms: 2

Foundation: Slab; crawl space for fee

Materials List Available: Yes

Price Category: B

Images provided by designer/architect.

Copyright by designer/architect.

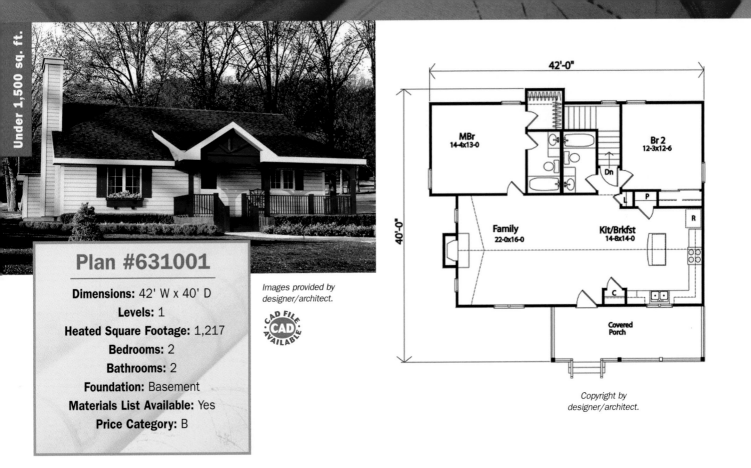

Plan #631001

Dimensions: 42' W x 40' D

Levels: 1

Heated Square Footage: 1,217

Bedrooms: 2

Bathrooms: 2

Foundation: Basement

Materials List Available: Yes

Price Category: B

Images provided by designer/architect.

CAD FILE AVAILABLE

Copyright by designer/architect.

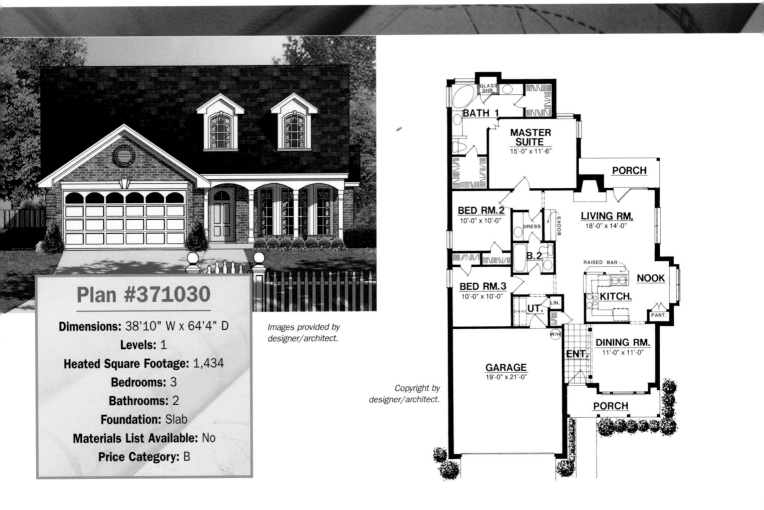

Plan #371030

Dimensions: 38'10" W x 64'4" D

Levels: 1

Heated Square Footage: 1,434

Bedrooms: 3

Bathrooms: 2

Foundation: Slab

Materials List Available: No

Price Category: B

Images provided by designer/architect.

Copyright by designer/architect.

Main Level Floor Plan

15'-8" X 12'-2"
4,70 X 3,55

10'-8" X 10'-0"
3,20 X 3,00

9'-4" 14'-4"
2,80 X 4,30

26'-0"
7,8 m

27'-8"
8,3 m

Upper Level Floor Plan

Copyright by designer/architect.

13'-8" X 11'-10"
4,10 X 3,55

10'-0" X 9'-8"
3,00 X 2,90

10'-0" X 10'-0"
3,00 X 3,00

Plan #181223

Dimensions: 27'8" W x 26' D

Levels: 2

Heated Square Footage: 1,440

Main Level Sq. Ft.: 720

Upper Level Sq. Ft.: 720

Bedrooms: 3

Bathrooms: 2

Foundation: Basement; crawl space or slab for fee

Materials List Available: Yes

Price Category: B

Images provided by designer/architect.

CAD FILE AVAILABLE

Plan #371049

Dimensions: 52' W x 45' D

Levels: 1

Heated Square Footage: 1,440

Bedrooms: 3

Bathrooms: 2

Foundation: Crawl space, slab or basement

Materials List Available: No

Price Category: B

Images provided by designer/architect.

CAD FILE AVAILABLE

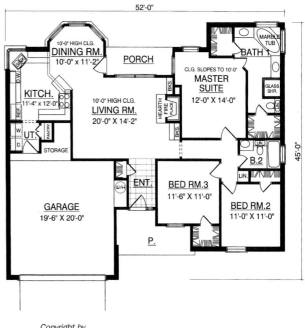

52'-0"

DINING RM.
10'-0" X 11'-2"
10'-0" HIGH CLG.

PORCH

BATH
MARBLE TUB

KITCH.
11'-4" x 12'-0"

LIVING RM.
20'-0" X 14'-2"
10'-0" HIGH CLG.

MASTER SUITE
12'-0" X 14'-0"
CLG. SLOPES TO 10'-0"

GLASS SHR.

UT.
PANTRY
STORAGE

ENT.

BED RM.3
11'-6" X 11'-0"

B.2

GARAGE
19'-6" X 20'-0"

BED RM.2
11'-0" X 11'-0"

P.

45'-0"

Copyright by designer/architect.

Plan #151529

Dimensions: 43' W x 66'6" D
Levels: 1
Heated Square Footage: 1,474
Bedrooms: 2
Bathrooms: 2
Foundation: Crawl space or slab
CompleteCost List Available: Yes
Price Category: B

This elegant design is reflective of the Arts and Crafts era. Copper roofing and carriage style garage doors warmly welcome guests into this split-bedroom plan.

Features:

- **Great Room:** With access to the grilling porch as a bonus, this large gathering area features a 10-ft.-high ceiling and a beautiful fireplace.

- **Kitchen:** This fully equipped island kitchen has a raised bar and a built-in pantry. The area is open to the great room and dining room, giving an open and airy feeling to the home.

- **Master Suite:** Located on the opposite side of the home from the secondary bedroom, this retreat offers a large sleeping area and two large closets. The master bath features a spa tub, a separate shower, and dual vanities.

- **Bedroom:** This secondary bedroom has a large closet and access to the full bathroom in the hallway.

Images provided by designer/architect.

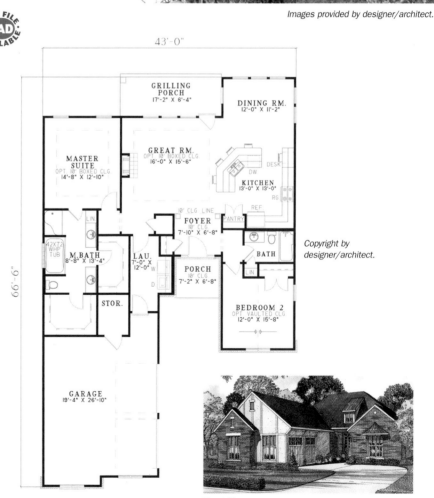

Copyright by designer/architect.

Front View

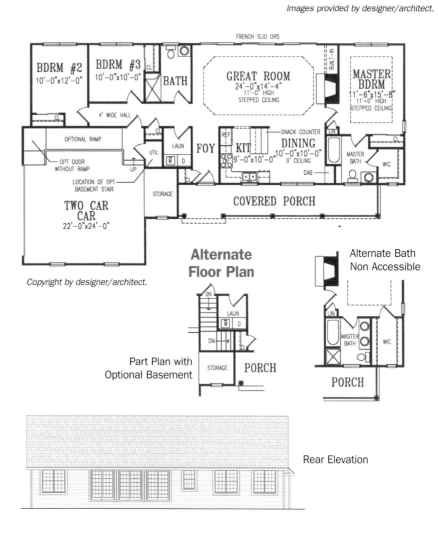

Images provided by designer/architect.

Plan #131017

Dimensions: 69'8" W x 39'4" D

Levels: 1

Heated Square Footage: 1,480

Bedrooms: 3

Bathrooms: 2

Foundation: Crawl space, slab, or basement

Materials List Available: Yes

Price Category: C

This fully accessible home is designed for wheelchair access to every area, giving everyone true enjoyment and freedom of movement.

Features:

- Great Room: Facing towards the rear, this great room features a volume ceiling that adds to the spacious feeling of the room.

- Kitchen: Designed for total convenience and easy work patterns, this kitchen also offers a view out to the covered front porch.

- Master Bedroom: Enjoy the quiet in this room which is sure to become your favorite place to relax at the end of the day.

- Additional Bedrooms: Both rooms have easy access to a full bath and feature nicely sized closet spaces.

- Garage: Use the extra space in this attached garage for storage.

Copyright by designer/architect.

Alternate Floor Plan

Part Plan with Optional Basement

Alternate Bath Non Accessible

Rear Elevation

Plan #351020

Dimensions: 54' W x 48' D

Levels: 1

Heated Square Footage: 1,488

Bedrooms: 3

Bathrooms: 3

Foundation: Basement

Materials List Available: Yes

Price Category: D

This is a lot of house for its size and is an excellent example of the popular split bedroom layout.

Features:

• Great Room: This large room is open to the dining room.

• Kitchen: This fully equipped kitchen has a peninsula counter and is open into the dining room.

• Master Suite: This private area, located on the other side of the home from the secondary bedrooms, features large walk-in closets and bath areas.

• Bedrooms: The two secondary bedrooms have large closets and share a hall bathroom.

Images provided by designer/architect.

Copyright by designer/architect.

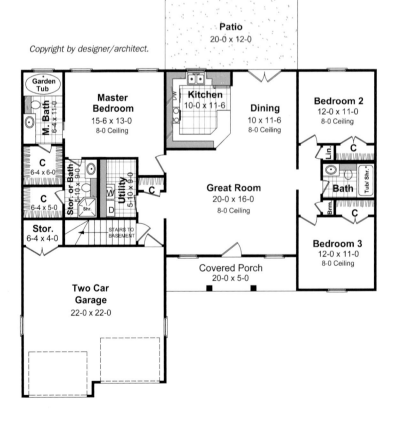

Plan #131013

Dimensions: 50' W x 41'8" D

Levels: 1

Heated Square Footage: 1,489

Bedrooms: 3

Bathrooms: 2

Foundation: Crawl space, slab, basement, or walkout

Materials List Available: Yes

Price Category: C

Images provided by designer/architect.

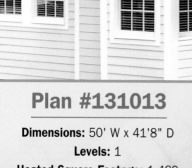

You'll love the Victorian details on the exterior of this charming ranch-style home.

Features:

• Front Porch: This porch is large enough so that you can sit out on warm summer nights to catch a breeze or create a garden of potted ornamentals.

• Great Room: Running from the front of the house to the rear, this great room is bathed in natural light from both directions. The volume ceiling adds a luxurious feeling to it, and the fireplace creates a cozy place on chilly afternoons.

• Kitchen: Cooking will be a pleasure in this kitchen, thanks to the thoughtful layout and well-designed work areas.

• Master Suite: Enjoy the quiet in this room, where it will be easy to relax and unwind, no matter what the time of day. The walk-in closet gives you plenty of storage space, and you're sure to appreciate both the privacy and large size of the master bath.

Copyright by designer/architect.

Rear Elevation

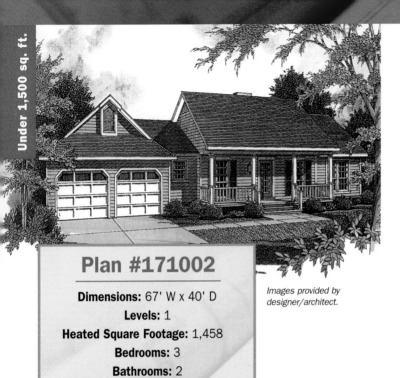

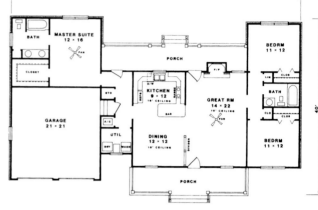

Plan #171002

Dimensions: 67' W x 40' D

Levels: 1

Heated Square Footage: 1,458

Bedrooms: 3

Bathrooms: 2

Foundation: Crawl space or slab

Materials List Available: Yes

Price Category: B

Images provided by designer/architect.

Copyright by designer/architect.

Main Level Floor Plan

Plan #151411

Dimensions: 44'2" W x 39' D

Levels: 1.5

Heated Square Footage: 1,472

Main Level Sq. Ft.: 1,140

Upper Level Sq. Ft.: 332

Bedrooms: 4

Bathrooms: 2

Foundation: Crawl space or slab

CompleteCost List Available: Yes

Price Category: B

Images provided by designer/architect.

CAD FILE AVAILABLE

Upper Level Floor Plan

Copyright by designer/architect.

Upper Level Floor Plan

9'-9" X 10'-0"
2,93 X 3,00

9'-9" X 10'-0"
2,93 X 3,00

12'-8" X 14'-8"
3,80 X 4,40

Images provided by designer/architect.

CAD FILE AVAILABLE CAD

10'-4" X 13'-4"
3,10 X 4,00

9'-8" X 10'-0"
2,90 X 3,00

12'-8" X 14'-8"
3,80 X 4,40

29'-8"
8,9 m

Main Level Floor Plan

Copyright by designer/architect.

28'-0"
8,4 m

Plan #181226

Dimensions: 28' W x 29'8" D
Levels: 2
Heated Square Footage: 1,485
Main Level Sq. Ft.: 735
Upper Level Sq. Ft.: 750
Bedrooms: 3
Bathrooms: 1½
Foundation: Basement; crawl space or slab for fee
Materials List Available: Yes
Price Category: B

Plan #341071

Dimensions: 72'7" W x 38'6" D
Levels: 1
Heated Square Footage: 1,500
Bedrooms: 3
Bathrooms: 2
Foundation: Crawl space; slab or basement for fee
Materials List Available: Yes
Price Category: C

Images provided by designer/architect.

CAD FILE AVAILABLE CAD

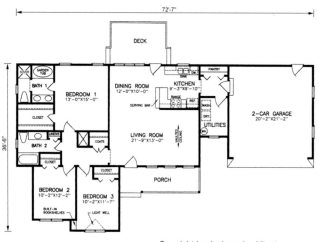

72'-7"

DECK

GARDEN TUB

BATH 1

BEDROOM 1
13'-0"X15'-0"

DINING ROOM
12'-0"X10'-0"

KITCHEN
9'-3"X9'-10"

PANTRY

SERVING BAR

RANGE

REF.

2-CAR GARAGE
20'-2"X21'-2"

36'-6"

BATH 2

LIVING ROOM
21'-9"X13'-0"

VAULTED CEILING

WASH
DRY

UTILITIES

CLOSET

COATS

BEDROOM 2
10'-2"X12'-2"

CLOSET

PORCH

BUILT-IN BOOKSHELVES

BEDROOM 3
10'-2"X11'-7"

LIGHT WELL

Copyright by designer/architect.

Images provided by designer/architect.

Plan #151035

Dimensions: 37'8" W x 38'4" D

Levels: 1.5

Heated Square Footage: 1,451

Main Level Sq. Ft.: 868

Upper Level Sq. Ft: 583

Bedrooms: 3

Bathrooms: 2

Foundation: Crawl space or slab

CompleteCost List Available: Yes

Price Category: B

Country living meets the modern day family in this well designed home.

Features:

- **Den:** The large stone fireplace is the focal point in this gathering area. Located just off the entry porch, the area welcomes you home.

- **Kitchen:** This efficiently designed kitchen has an abundance of cabinets and counter space. The eat-at counter, open to the den, adds extra space for family and friends.

- **Grilling Porch:** On nice days, overflow your dinner guests onto this rear covered grilling porch. From the relaxing area you can watch the kids play in the backyard.

- **Upper Level:** Two bedrooms, with large closets, and a full bathroom occupy this level. The dormers in each of the bedrooms add more space to these rooms.

Upper Level Floor Plan

BATH 7'-8" X 7'-0"

6'4" WALL   6'4" WALL

8' LINE

BEDROOM 2 13'-4" X 14'-6"

BEDROOM 3 11'-4" X 14'-5"

8' LINE   8' LINE

4' WALL   4' WALL

Main Level Floor Plan

37'-8"

38'-4"

KITCHEN 9'-4" X 10'-10"

REF PANTRY

DINING 10'-0" X 13'-6"

GRILLING PORCH 17'-8" X 6'-0"

SUPPLY ROOM   STORAGE

BATH 7'-6" X 5'-0"

STACK W/D

DEN 15'-6" X 18'-10"

BEDROOM 1 11'-4" X 11'-0"

8' COVERED PORCH

Images provided by designer/architect.

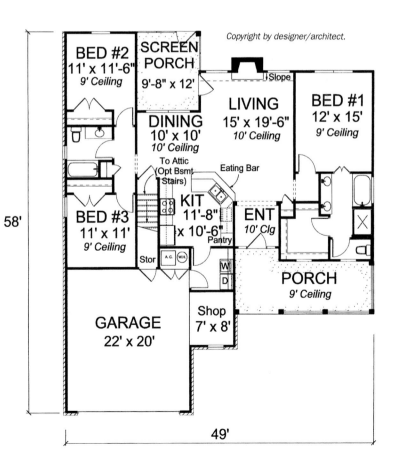

Images provided by designer/architect.

Plan #121199

Dimensions: 49' W x 58' D

Levels: 1

Heated Square Footage: 1,416

Bedrooms: 3

Bathrooms: 2

Foundation: Slab

Materials List Available: Yes

Price Category: B

Multiple porches, a home workshop, and an eating bar set this one-story plan apart from the rest.

Features:

- Porches: At the front of the house, an ample 9-ft.-high ceiling covers this large open porch. At the rear, the screened-in porch connects to the dining room, which is perfect for enjoying a meal outside.

- Kitchen: This functional kitchen is open to the dining and living rooms. A snack bar connects the spaces.

- Shop: Located off of the two-car garage, the shop provides a place to work on a project or just get away and unwind.

- Bedrooms: All three bedrooms in this house feature 9-ft.-high ceilings. The master suite has access to a private bath, while the other two bedrooms share a centrally located bathroom.

Copyright by designer/architect.

BED #2 11' x 11'-6" 9' Ceiling

SCREEN PORCH 9'-8" x 12'

LIVING 15' x 19'-6" 10' Ceiling

BED #1 12' x 15' 9' Ceiling

DINING 10' x 10' 10' Ceiling

To Attic (Opt Bsmt Stairs)

Eating Bar

BED #3 11' x 11' 9' Ceiling

KIT 11'-8" x 10'-6"

Pantry

ENT 10' Clg

Stor

A.C. W.H.

W D

PORCH 9' Ceiling

GARAGE 22' x 20'

Shop 7' x 8'

58'

49'

Plan #161079

Dimensions: 66'4" W x 44'10" D
Levels: 1
Heated Square Footage: 1,498
Bedrooms: 3
Bathrooms: 2
Foundation: Basement
Materials List Available: Yes
Price Category: B

Images provided by designer/architect.

This three-bedroom one-story house enjoys step-saving convenience, plus a beautiful stone-and-siding facade with a covered porch.

Features:

- Great Room: This gathering area, with a gas fireplace and sloped ceiling, is visible from the foyer, breakfast room, and kitchen, creating a large open area.

- Kitchen: This large kitchen, with its snack bar, and the breakfast area both open generously to the great room for a continuous traffic flow.

- Master Suite: This suite enjoys a luxurious bath, large walk-in closet, and raised ceiling.

- Basement: This full basement shows a rough-in for a bathroom and offers space for a future living area.

Copyright by designer/architect.

Rear Elevation

Plan #441018

Dimensions: 36' W x 44' D
Levels: 2
Heated Square Footage: 1,500
Main Level Sq. Ft.: 716
Upper Level Sq. Ft.: 784
Bedrooms: 3
Bathrooms: 2½
Foundation: Crawl space
Materials List Available: Yes
Price Category: C

Images provided by designer/architect.

A trio of gables and a porch entry create a charming exterior for this home. With a compact footprint especially suited for smaller lots, it offers all the amenities important to today's sophisticated homebuyer.

Features:

- Great Room: From the entry, view this spacious two-story room, which features a fireplace and a wall of windows overlooking the porch.

- Dining Room: A French door to the porch is located in this room, along with a planning desk and a large pantry.

- Kitchen: Family will gravitate to this corner kitchen. It offers plenty of cabinet space and countertops including a center island, complete with a breakfast bar to add more space and convenience.

- Master Suite: Located upstairs, this vaulted suite features a walk-in closet and private bathroom.

CAD FILE AVAILABLE

Main Level Floor Plan

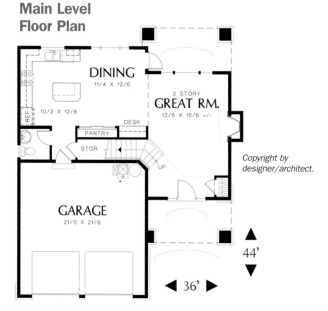

Copyright by designer/architect.

DINING 11/4 X 12/6

10/2 X 12/6

REF.

2 STORY GREAT RM. 13/6 X 16/6 +/-

DESK

PANTRY

STOR

UP

GARAGE 21/0 X 21/6

44'

36'

Upper Level Floor Plan

VAULTED MASTER 11/8 X 14/4

GREAT RM. BELOW

DN

LINEN

FOYER BELOW

PLANT SHELF

BR. 2 10/4 X 13/4 +/-

BR. 3 10/4 X 11/0 +

Plan #131003

Dimensions: 60' W x 39'10" D

Levels: 1

Heated Square Footage: 1,466

Bedrooms: 3

Bathrooms: 2

Foundation: Crawl space, slab, or basement

Materials List Available: Yes

Price Category: C

This home, as shown in the photograph, may differ from the actual blueprints. For more detailed information, please check the floor plans carefully.

Victorian styling adds elegance to this compact and easy-to-maintain ranch design.

Images provided by designer/architect.

Features:

- Ceiling Height: 8 ft.

- Foyer: Bridging between the front door and the great room, this foyer is a surprise feature.

- Great Room: A 10-ft. ceiling adds to the spacious feeling of this room, while the corner fireplace gives it an intimate feeling. Sliding glass doors at the rear of the room open to the backyard.

- Dining Room: This formal room adjoins the great room, allowing guests and family to flow between the rooms.

- Breakfast Room: Turrets add a Victorian feeling to this room that's just off the kitchen and overlooks the front porch.

- Master Suite: Privacy is assured in this suite, which is separated from the main part of the house. A separate toilet room and large walk-in closet add convenience to its beauty.

Kitchen

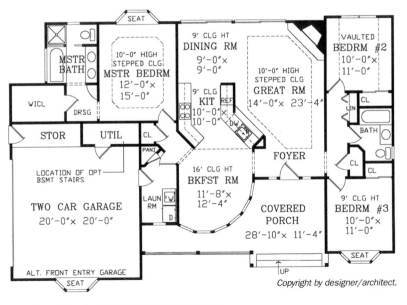

Copyright by designer/architect.

Front View

Foyer/Kitchen/Breakfast Room

Breakfast Room

Great Room

Great Room

Today's Fireplace Technology

Handsome and romantic, but drafty. Thirty years ago, you might have described a traditional fireplace in this way. But that was before technological advancements finally made fireplaces more efficient. Now, not only can you expect your fireplace to provide ambiance and warmth, you can relax knowing that your energy dollars aren't going up in smoke. Over the centuries, people had tried to improve the efficiency of the fireplace so that it would generate the maximum heat possible from the wood consumed. But real strides didn't come until the energy crisis of the early 1970s. That's when designers of fireplaces and stoves introduced some significant innovations. Today, fireplaces are not only more efficient, but cleaner and easier to use.

The traditional fireplace is an all-masonry construction, consisting of only bricks and mortar. However, new constructions and reconstructions of masonry fireplaces often include either a metal or a ceramic firebox. This type of firebox has double walls. The space between these walls is where cool air heats up after being drawn in through openings near the floor of the room. The warm air exits through openings near the top of the firebox. Although a metal firebox is more efficient than an all-masonry firebox, it doesn't radiate heat very effectively, and the heat from the fireplace is distributed by convection—that is, the circulation of warmed air. This im–provement in heating capacity comes from the warm air emitted by the upper openings. But that doesn't keep your feet toasty on a cold winter's night—remember, warm air rises.

A more recent development is the ceramic firebox, which is engineered from modern materials such as the type used in kilns. Fires in ceramic fireboxes burn hotter, cleaner, and more efficiently than in all-masonry or metal fireboxes. The main reason is that the back and the walls of a ceramic firebox absorb, retain, and reflect heat effectively. This means that during the time the fire is blazing, more heat radiates into the room than with the other fireboxes. Heat radiation is boosted by the fact that most ceramic units are made with

The warm glow of a realistic-looking modern zero-clearance gas fire, below, can make the hearth the heart of any room in the house.

Zero-Clearance Fireplace

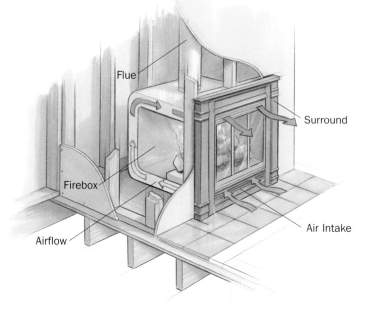

Flue

Surround

Firebox

Air Intake

Airflow

Traditional Masonry Fireplace

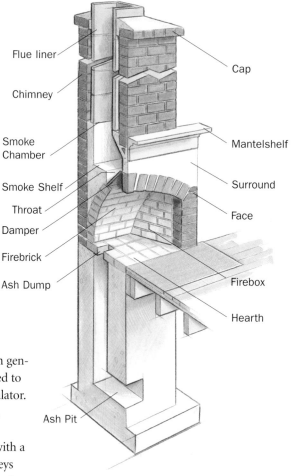

Flue liner

Cap

Chimney

Smoke Chamber

Mantelshelf

Smoke Shelf

Surround

Throat

Face

Damper

Firebrick

Firebox

Ash Dump

Hearth

Ash Pit

thick walls, and so the fire itself is not set as deeply into the hearth as it is with all-masonry or metal fireboxes. As a bonus, because heat is absorbed and retained by the material, the firebox actually radiates a significant amount of heat many hours after the fire has died down. By contrast, a metal firebox cools quickly once the heat source goes out.

In this type of efficient fireplace construction, a metal firebox is usually less expensive than a ceramic one, but the metal does break down over time, in a process professionals refer to as burnout. In addition, an air-circulating metal firebox can only be installed in masonry constructions that are built with ports for the intake of cool air and the discharge of warmed air, or in masonry fireplaces in which such ports can be added. On the other hand, ceramic fireboxes can be installed in any type of masonry fireplace and are not subject to burnout.

Manufactured Fireplaces

The metal fireplaces that are made today can be zero-clearance or freestanding. The zero-clearance units are so named because they can be installed safely against combustible surfaces such as wood. Any of a number of methods are used to keep the

outer jacket cool enough, but in general, these fireplaces are designed to use cool air as the primary insulator. Many manufactured fireplaces, including zero-clearance units, are made with fireboxes lined with a refractory material. The chimneys are also made of metal, and a variety of designs use noncombustible material or air as insulation to keep the outer surface at a safe temperature.

New-technology and traditional fireplaces are shown above. Woodstove-like inserts, below and opposite, make fireplaces more efficient.

The Advantages of a Manufactured Unit

There are some important pluses to choosing a zero-clearance manufactured fireplace. First is the price, which is relatively low, and second is the easy and quick installation. Also, these units are lightweight and can be installed over almost any type of flooring, including wood. This means they do not need elaborate foundations, which is another cost-saver. Manufactured fireplaces are also extremely efficient, and many are designed to provide both radiated heat from the firebox and convection heat from ducting.

Manufactured freestanding fireplaces are, in effect, stoves. They are available in an array of colors, finishes, shapes, and sizes. Like zero-clearance factory-built fireplaces, freestanding models are lightweight, offering the same advantages: no need for heavy masonry or additional reinforcement of flooring. And you have a choice of either a wood-burning or gas-powered unit. Heat efficiency is maximized because, in addition to the firebox, the chimney and all

sides of the unit radiate heat into the room. Freestanding units may be the least expensive option because installation requires only a chimney hole and, depending on the type of flooring, a noncombustible pad. A major disadvantage is the space required for placement, because you cannot install most of these units near a combustible wall. Also, a freestanding fireplace is probably not the best choice for families with young children because so much heat is radiated from the exposed surfaces.

Hybrids

If you're looking for a way to get improved efficiency from a masonry fireplace, consider a gas insert (actually a prefabricated firebox equipped with gas logs). You can purchase either a venting insert or one that's nonventing. But be prepared to pay $1,500 to several thousand dollars for the unit in addition to the cost of installation. For a fraction of that amount you can simply replace real wood logs with ceramic logs powered by gas. Like inserts, these logs may or may not require venting. Consult

an experienced plumber or heating contractor, and remember that once you convert to gas you cannot burn wood.

Improving a masonry fireplace on the inside by installing a metal firebox might also be an inspiration to think of the fireplace and mantel in a new design way. Pairing two or more finishing materials, such as metal and masonry, can make your fireplace a hybrid in more than one way. For example, combine a stone base with a metal hood and chimney to create a custom-designed fireplace that works as a room divider in a large space. The design options in terms of materials and technology are seemingly endless.

If you have plans for building an innovative custom design, carefully review them with an expert in fireplace construction and maintenance to make sure you're not doing something hazardous. Also, don't forget to check with your local building inspector so that you don't waste time and money on a project that may not comply with codes and regulations set forth where you live.

Enhancing the Basics

You can improve the efficiency of any manufactured fireplace, and of masonry and hybrid constructions as well, with a few extras. In a masonry fireplace, a device commonly referred to as a fresh-air intake accessory or an outside air kit may improve performance. A fresh-air accessory makes use of outside air instead of heated room air for combustion, thus improving the fireplace's efficiency. There is another way to make your fireplace more efficient that isn't high tech at all, however. Simply replace the traditional grate or firebasket with a superior design—one that provides greater air circulation and allows a better placement of logs. Another type, a heat-exchanger grate, works with a fan. The device draws in the room's air, reheats it quickly, and then forces it back into the room.

Capitalizing on Technology

Wood is the traditional fuel for a fireplace, and today's manufactured fireplaces offer designs that make the most of your cord of hardwood. However, wood is not the only fuel option. In fact, in some places, it's not an option at all. There are manufactured units that offer a choice of natural gas or propane as a fuel source, which heats ceramic logs designed to realistically simulate wood. The fire, complete with glowing embers, is often difficult to distinguish from one burning real wood.

In some areas of the country, fireplace emission regulations have become strict—in places such as much of Colorado and parts of Nevada and California so strict that new construction of wood-burning fireplaces has been outlawed. In these areas, manufactured units using alternative fuels allow homeowners all the benefits of a wood-burning fireplace without the adverse impact on air quality.

Most of the units available today also offer a variety of amenities, including built-in thermostatic control and remote-control devices for turning the fire on and off and regulating heat output.

The Importance of a Clean Sweep

Finally, one of the most important factors in the use of a fireplace or stove is the regular inspection and cleaning of the stovepipe, flue, and chimney. To understand why, remember that the burning of wood results in the combustion of solids as well as combustible gases. However, not everything that goes into the firebox is burned, no matter how efficient the appliance. One of the by-products of wood burning is the dark brown or black tar called creosote, a flammable substance that sticks to the linings of chimney flues.

Although the burning temperature of creosote is high, it can ignite and cause a chimney fire. It may be brief and without apparent damage, but a chimney fire may also be prolonged or intense and result in significant fire and smoke damage or, at worst, the loss of your home if the creosote buildup is great enough. Creosote causes other problems, too. It decreases the inside diameter of stovepipes and flues, causing slower burning. This makes burning less efficient and contributes to further deposits of creosote. In addition, because creosote is acidic, it corrodes mortar, metal, and eventually even stainless-steel and ceramic chimney liners.

To prevent costly and dangerous creosote buildup, have your chimney professionally cleaned by a qualified chimney sweep. How often depends on the amount of creosote deposited during the burning season, and this, in turn, depends largely on how and what kind of wood you burn. Professional sweeps usually recommend at least annual cleaning. Depending on where you live, you'll spend about $150, perhaps less, for a cleaning.

You'll enjoy a warm glow at the highest efficiency if you use a glass-front wood-burning or gas-fueled, right, fireplace insert.

Fireside Arrangements

Creating an attractive, comfortable setting around a fireplace should be easy. Who doesn't like the cozy ambiance of relaxing in front of a fire? But there are times when the presence of a fireplace in a room poses problems with the layout. A fireplace can take up considerable floor and wall space, and like any other permanent feature or built-in piece of furniture, its size or position can limit the design possibilities.

The Fireplace and the Space

What is the room's size and shape—large, small, square, long and narrow, L-shaped?

Where is the fireplace located—in the center of a wall, to the side, or in a corner? What other permanent features, such as windows, doors, bookcases, or media units, will you have to work with in your arrangement? How much clearance can you allow around the furniture for easy passage? How close do you want to be to the fire? Think of these questions as you consider the design basics presented below.

Scale and Proportion. Remember the importance of spatial relationships. For example, a fireplace may seem large in a room with a low ceiling; conversely, it may appear small in a room with a vaulted ceil-

ing. Size is relative. Applied to objects on the mantel or the wall above the fireplace, correct scale and proportion happen when the objects are the appropriate size for the wall or the fireplace.

Balance. Sometimes the architectural features of a mantel or surround are so strong, you'll have to match them with furnishings of equal visual weight. Or they may be so ornate or plain that you'll have to play them up or tone them down to make them work with the rest of the decor. That's balance. But balance also refers to arrangements: symmetrical, asymmetrical, and radial.

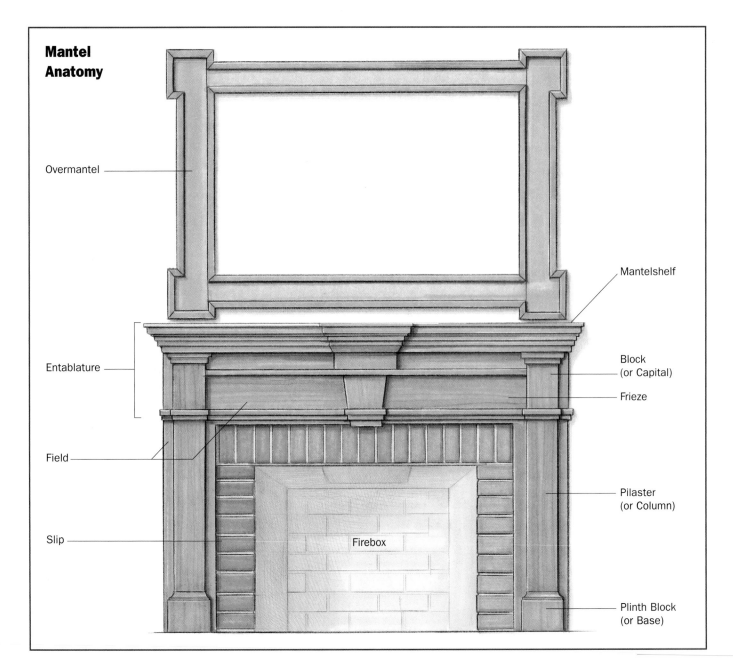

Mantel Anatomy

Overmantel

Entablature

Field

Slip

Mantelshelf

Block (or Capital)

Frieze

Pilaster (or Column)

Firebox

Plinth Block (or Base)

Line. Shape depends on line. Different types of lines suggest various qualities. Pay attention to the lines when you're creating arrangements and relationships among objects. Some lines are inherent in a room or an architectural feature, but you can modify them. For example: vertical lines are stately and dignified, which is just the look you want for your fireplace, but unfortunately, it's rather wide and squat instead. Solution? Create an arrangement above the fireplace that extends high on the wall, or hang a tall mirror or frame over than mantel.

What if the fireplace is too tall? Does it overwhelm the rest of the furniture? Add horizontal lines by moving seating pieces farther apart to the right and left of the hearth. Install wall art on the sides of the fireplace.

If the room is boxy, avoid grouping pieces at right angles to the fireplace and each other. Instead, de-emphasize the boxy shape by placing them on the diagonal to open the square. Use upholstered pieces with rounded arms or curvaceous cushions, legs, or frames. Create a radial arrangement. With the hearth as the central point, create a semicircular hub of furnishings that include seating and a small table or two.

Rhythm. Keep the eye moving at a measured pace by repeating motifs, colors, or shapes. For example, you might pick up the color from a tiled surround to use as an accent color in fabrics on upholstered pieces, curtains, pillows, throws, or other decorative accessories. Or repeat architectural features of the fireplace with other similar elements in the room, such as molding or other woodwork details.

Variety. Don't go overboard trying to match everything exactly. The most interesting rooms and arrangements mix objects of different sizes, shapes, lines, and sometimes even styles (as long as they are compatible).

Harmony. Create harmony among all of the parts of your design by connecting all of the elements either by color or motif. For example, in a display of family photos the frames may all be different shapes, styles, and heights, but because each one is made of brass, the overall appearance looks harmonious. Or you could assemble a wall vignette of frames over the fireplace, all different in finish but tied together by the subject matter of each one—all landscapes, for example, or all pink cabbage roses. Unifying diverse items in this way creates a finished-looking scheme.

How to Make a Hinged Fireboard

You'll need a hinged three-panel wooden fireplace screen, which you can buy or make. If you buy one, you'll have to sand and prime it thoroughly before applying the new finish over the existing one. Ideally, it's best to work on unfinished wood.

The screen used for this project features two 9 x 36-inch side panels and one 26 x 36-inch center panel that were cut from a ¾-inch-thick sheet of plywood. If you aren't handy with a circular saw or table saw, ask your local lumber supplier to cut the panels to your desired dimensions. Attach the side and center panels with two-way (piano) hinges, which are easy to install. Simply mark their location along the inside edges of the panel pieces, drill pilot holes, and then screw the hinges into place. To finish, prime the boards; then paint or stencil a design onto each panel. For Victorian authenticity, decoupage the panels with a motif cut out of a piece of fabric, wallpaper, old greeting cards, or postcards.

Symmetrical versus Asymmetrical Arrangements

If you like the symmetry of classic design, balance your arranged pieces accordingly. For example, position two sofas or love seats of the same size perpendicular to the fireplace and exactly opposite each other. Or place a single sofa parallel with the fireplace, with two chairs opposite one another and equidistant from both the sofa and the hearth. Try out a low coffee table or an oversize ottoman in the center of the arrangement. Leave the peripheral areas outside the main grouping for creating small impromptu conversation areas during parties and gatherings or to accommodate a modest dining area or home-office station.

If your design sense is less formal or contemporary, try an asymmetrical grouping in front of the fire. Turn seating pieces at a 45-degree angle from the hearth.

In a large open space, locate seating not directly in front of the hearth but slightly off to the side. Counterbalance the arrangement with a large table and chairs, a hutch, bookcases, or any element of relatively equal weight. This layout works especially well when the ceiling is vaulted (as most great rooms are) or when the hearth is massive. In many contemporary homes, especially where there is a zero-clearance unit, the fireplace is not on an outside wall, nor is it necessarily in a central location. This means you can put the fireplace almost anywhere.

Comfortable Arrangements

You may want an intimate environment in front of the fire, but the room is so large that it feels and looks impersonal. Large rooms afford lots of leeway for arranging, but people often make the mistake of pushing all of the furniture against the walls. If that's what you're doing, pull the major seating pieces closer together and near the fire, keeping a distance of only 4 to 10 feet between sofas and chairs. For the most comfortable result, create one or more small groupings that can accommodate up to four to six people in different areas of the room.

A raised hearth, above, reinforces the idea of a fireplace as a focal point, and it provides seating near the fire. Place other furniture to the sides of the hearth.

Modular Seating. Instead of a standard sofa and chairs, consider the convenience of modular seating, too, which comes in any number of armless and single-arm end pieces. The advantage of these separate upholstered units is that you can easily add, take away, or rearrange the modules to suit any of your layout or seating needs. Create an L or a U arrangement in front of the fire; subtract pieces, moving one or two outside of the area for an intimate grouping. Use an area rug to further define the space. Or put the pieces together to make one large arrangement in any configuration. Versatile furnishings such as an ottoman with a hinged top or an antique trunk can double as seating, a low table, or storage.

A Quick Guide to Buying Firewood

How much wood you need to buy in a season depends on a number of factors, but there are three major variables: how often and how long you burn fires; the efficiency of your fireplace or stove; and the type of wood you burn. In general, hard, dense woods are ideal for fuel. As a rule of thumb, the wood from deciduous trees is best. (Deciduous trees are those that shed their leaves annually.) These include oak, maple, walnut, birch, beech, ash, and the wood from fruit trees such as cherry and apple.

Avoid burning wood from evergreens—those cone-bearing (coniferous) trees with needles instead of leaves. The wood of coniferous trees is soft and it will burn faster, so a greater volume of wood will be consumed per hour compared with hardwood. A greater problem with softwoods, however, is the resin content. Resin is the gummy substance that's used in the manufacture of some wood stains and shellacs, and when resin is burned it gives off a byproduct called creosote. Creosote, which is flammable, accumulates in flues and chimneys, and this buildup represents a potential fire hazard.

The wood you purchase should also be seasoned, which means that the tree should have been cut down at least six months or, preferably, a year prior to the burning of the wood. Ideally, the wood should be cut and split soon after the tree is felled, allowing for more effective drying. The moisture in unseasoned (or green) wood tends to have a cooling effect, preventing complete combustion and making it harder to keep a fire blazing. A low-burning fire also increases creosote. (It's okay to burn green wood occasionally, but make sure to use small logs or split sticks and add them to an already hot fire.)

Mantel Vignettes

A grouping of objects on your mantel can be as simple or complex as you like. To make your display lively, choose a variety of shapes and sizes. For dramatic impact, group related objects that you can link in theme or color.

Remember that a symmetrical arrangement has classical overtones and will reinforce the formality of traditional designs. Stick with similar objects: a pair of Chinese ginger jars or antique silver candlesticks arranged in mirror fashion on either side of the mantel equidistant from the center, for example. Or keep the look simple by placing a single but important object in the center; it could be a mantel clock, a floral arrangement, or some other objet d'art.

Asymmetry, on the other hand, brings a different dynamic to a mantel vignette with mismatched pieces. Try placing a large object to one side of the mantel, and then balance that piece by massing several small objects or a different type of object of similar scale on the opposite side. An example might be an arrangement of books of varying heights and sizes at one end of the mantel and a simple large vase at the other end. Or you might oppose tall thin candlesticks with one fat candle.

A simple brick wall, left, serves as a backdrop for a gleaming fireplace insert.

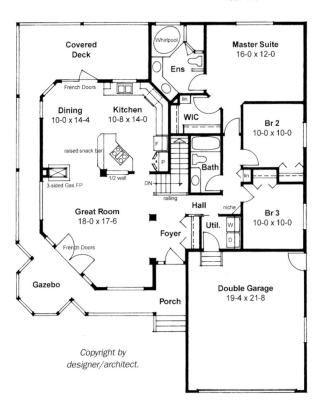

Plan #281022

Dimensions: 48' W x 58' D

Levels: 1

Heated Square Footage: 1,506

Bedrooms: 3

Bathrooms: 2

Foundation: Basement

Materials List Available: Yes

Price Category: C

• Master Suite: Close to the secondary bedrooms, this master suite includes a spacious walk-in closet, a whirlpool tub, and a dual-sink vanity.

Rear View

You'll spend hours enjoying the sunshine on this home's wraparound porch and gazebo.

CAD FILE AVAILABLE

Features:

• Porch: Stretching from the front to the back of the house, this porch has a gazebo on one corner and becomes a covered deck at the back.

• Great Room: This beautiful great room includes a three-sided fireplace and French doors that open out onto the porch by the gazebo.

• Kitchen: Divided from the dining room and great room by an island with a raised snack bar, this kitchen also has French doors nearby that open out to the covered deck, a wonderful location for outdoor meals.

Covered Deck

Whirlpool

Master Suite
16-0 x 12-0

Ens

French Doors

Dining
10-0 x 14-4

Kitchen
10-8 x 14-0

WIC

lin

Br 2
10-0 x 10-0

raised snack bar

F

P

Bath

lin

3-sided Gas FP

1/2 wall

DN

railing

Great Room
18-0 x 17-6

Hall

niche

Br 3
10-0 x 10-0

Foyer

Util.

W

D

French Doors

Gazebo

Porch

Double Garage
19-4 x 21-8

Copyright by designer/architect.

Plan #401008

Dimensions: 87' W x 44' D

Levels: 1

Heated Square Footage: 1,541

Bedrooms: 3

Bathrooms: 2

Foundation: Basement

Materials List Available: Yes

Price Category: C

This popular design begins with a wraparound covered porch made even more charming by turned wood spindles.

CAD FILE AVAILABLE

Features:

- **Great Room:** The entry opens directly into this great room, which is warmed by a woodstove.

- **Dining Room:** This room offers access to a screened porch for outdoor after-dinner leisure.

- **Kitchen:** This country kitchen features a center island and a breakfast bay for casual meals.

- **Bedrooms:** Family bedrooms share a full bath that includes a soaking tub.

Images provided by designer/architect.

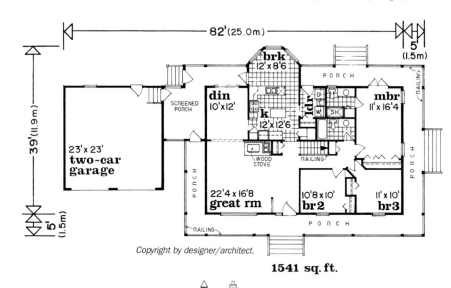

Copyright by designer/architect.

1541 sq. ft.

Rear Elevation

Left Side Elevation

Right Side Elevation

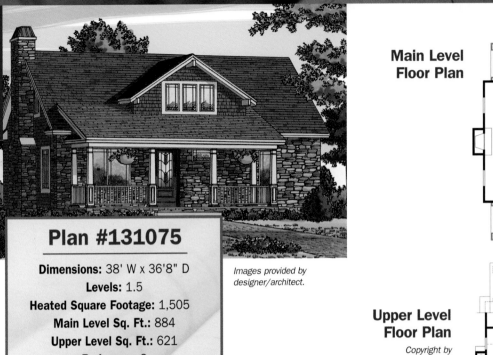

Main Level Floor Plan

COVERED PORCH
35'-0"x 7'-0"

9'-1" CLG
EAT-IN KITCHEN
12'-0"x 9'-8"

9'-1" CLG
MASTER BEDRM
11'-8"x 14'-8"

REF DW S

9'-1" CLG
GREAT RM
13'-0"x 22'-0"

W/D LAV

CL

DN TO OPT BASEMENT

FOYER

UP

WICL
5'-6"x 6'-4"

BATH

COVERED PORCH
27'-0"x 7'-0"

Upper Level Floor Plan

Copyright by designer/architect.

BATH

5'-1" PL. HT.

5'-1" PL. HT.

8'-1" CLG
BEDRM #3
13'-0"x 12'-0"

CL CL

8'-1" CLG
BEDRM #2
15'-0"x 12'-0"

5'-1" PL. HT.

BALC

DN

5'-1" PL. HT.

Plan #131075

Dimensions: 38' W x 36'8" D

Levels: 1.5

Heated Square Footage: 1,505

Main Level Sq. Ft.: 884

Upper Level Sq. Ft.: 621

Bedrooms: 3

Bathrooms: 2½

Foundation: Crawl space, slab or basement

Materials List Available: Yes

Price Category: C

Images provided by designer/architect.

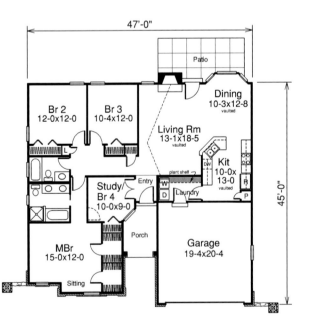

47'-0"

Patio

Br 2
12-0x12-0

Br 3
10-4x12-0

Living Rm
13-1x18-5
vaulted

Dining
10-3x12-8
vaulted

plant shelf

L

Entry

W

Kit
10-0x
13-0
vaulted

D

Laundry

P

Study/
Br 4
10-0x9-0

45'-0"

MBr
15-0x12-0

Porch

Garage
19-4x20-4

Sitting

Copyright by designer/architect.

Plan #321224

Dimensions: 47' W x 45' D

Levels: 1

Heated Square Footage: 1,519

Bedrooms: 4

Bathrooms: 2

Foundation: Crawl space, slab or basement

Materials List Available: Yes

Price Category: C

Images provided by designer/architect.

CAD FILE AVAILABLE

Copyright by
designer/architect.

Storage
19-4x5-4

Carport
20-0x22-0

Patio

Owner's Bedroom
17-9x13-8

66-6

Laun.
6-0x7-8

Kitchen
10-8x13-9

Greatroom
14-5x17-5

Bath

Bath

Dining
10-0x11-9

Foyer

Bedroom
11-2x12-0

Bedroom
10-7x11-4

Porch
18-0x6-0

51-5

Plan #311052

Dimensions: 51'5" W x 66'6" D
Levels: 1
Heated Square Footage: 1,539
Bedrooms: 3
Bathrooms: 2
Foundation: Crawl space or slab
Material List Available: Yes
Price Category: C

Images provided by designer/architect.

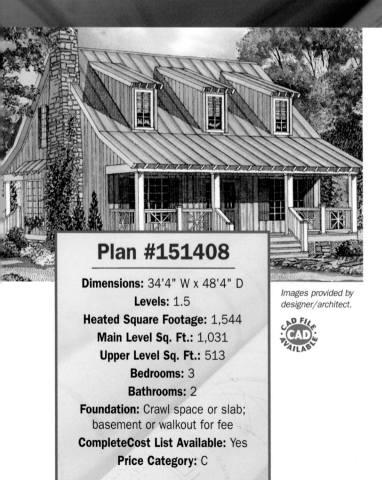

34'-4"

GRILLING PORCH
32'-0" X 8'-0"

SUPPLY ROOM

KITCHEN
12'-2" X 11'-4"

BEDROOM 2
11'-0" X 8'-8"

DINING
9'-0" X 14'-2"

48'-4"

BATH

GREAT ROOM
20'-0" X 17'-6"

BEDROOM 1
11'-0" X 11'-6"

COVERED PORCH
32'-0" X 8'-0"

Main Level Floor Plan

Plan #151408

Dimensions: 34'4" W x 48'4" D
Levels: 1.5
Heated Square Footage: 1,544
Main Level Sq. Ft.: 1,031
Upper Level Sq. Ft.: 513
Bedrooms: 3
Bathrooms: 2
Foundation: Crawl space or slab; basement or walkout for fee
CompleteCost List Available: Yes
Price Category: C

Images provided by designer/architect.

CAD FILE AVAILABLE

Upper Level Floor Plan

Copyright by designer/architect.

STRG.

BATH

STRG.

LOFT
20'-0" X 8'-0"

BEDROOM 3
11'-0" X 19'-6"

Plan #251004

Dimensions: 50'9" W x 42'1" D
Levels: 1
Heated Square Footage: 1,550
Bedrooms: 3
Bathrooms: 2
Foundation: Crawl space, slab
Materials List Available: Yes
Price Category: C

Images provided by designer/architect.

Combine the old-fashioned appeal of a country farmhouse with all the comforts of modern living.

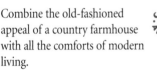

Features:

- Ceiling Height: 9 ft.
- Foyer: When guests enter this inviting foyer, they will be greeted by a view of the lovely family room.
- Family Room: Usher family and friends into this welcoming family room, where they can warm up in front of the fireplace. The room's 12-ft. ceiling enhances its sense of spaciousness.

- Kitchen: Gather around and keep the cook company at the snack bar in this roomy kitchen. There's still plenty of counter space for food preparation, thanks to the kitchen island.
- Master Bedroom: This elegant master bedroom features a large walk-in closet and a 9-ft. recessed ceiling.
- Master Bath. This master bath includes a double vanity, a tub, and a walk-in shower.
- Garage: This attached garage provides plenty of extra storage space, as well as parking for two cars.

Copyright by designer/architect.

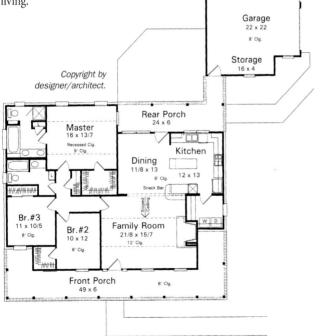

SMARTtip

Shaker Style in Your Bathroom

This warm, likable style fits in perfectly with a country home because of its old-fashioned values. But it blends in well with contemporary interiors, too, because of its clean lines and plain geometric shapes. In fact, adding a few Shaker elements can warm up the sometimes cold look of a thoroughly modern room.

Plan #191037

Dimensions: 57'4" W x 65' D
Levels: 1
Heated Square Footage: 1,575
Bedrooms: 3
Bathrooms: 2
Foundation: Crawl space, slab
Materials List Available: No
Price Category: C

Images provided by designer/architect.

This home seems to expand from the inside out and has everything the growing family needs.

Features:

- **Great Room:** Gather with guests around the fireplace for conversation or relax with the family in front of the television in this welcoming space.

- **Kitchen:** This area is surrounded by storage and workspace, which includes a center island. Transition easily from the kitchen to the dining room or patio for meals.

- **Master Suite:** A window-flanked whirlpool tub, dual sinks, standing shower, and walk-in closet all make for a relaxing atmosphere in the master bath.

- **Secondary Bedrooms:** Two additional bedrooms are separated from the rest of the house by a small hallway. A compartmentalized full bathroom is shared between the two.

- **Garage:** This two-car garage has extra storage areas, one accessible from the inside, the other accessible from the outside.

Copyright by designer/architect.

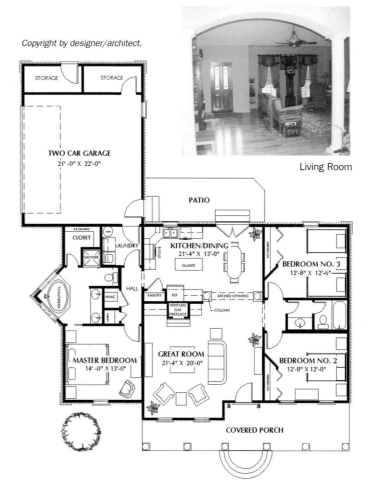

Living Room

Plan #441003

Dimensions: 50' W x 48' D
Levels: 1
Heated Square Footage: 1,580
Bedrooms: 3
Bathrooms: 2½
Foundation: Crawl space;
slab or basement available for fee
Materials List Available: No
Price Category: C

Craftsman styling with modern floor planning—that's the advantage of this cozy design. Covered porches at front and back enhance both the look and the livability of the plan.

Features:

- Great Room: This vaulted entertaining area boasts a corner fireplace and a built-in media center. The area is open to the kitchen and the dining area.

- Kitchen: This large, open island kitchen will please the chef in the family. The raised bar is open to the dining area and the great room.

- Master Suite: Look for luxurious amenities such as double sinks and a separate tub and shower in the master bath. The master bedroom has a vaulted ceiling and a walk-in closet with built-in shelves.

- Bedrooms: Two secondary bedrooms are located away from the master suite. Each has a large closet and access to a common bathroom.

Images provided by designer/architect.

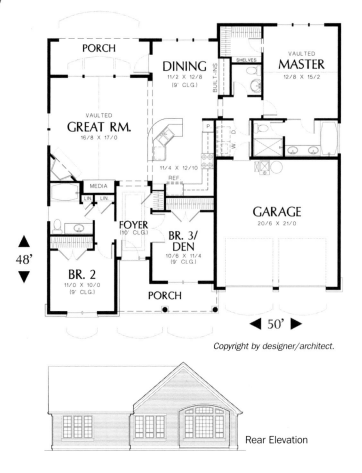

Copyright by designer/architect.

Rear Elevation

Images provided by designer/architect.

Plan #181217

Dimensions: 38' W x 35' D
Levels: 2
Heated Square Footage: 1,588
Main Level Sq. Ft.: 778
Upper Level Sq. Ft.: 810
Bedrooms: 3
Bathrooms: 1½
Foundation: Basement
Materials List Available: Yes
Price Category: C

Growing families will embrace all the charm and comfort of this Victorian-style three-bedroom home.

Features:

- **Style:** Timeless exterior styling begins with a covered front porch and beautiful windows, including a bright bay.

- **Entry:** Double windows in the closed front entrance infuse this space with cheerful natural light.

- **Kitchen:** A circular lunch counter rounds off this U-shaped kitchen, which has a nearby laundry and half bath.

- **Bathroom:** This upstairs full bath features a separate shower and tub for bathing in beauty and luxurious comfort.

Copyright by designer/architect.

Main Level Floor Plan

Upper Level Floor Plan

Plan #281021

Dimensions: 46' W x 60'6" D

Levels: 1

Heated Square Footage: 1,546

Bedrooms: 3

Bathrooms: 2

Foundation: Basement

Materials List Available: Yes

Price Category: C

Images provided by designer/architect.

CAD FILE AVAILABLE

Copyright by designer/architect.

Rear View

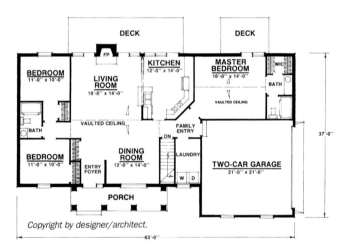

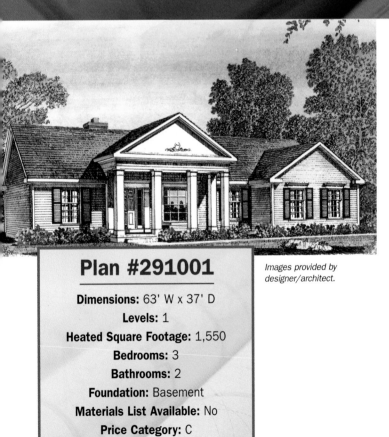

Plan #291001

Images provided by designer/architect.

Dimensions: 63' W x 37' D

Levels: 1

Heated Square Footage: 1,550

Bedrooms: 3

Bathrooms: 2

Foundation: Basement

Materials List Available: No

Price Category: C

Copyright by designer/architect.

Rear View

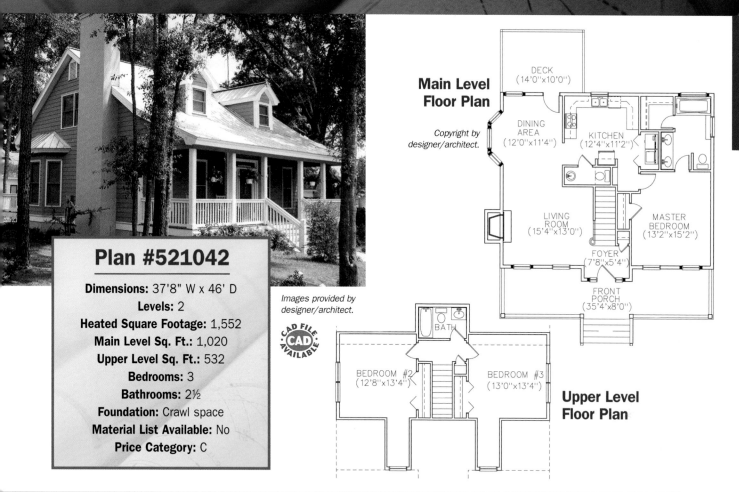

Main Level Floor Plan

Copyright by designer/architect.

DECK (14'0"x10'0")

DINING AREA (12'0"x11'4")

KITCHEN (12'4"x11'2")

LIVING ROOM (15'4"x13'0")

MASTER BEDROOM (13'2"x15'2")

FOYER (7'8"x5'4")

FRONT PORCH (35'4"x8'0")

Images provided by designer/architect.

CAD FILE AVAILABLE

BATH

BEDROOM #2 (12'8"x13'4")

BEDROOM #3 (13'0"x13'4")

Upper Level Floor Plan

Plan #521042

Dimensions: 37'8" W x 46' D
Levels: 2
Heated Square Footage: 1,552
Main Level Sq. Ft.: 1,020
Upper Level Sq. Ft.: 532
Bedrooms: 3
Bathrooms: 2½
Foundation: Crawl space
Material List Available: No
Price Category: C

Plan #251007

Dimensions: 41' W x 35' D
Levels: 2
Heated Square Footage: 1,597
Main Level Sq. Ft.: 982
Upper Level Sq. Ft.: 615
Bedrooms: 4
Bathrooms: 2½
Foundation: Basement
Materials List Available: Yes
Price Category: C

Images provided by designer/architect.

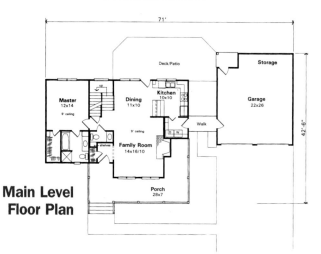

Upper Level Floor Plan

Copyright by designer/architect.

down

Br.#4 12x10

Br.#3 10x11/8

Desk

Br.#2 10/8x11/8

roof

71'

Deck/Patio

Storage

Master 12x14 9' ceiling

Dining 11x10

Kitchen 10x10

Garage 22x26

Walk

9' ceiling

D W

shelves

Family Room 14x16/10

42'-6"

Porch 28x7

Main Level Floor Plan

Copyright by designer/architect.

DECK (17'0"x6'0")

LIVING ROOM 16'4"x21'4")

DINING AREA

KITCHEN (16'4"x10'6")

FOYER

FRONT PORCH (8'0"x19'8")

SCREENED PORCH (21'0"x11'4")

MASTER BEDROOM (15'4"x12'0")

BEDROOM #2 (12'8"x12'0")

BEDROOM #3 (10'8"x13'0")

Plan #521040

Dimensions: 42'2" W x 57' D
Levels: 1
Heated Square Footage: 1,555
Bedrooms: 3
Bathrooms: 2½
Foundation: Slab
Material List Available: No
Price Category: C

CAD FILE AVAILABLE CAD

Images provided by designer/architect.

This home, as shown in the photographs, may differ from the actual blueprints. For more detailed information, please check the floor plans carefully.

Front View

Rear View

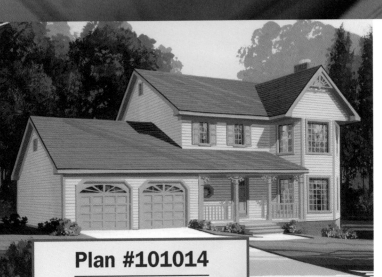

Plan #101014

Dimensions: 52' W x 28' D
Levels: 2
Heated Square Footage: 1,598
Main Level Sq. Ft.: 812
Upper Level Sq. Ft.: 786
Bedrooms: 3
Bathrooms: 2½
Foundation: Crawl space, slab
Materials List Available: No
Price Category: D

Images provided by designer/architect.

Main Level Floor Plan

DECK

STORAGE

KITCHEN 10 x 12

BREAKFAST 9 x 10

DINING 12 x 11

FAMILY ROOM 14 x 16

W D

UP

GARAGE 20 x 21

28

52

Upper Level Floor Plan

Copyright by designer/architect.

BEDROOM 2 12 x 11

BEDROOM 3 11 x 10

DN

MASTER BEDROOM 14 x 15

VAULT

Main Level Floor Plan

SCREENED PORCH (10'0"x10'0")
MASTER BEDROOM (16'4"x12'0")
DINING AREA (10'0"x14'8")
KITCHEN (12'8"x9'0")
LAUNDRY
LIVING ROOM (18'0"x13'8")
FRONT WRAP AROUND PORCH

Images provided by designer/architect.

Upper Level Floor Plan

Copyright by designer/architect.

BEDROOM #2 (11'4"x10'0")
BEDROOM #3 (11'8"x10'0")

Plan #521036

Dimensions: 36' W x 43'8" D
Levels: 2
Heated Square Footage: 1,578
Main Level Sq. Ft.: 1,080
Upper Level Sq. Ft.: 498
Bedrooms: 3
Bathrooms: 2½
Foundation: Crawl space
Material List Available: No
Price Category: C

CAD FILE AVAILABLE

Plan #211030

Dimensions: 75' W x 37' D
Levels: 1
Heated Square Footage: 1,600
Bedrooms: 3
Bathrooms: 2
Foundation: Slab
Materials List Available: Yes
Price Category: D

Images provided by designer/architect.

SMARTtip

Brackets in Window Treatments

Although it is rarely noticed, a bracket plays an important role in supporting rods and poles. If a treatment rubs against a window frame, an extension bracket solves the problem. It projects from the wall at an adjustable length, providing enough clearance. A hold-down bracket anchors a cellular shade or a blind to the bottom of a door, preventing the treatment from moving when the door is opened or closed.

Copyright by designer/architect.

br 2 12 x 12
living 18 x 18
mbr 14 x 12
sitting
sto 11 x 9
br 3 12 x 12
dining 12 x 11
kit 12x10
sew util 9x8
garage 22 x 22
entry
porch 42 x 7
work bench

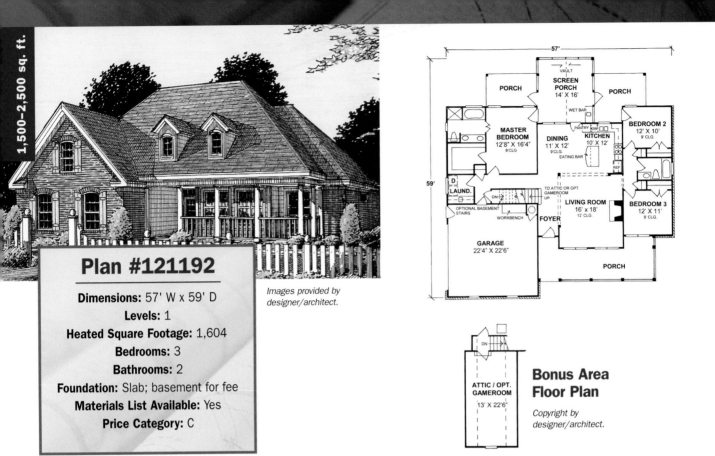

PORCH

SCREEN PORCH 14' X 16'

PORCH

VAULT

WET BAR

MASTER BEDROOM 12'8" X 16'4" 9'CLG.

DINING 11' X 12' 9'CLG.

PANTRY

KITCHEN 10' X 12'

EATING BAR

BEDROOM 2 12' X 10' 9' CLG.

REF

57'

59'

D

LAUND.

DN

OPTIONAL BASEMENT STAIRS

WORKBENCH

TO ATTIC OR OPT. GAMEROOM UP

LIVING ROOM 16' x 18' 12' CLG.

FOYER

BEDROOM 3 12' X 11' 9' CLG.

GARAGE 22'4" X 22'6"

PORCH

Images provided by designer/architect.

DN

ATTIC / OPT. GAMEROOM 13' X 22'6"

Bonus Area Floor Plan

Copyright by designer/architect.

Plan #121192

Dimensions: 57' W x 59' D

Levels: 1

Heated Square Footage: 1,604

Bedrooms: 3

Bathrooms: 2

Foundation: Slab; basement for fee

Materials List Available: Yes

Price Category: C

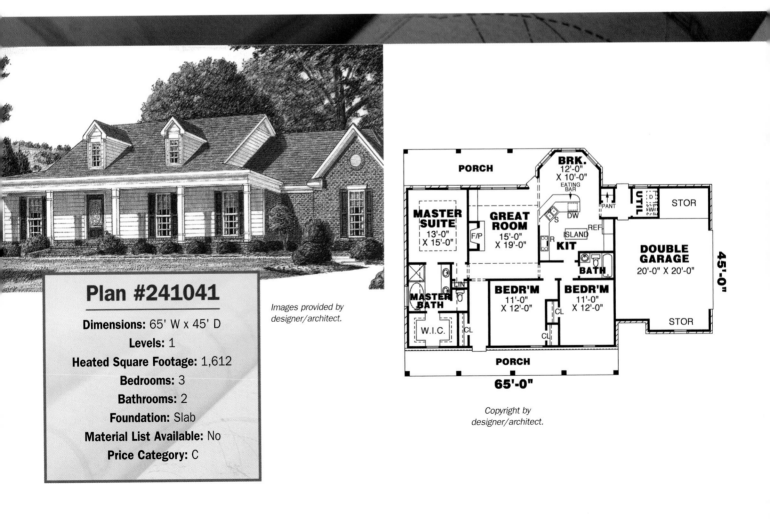

Images provided by designer/architect.

PORCH

BRK. 12'-0" X 10'-0"

EATING BAR

UTIL

STOR

MASTER SUITE 13'-0" X 15'-0"

F/P

GREAT ROOM 15'-0" X 19'-0"

KIT

ISLAND

S

DW

R

REF

PANT

BATH

DOUBLE GARAGE 20'-0" X 20'-0"

45'-0"

MASTER BATH

LIN

BEDR'M 11'-0" X 12'-0"

CL

BEDR'M 11'-0" X 12'-0"

CL

STOR

W.I.C.

CL

CL

PORCH

65'-0"

Copyright by designer/architect.

Plan #241041

Dimensions: 65' W x 45' D

Levels: 1

Heated Square Footage: 1,612

Bedrooms: 3

Bathrooms: 2

Foundation: Slab

Material List Available: No

Price Category: C

Main Floor Plan

SCREENED PORCH
14'-0" X 10'-0"

KITCHEN
12'-9" X 14'-1"

DINING ROOM
13'-7" X 12'-0"

COVERED PATIO

HALF BATH

BUILT-IN BOOKCASE

PREFAB GAS LOG FIREPLACE

FAMILY ROOM
13'-7" X 16'-9"

GARAGE
20'-3" X 21'-0"

PORCH

35'-0"

44'-4"

BEDROOM 3
10'-3" X 10'-1"

BEDROOM 2
10'-9" X 10'-1"

CLOSET

BATH 1

CLOSET

LINENS

BATH 2

WOOD HANDRAIL

DOWN 16 RISERS

WASH DRY

BEDROOM 1
13'-7" X 13'-7"

UNFINISHED REC. ROOM
11'-10" X 12'-0"

Upper Level Floor Plan

Copyright by designer/architect.

Plan #341057

Dimensions: 35' W x 44'4" D

Levels: 2

Heated Square Footage: 1,642

Main Level Sq. Ft.: 762

Upper Level Sq. Ft.: 880

Bedrooms: 3

Bathrooms: 2½

Foundation: Crawl space; slab or basement for fee

Materials List Available: Yes

Price Category: C

Images provided by designer/architect.

CAD FILE AVAILABLE
CAD

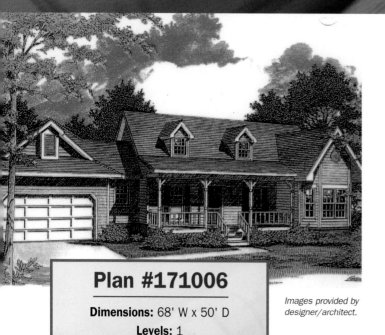

MASTER SUITE
15 × 16

BATH
10 × 10

CLOSET

PORCH
42 × 6

GARAGE
21 × 22

1/2 BATH

DINING
10 × 11

GREAT RM
16 × 24

BEDRM
11 × 12

UTILITY

KITCHEN
11 × 14

BATH

BEDRM
12 × 12

PORCH
28 × 6

68'

50'

Copyright by designer/architect.

Plan #171006

Dimensions: 68' W x 50' D

Levels: 1

Heated Square Footage: 1,648

Bedrooms: 3

Bathrooms: 2½

Foundation: Crawl space, slab

Materials List Available: Yes

Price Category: C

Images provided by designer/architect.

SMARTtip

Window Shades

While decorative hems add interest to roller shades, they also increase the cost. If you're handy with a glue gun, choose one of the trims available at fabric and craft stores, and consider attaching it yourself. Give your shades fancy pulls for an inexpensive dash of pizzazz.

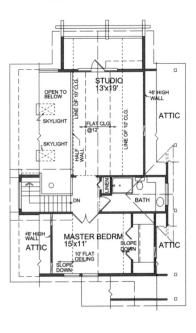

Images provided by designer/architect.

Plan #491008

Dimensions: 36' W x 50'6" D

Levels: 2

Heated Square Footage: 1,644

Main Level Sq. Ft.: 955

Upper Level Sq. Ft.: 689

Bedrooms: 2

Bathrooms: 2

Foundation: Crawl space

Materials List Available: Yes

Price Category: C

This sweet cabin-style home has everything you want and need to relax in a cozy retreat.

Features:

- **Outdoor Space:** The wraparound porch welcomes neighbors for a spell of calm conversation or quiet stargazing.

- **Great Room:** Warmed by a romantic wood stove and with half of the room sunlit and spanning both stories, this great room is sure to enchant you and your guests.

- **Kitchen:** An efficient space, this kitchen has enough workspace and storage to keep even the expert chef happy. Warm, inviting scents will drift over the breakfast bar and fill the home.

- **Second Floor:** This is a space that is entirely your own. The master bedroom sits away from the din of daily life so you have peace and quiet, day or night. A full bathroom and a studio, to be molded to your needs, means having everything you need within arm's reach.

CAD FILE AVAILABLE

Main Level Floor Plan

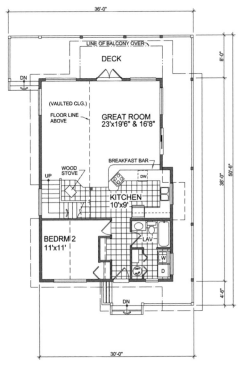

Upper Level Floor Plan

Copyright by designer/architect.

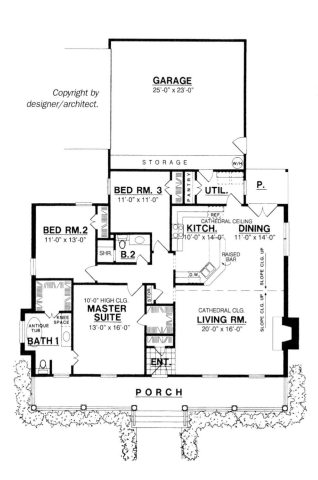

Plan #371053

Dimensions: 51'2" W x 66'7" D

Levels: 1

Heated Square Footage: 1,654

Bedrooms: 3

Bathrooms: 2

Foundation: Slab

Materials List Available: No

Price Category: C

Images provided by designer/architect.

A cozy country porch and large inviting windows are the perfect way to say, "I'm home." This country charmer has everything you need.

Features:

- Kitchen: This large kitchen boasts a cathedral ceiling and a raised bar.

- Dining Room: This room has a cathedral ceiling and is open to the living room and kitchen.

- Living Room: The fireplace and cathedral ceiling give this room an inviting feeling.

- Master Suite: This private retreat features two walk-in closets. The old-fashioned bath with an antique tub is perfect for relaxing.

Copyright by designer/architect.

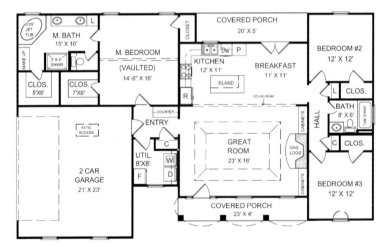

Images provided by designer/architect.

Plan #351033

Dimensions: 64' W x 39' D

Levels: 1

Heated Square Footage: 1,654

Bedrooms: 3

Bathrooms: 2

Foundation: Crawl space, slab, or basement

Materials List Available: Yes

Price Category: E

This gorgeous three-bedroom brick home would be the perfect place to raise your family.

Features:

- Great Room: This terrific room has a gas fireplace with built-in cabinets on either side.

- Kitchen: This island kitchen with breakfast area is open to the great room.

- Master Suite: This private room features a vaulted ceiling and a large walk-in closet. The bath area has a walk-in closet, jetted tub, and double vanities.

- Bedrooms: The two additional bedrooms share a bathroom located in the hall.

Copyright by designer/architect.

Plan #171023

Dimensions: 74' W x 41' D
Levels: 1
Heated Square Footage: 1,684
Bedrooms: 3
Bathrooms: 2
Foundation: Crawl space or slab
Materials List Available: Yes
Price Category: C

Images provided by designer/architect.

This beautifully designed home will be a perfect place to raise your family.

Features:

- **Great Room:** This large gathering area features a corner fireplace and an 11-ft.-high ceiling. Its direct access to the rear porch enables the room to expand on nice summer days.

- **Kitchen:** Featuring plenty of workspace and storage, this kitchen is adjacent to the dining room, simplyfying mealtime transitions.

- **Master Suite:** This spacious area features a walk-in closet to simplify the process of getting ready in the morning. The master bath features a stall shower and a garden tub.

- **Secondary Bedrooms:** Both of the two additional bedrooms have ample closet space and access to a full bathroom.

**Bonus Area
Floor Plan**

Copyright by designer/architect.

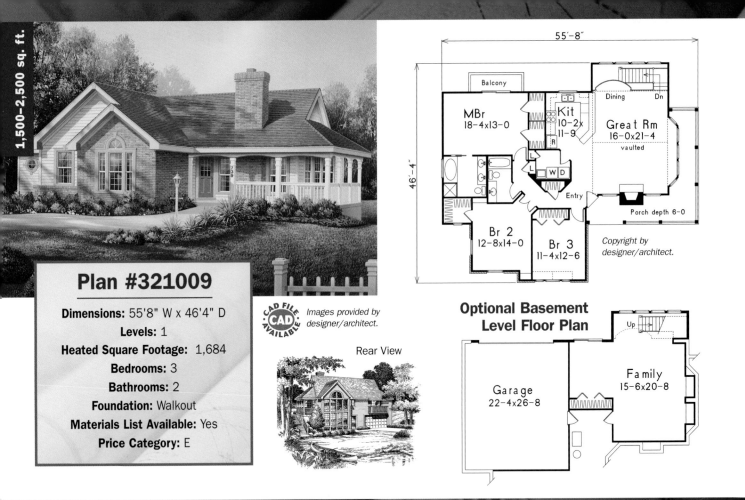

1,500-2,500 sq. ft.

Plan #321009

Dimensions: 55'8" W x 46'4" D

Levels: 1

Heated Square Footage: 1,684

Bedrooms: 3

Bathrooms: 2

Foundation: Walkout

Materials List Available: Yes

Price Category: E

CAD FILE AVAILABLE

Images provided by designer/architect.

Rear View

Optional Basement Level Floor Plan

Plan #161024

Dimensions: 54'4" W x 26'8" D

Levels: 2

Heated Square Footage: 1,698

Main Level Sq. Ft.: 868

Upper Level Sq. Ft.: 830

Bonus Space Sq. Ft.: 269

Bedrooms: 3

Bathrooms: 2½

Foundation: Basement

Materials List Available: No

Price Category: C

Images provided by designer/architect.

This home, as shown in the photograph, may differ from the actual blueprints. For more detailed information, please check the floor plans carefully.

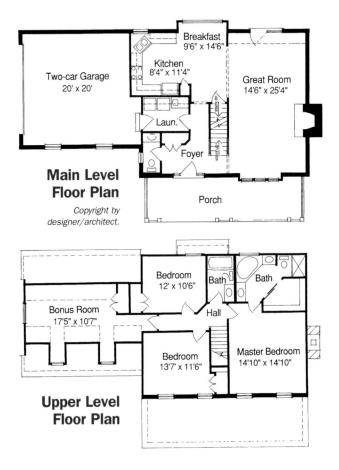

Main Level Floor Plan

Copyright by designer/architect.

Upper Level Floor Plan

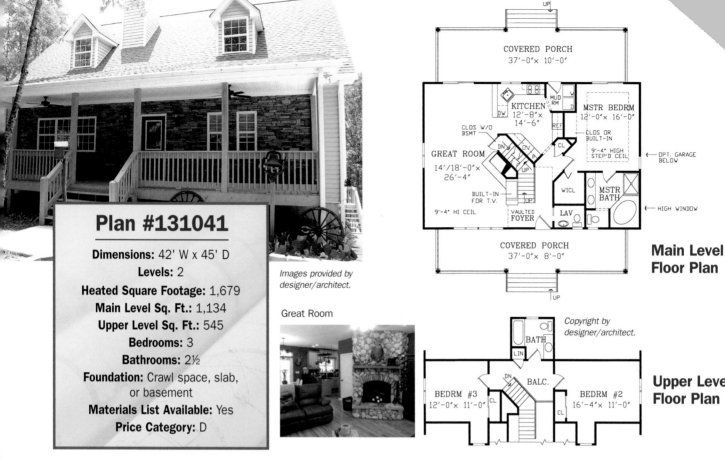

COVERED PORCH
37'-0" x 10'-0"

KITCHEN
12'-8" x 14'-6"

MUD RM

MSTR BEDRM
12'-0" x 16'-0"

CLOS W/O BSMT

CLOS OR BUILT-IN

GREAT ROOM
14'/18'-0" x 26'-4"

9'-4" HIGH STEP'D CEIL

9'-4" HI CEIL

BUILT-IN FOR T.V.

WICL

MSTR BATH

VAULTED FOYER

LAV

← OPT. GARAGE BELOW

← HIGH WINDOW

COVERED PORCH
37'-0" x 8'-0"

Main Level Floor Plan

Plan #131041

Dimensions: 42' W x 45' D

Levels: 2

Heated Square Footage: 1,679

Main Level Sq. Ft.: 1,134

Upper Level Sq. Ft.: 545

Bedrooms: 3

Bathrooms: 2½

Foundation: Crawl space, slab, or basement

Materials List Available: Yes

Price Category: D

Images provided by designer/architect.

Great Room

Copyright by designer/architect.

BATH

LIN

BEDRM #3
12'-0" x 11'-0"

DN

BALC.

BEDRM #2
16'-4" x 11'-0"

Upper Level Floor Plan

NOOK
8/8 X 8/10

DINING
9/10 X 10/4

VAULTED MASTER
16/0 X 11/10

TWO STORY GREAT RM.
15/10 X 19/8

SPA

LINEN

Main Level Floor Plan

GARAGE
19/4 X 21/8

◄ 40' ►

53'

Plan #441017

Dimensions: 40' W x 53' D

Levels: 1.5

Heated Square Footage: 1,707

Main Level Sq. Ft.: 1,230

Upper Level Sq. Ft.: 477

Bedrooms: 3

Bathrooms: 2½

Foundation: Crawl space; slab or basement available for fee

Materials List Available: Yes

Price Category: C

Images provided by designer/architect.

CAD FILE AVAILABLE

BR. 3
12/6 X 12/2

BR. 2
10/9 X 12/2

OPEN TO GREAT RM. BELOW

DN

BONUS RM.
13/6 X 12/6

ATTIC STORAGE

Upper Level Floor Plan

Copyright by designer/architect.

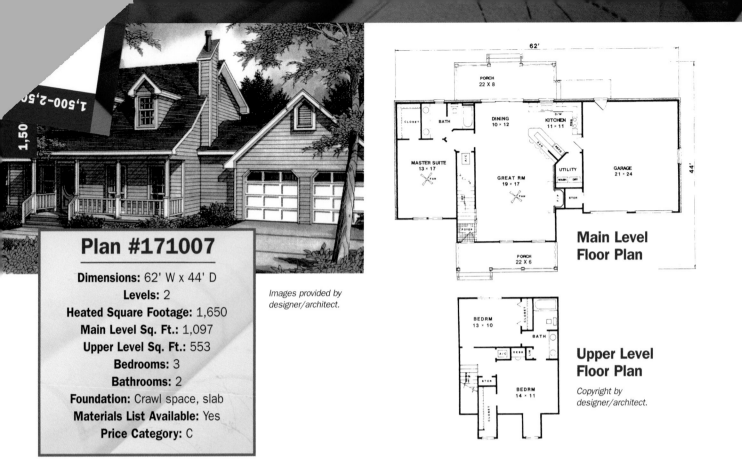

Plan #171007

Dimensions: 62' W x 44' D
Levels: 2
Heated Square Footage: 1,650
Main Level Sq. Ft.: 1,097
Upper Level Sq. Ft.: 553
Bedrooms: 3
Bathrooms: 2
Foundation: Crawl space, slab
Materials List Available: Yes
Price Category: C

Images provided by designer/architect.

Main Level Floor Plan

Upper Level Floor Plan

Copyright by designer/architect.

Plan #371032

Dimensions: 55'6" W x 46' D
Levels: 1
Heated Square Footage: 1,659
Bedrooms: 3
Bathrooms: 2
Foundation: Slab
Materials List Available: No
Price Category: C

Images provided by designer/architect.

CAD FILE AVAILABLE

Bonus Area Floor Plan

Copyright by designer/architect.

Upper Level Floor Plan

BEDROOM #2 (10'0"x11'8")
BEDROOM #4 (11'2"x10'0")
BEDROOM #3 (10'0"x11'6")

Main Level Floor Plan

Copyright by designer/architect.

MASTER BEDROOM (14'4"x11'8") +BAY
COVERED PORCH (10'8"X 12'0")
LAUNDRY ROOM
DINING AREA (13'4"x10'0")
LIVING ROOM (16'1"x16'10")
KITCHEN (9'6"x10'6")
ENTRY
FRONT PORCH (23'8"X8'0")

Plan #521030

Dimensions: 41'8" W x 41' D
Levels: 2
Heated Square Footage: 1,660
Main Level Sq. Ft.: 1,034
Upper Level Sq. Ft.: 626
Bedrooms: 4
Bathrooms: 2½
Foundation: Crawl space
Material List Available: No
Price Category: C

Images provided by designer/architect.

CAD FILE AVAILABLE

Plan #121482

Dimensions: 54' W x 37' D
Levels: 1.5
Heated Square Footage: 1,671
Main Level Sq. Ft.: 1,087
Upper Level Sq. Ft.: 584
Bedrooms: 3
Bathrooms: 2½
Foundation: Slab
Materials List Available: Yes
Price Category: C

Images provided by designer/architect.

CAD FILE AVAILABLE

54'

GARAGE 20'8" X 21'4"
KITCHEN 11' X 9' 9' CLG.
DINING ROOM 10'8" X 11 9' CLG.
LAUN. W D
EATING BAR
ISLAND
REF
OPTIONAL BASEMENT STAIRS
LIVING ROOM 16' X 20' 18' CLG.
DN
RAIL
UP
MASTER BEDROOM 12'4" X 15' 9' CLG.
SLOPE 16' TO 18'
PORCH 11' CLG.

37'

Main Level Floor Plan

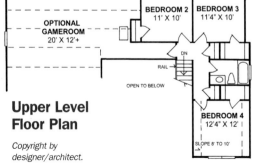

Upper Level Floor Plan

OPTIONAL GAMEROOM 20' X 12'+
BEDROOM 2 11' X 10'
BEDROOM 3 11'4" X 10'
DN
RAIL
OPEN TO BELOW
BEDROOM 4 12'4" X 12'
SLOPE 8' TO 10'

Copyright by designer/architect.

Plan #311051

Dimensions: 56'6" W x 68'6" D

Levels: 1

Heated Square Footage: 1,680

Bedrooms: 3

Bathrooms: 2

Foundation: Crawl space, slab, or basement

Material List Available: Yes

Price Category: C

Images provided by designer/architect.

Basement Stair Location

Copyright by designer/architect.

Greatroom 16-8x17-6
16-3 ceiling

Storage 21-4x7-4

Carport 22-0x22-0

Patio 18-0x12-0

68-6

Bedroom 11-6x11-6 9' ceiling

Pantry

Dining 12-0x11-6 9' ceiling

Kitchen 9-10x11-6

M.Bath

Bedroom 11-6x13-6 9' ceiling

Bath

Greatroom 21-10x17-6 16-3 ceiling

Owner's Bedroom 15-6x17-6 9' ceiling

Porch 39-4x8-6

56-6

Plan #631065

Dimensions: 78'8" W x 39'8" D

Levels: 1

Heated Square Footage: 1,682

Bedrooms: 3

Bathrooms: 2

Foundation: Basement

Materials List Available: Yes

Price Category: C

Images provided by designer/architect.

CAD FILE AVAILABLE

78'-8"

MBr 13-0x15-0 Vaulted Clg

Dining 10-11x11-0

Klt. 10-6x 11-0

Garage 21-4x25-4

39'-8"

Br 2 10-0x12-3

Br 3 10-0x12-3

Family 21-9x15-8

Covered Porch 24-0x8-0

Copyright by designer/architect.

Rear View

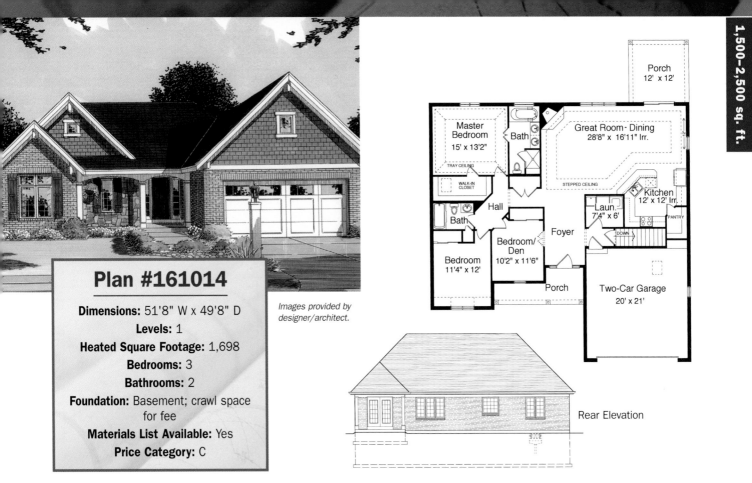

Images provided by designer/architect.

Rear Elevation

Plan #161014

Dimensions: 51'8" W x 49'8" D

Levels: 1

Heated Square Footage: 1,698

Bedrooms: 3

Bathrooms: 2

Foundation: Basement; crawl space for fee

Materials List Available: Yes

Price Category: C

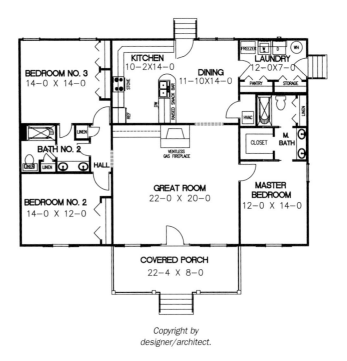

Images provided by designer/architect.

Copyright by designer/architect.

Plan #191024

Dimensions: 50' W x 42' D

Levels: 1

Heated Square Footage: 1,700

Bedrooms: 3

Bathrooms: 2

Foundation: Crawl space or basement

Materials List Available: No

Price Category: C

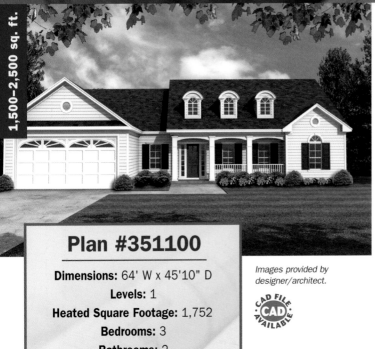

1,500–2,500 sq. ft.

Plan #351100

Dimensions: 64' W x 45'10" D

Levels: 1

Heated Square Footage: 1,752

Bedrooms: 3

Bathrooms: 2

Foundation: Crawl space or slab

Materials List Available: Yes

Price Category: E

Images provided by designer/architect.

CAD FILE CAD AVAILABLE

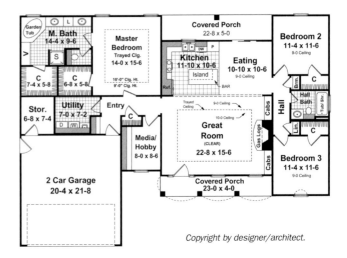

Copyright by designer/architect.

Plan #121006

Dimensions: 46' W x 58' D

Levels: 1

Heated Square Footage: 1,762

Bedrooms: 3

Bathrooms: 2

Foundation: Slab;
crawl space or basement for fee

Materials List Available: Yes

Price Category: C

Images provided by designer/architect.

CAD FILE CAD AVAILABLE

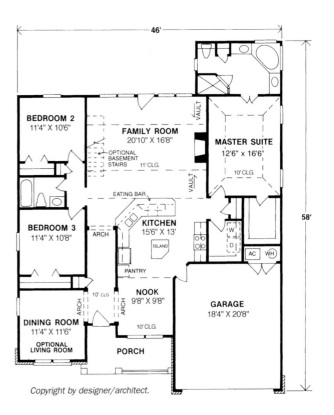

Copyright by designer/architect.

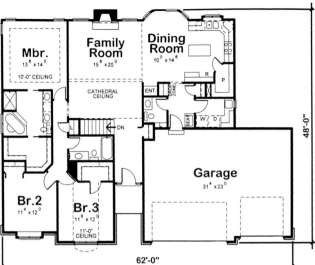

Plan #121331

Dimensions: 62' W x 48' D

Levels: 1

Heated Square Footage: 1,763

Bedrooms: 3

Bathrooms: 2½

Foundation: Basement

Materials List Available: Yes

Price Category: G

Images provided by designer/architect.

CAD FILE AVAILABLE

Copyright by designer/architect.

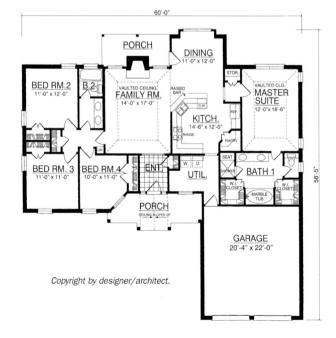

Plan #371036

Dimensions: 60' W x 58'5" D

Levels: 1

Heated Square Footage: 1,764

Bedrooms: 4

Bathrooms: 2

Foundation: Slab

Materials List Available: No

Price Category: C

Images provided by designer/architect.

CAD FILE AVAILABLE

Copyright by designer/architect.

Plan #131002

Dimensions: 70'1" W x 60'7" D
Levels: 1
Heated Square Footage: 1,709
Bedrooms: 3
Bathrooms: 2½
Foundation: Slab or basement
Materials List Available: Yes
Price Category: D

CAD FILE AVAILABLE

Images provided by designer/architect.

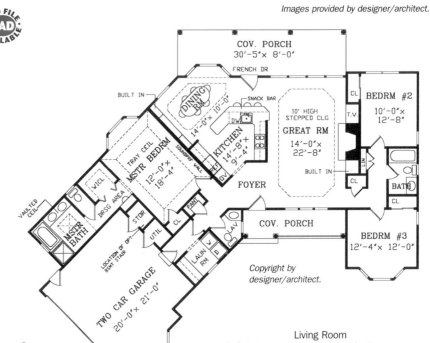

COV. PORCH 30'-5" x 8'-0"

FRENCH DR

BUILT IN

DINING RM 14'-0" x 10'-0"

SNACK BAR

KITCHEN 14'-8" x 9'-4"

TRAY CEIL

MSTR BEDRM 12'-0" x 18'-4"

10' HIGH STEPPED CLG

GREAT RM 14'-0" x 22'-8"

BEDRM #2 10'-0" x 12'-8"

T.V.

CL

BUILT IN

LIN

FOYER

VAULTED CEIL

WICL

DR.SG AREA

BATH

CL

CL

MSTR BATH

STOR

PANT

CL

COV. PORCH

BEDRM #3 12'-4" x 12'-0"

LOCATION OF OPT. BSMT STAIR

UTIL

LAUN RM

LAV

Copyright by designer/architect.

TWO CAR GARAGE 20'-0" x 21'-0"

Rear View

You'll love the way this angled ranch brings out the best in a corner lot or on a slope.

Features:

- Ceiling Height: 8 ft.

- Front Porch: Hang baskets of plants from the roof of this porch, which is just the right size for a couple of rockers and a side table.

- Dining Room: Well-placed windows flood this room with sunlight during the day and a built-in cabinet gives ample storage space for all your china, linens, and collectables.

- Foyer: Open to the great room, the foyer gives a lovely area to greet your visitors.

- Great Room: A built-in media center surrounds the fireplace where friends and family are sure to gather.

- Master Suite: You'll love the privacy of this somewhat isolated but easily accessed room. Decorate to show off the large bay window and tray ceiling, and enjoy the luxury of a separate toilet room.

Living Room

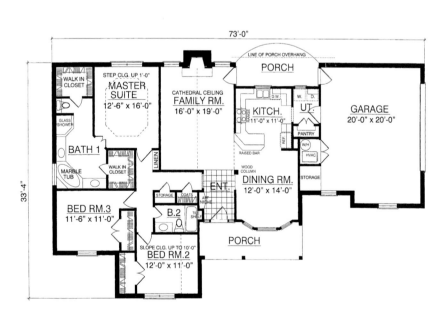

Images provided by designer/architect.

Plan #371033

Dimensions: 73' W x 33' 4" D

Levels: 1

Heated Square Footage: 1,724

Bedrooms: 3

Bathrooms: 2

Foundation: Crawl space or slab

Materials List Available: No

Price Category: C

This beautiful brick-and-stone country home will be the envy of the neighborhood.

Features:

- Front Porch: This charming yet functional porch welcomes you home.

- Family Room: This large room, with its cathedral ceiling and cozy fireplace, is ideal for entertaining.

- Kitchen: This gourmet kitchen has all the necessities you will ever need, including a raised bar area.

- Master Suite: This cozy area features a stepped ceiling. The luxurious bath boasts a marble tub and two walk-in closets.

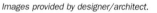

Copyright by designer/architect.

Images provided by designer/architect.

Plan #441004

Dimensions: 55' W x 48' D

Levels: 1

Heated Square Footage: 1,728

Bedrooms: 2

Bathrooms: 2

Foundation: Crawl space; slab or basement available for fee

Materials List Available: No

Price Category: C

Empty nesters and first-time homeowners will adore the comfort within this charming home. Rooms benefit from the many windows, which welcome light into the home.

Features:

- **Great Room:** This vaulted room is equipped with a media center and fireplace. Windows span across the back of the room and the adjoining dining room, extending the perceived area and offering access to the covered patio.

- **Kitchen:** Taking advantage of corner space, this kitchen provides ample cabinets and countertops to store goods and prepare meals. Every chef will appreciate the extra space afforded by the pantry.

- **Master Suite:** This luxurious escape has a large sleeping area with views of the backyard. The master bath features a spa tub, dual vanities, and a walk-in closet.

- **Garage:** This front-loading two-car garage has a shop area located in the rear.

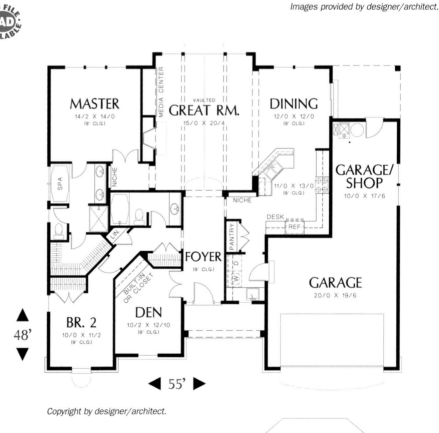

Copyright by designer/architect.

Rear Elevation

Plan #181074

Dimensions: 42' W x 40' D

Levels: 2

Heated Square Footage: 1,760

Main Level Sq. Ft.: 880

Upper Level Sq. Ft.: 880

Bedrooms: 3

Full Baths: 2½

Foundation: Basement; crawl space, slab and walk out for fee

Materials List Available: Yes

Price Category: D

A front porch and a standing-seam metal roof add to the country charm of this home.

CAD FILE AVAILABLE

Images provided by designer/architect.

Features:

- Great Room: Imagine coming home from a hard day of working or chauffeuring the kids and being welcomed by comfy couch and warm fire. This is the perfect room to help you unwind.

- Kitchen: From culinary expert to family cook, everyone will find this kitchen's workspaces and storage just what they need to create special meals. A sun-drenched family area shares the space and opens onto the future patio.

- Second Floor: For a restful atmosphere, the bedrooms are separated from the hum of daily life. The spacious master bedroom receives light from the bay windows. The area features a walk-in closet and a private bathroom. The two additional bedrooms share access to a Jack-and-Jill bathroom.

- Garage: A single-car garage adds convenience to this plan. It can be used as additional storage space.

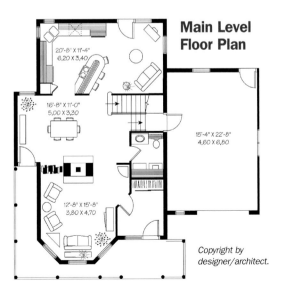

Main Level Floor Plan

20'-8" X 11'-4"
6,20 X 3,40

16'-8" X 11'-0"
5,00 X 3,30

15'-4" X 22'-8"
4,60 X 6,80

12'-8" X 15'-8"
3,80 X 4,70

Copyright by designer/architect.

Upper Level Floor Plan

13'-4" X 9'-0"
4,00 X 2,70

11'-0" X 11'-0"
3,30 X 3,30

15'-4" X 15'-4"
4,60 X 4,60

12'-8" X 15'-8"
3,80 X 4,70

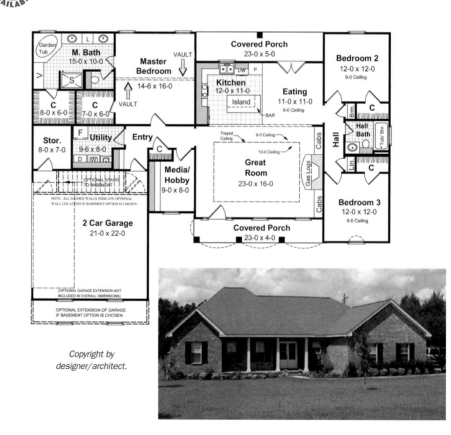

Images provided by designer/architect.

Plan #351003

Dimensions: 64' W x 45'10" D

Levels: 1

Heated Square Footage: 1,751

Bedrooms: 3

Bathrooms: 2

Foundation: Crawl space, slab, or basement

Materials List Available: Yes

Price Category: D

CAD FILE AVAILABLE

This beautiful three-bedroom brick house with a covered porch is perfect for today's family.

Features:

- Great Room: This gathering room features a tray ceiling, a gas fireplace, and built-in cabinets.

- Kitchen: This island kitchen with a raised bar is open to the great room and eating area.

- Master Suite: This primary bedroom features a vaulted ceiling and large walk-in closet. The private bath boasts a double vanity, corner tub, and walk-in closet.

- Bedrooms: Two additional bedrooms are located on the other side of the home from the master suite and share a common bathroom.

Copyright by designer/architect.

Dining Room

Kitchen

Great Room

Master Bathroom

Rear View

Plan #111046

Dimensions: 37' W x 57' D
Levels: 2
Heated Square Footage: 1,768
Main Level Sq. Ft.: 1,247
Upper Level Sq. Ft.: 521
Bedrooms: 3
Bathrooms: 2½
Foundation: Crawl space
Materials List Available: No
Price Category: D

Images provided by designer/architect.

Main Level Floor Plan

Wood Deck 12'6"x 8'
Covered Porch 12'2"x 10'
Ext. Storage
Master Bath
WIC
Breakfast 11'10"x 9'6'
Utility
Master Bedroom 12'6"x 15'6'
1/2 Ba.
Kitchen 10'x 11'6'
Living 14'4"x 17'6'
Dining 13'x 12'
Porch 32'x 5'

Upper Level Floor Plan

Bedroom 12'6"x 14'
Bedroom 10'6"x 13'2'
Balcony
Ba.

Copyright by designer/architect.

Plan #171009

Dimensions: 68' W x 50' D
Levels: 1
Heated Square Footage: 1,771
Bedrooms: 3
Bathrooms: 2
Foundation: Crawl space, slab
Materials List Available: Yes
Price Category: C

Images provided by designer/architect.

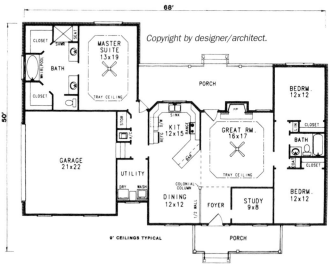

Copyright by designer/architect.

68'
50'
CLOSET
SEAT
SHWR
MASTER SUITE 13 x 19
TRAY CEILING
PORCH
BEDRM. 12 x 12
BATH
WHIRLPOOL
CLOSET
GARAGE 21x22
STOR
SINK
D/W
REFG
KIT 12 x15
RANGE
BAR
GREAT RM. 16 x17
TRAY CEILING
CLOSET
BATH
CLOSET
BEDRM. 12 x 12
UTILITY
DRY
WASH
COLONIAL COLUMN
DINING 12 x 12
FOYER
STUDY 9 x8
PORCH
9' CEILINGS TYPICAL

SMARTtip

Deck Awnings

Awnings come in bright colors. As light filters through, it will cast a hue to anything under the deck. Warm colors, such as red or pink, will create a rosy glow; cool colors, such blues or greens, will enhance the shade.

Images provided by designer/architect.

Copyright by designer/architect.

Rear Elevation

Plan #161164

Dimensions: 65'3" W x 49' D

Levels: 1

Heated Square Footage: 1,776

Bedrooms: 3

Bathrooms: 2

Foundation: Basement or walkout; crawl space or slab for fee

Material List Available: Yes

Price Category: C

CAD FILE AVAILABLE

Main Level Floor Plan

Bonus Room Above Garage

Upper Level Floor Plan

Copyright by designer/architect.

Plan #151016

Dimensions: 60'2" W x 39'10" D

Levels: 1.5

Heated Square Footage: 1,783; 2,107 with bonus

Main Level Sq. Ft.: 1,124

Upper Level Sq. Ft.: 659

Bonus Room Sq. Ft.: 324

Bedrooms: 3

Bathrooms: 2½

Foundation: Crawl space, slab, or basement

CompleteCost List Available: Yes

Price Category: C

Images provided by designer/architect.

CAD FILE AVAILABLE

1,500–2,500 sq. ft.

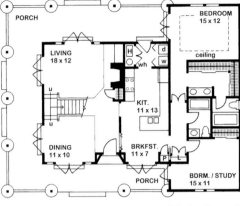

Plan #381063

Dimensions: 52' W x 40' D

Levels: 2

Heated Square Footage: 1,785

Main Level Sq. Ft.: 1,355

Upper Level Sq. Ft.: 430

Bedrooms: 3

Bathrooms: 3

Foundation: Crawl space

Materials List Available: Yes

Price Category: C

Images provided by designer/architect.

PORCH

LIVING
18 x 12

BEDROOM
15 x 12

ceiling

KIT.
11 x 13

DINING
11 x 10

BRKFST.
11 x 7

PORCH

BDRM. / STUDY
15 x 11

Main Level Floor Plan

Upper Level Floor Plan

Copyright by designer/architect.

seat

BR./ DEN
10 x 16

OPEN

BEDROOM
10 x 11

OPEN

OPEN

storage

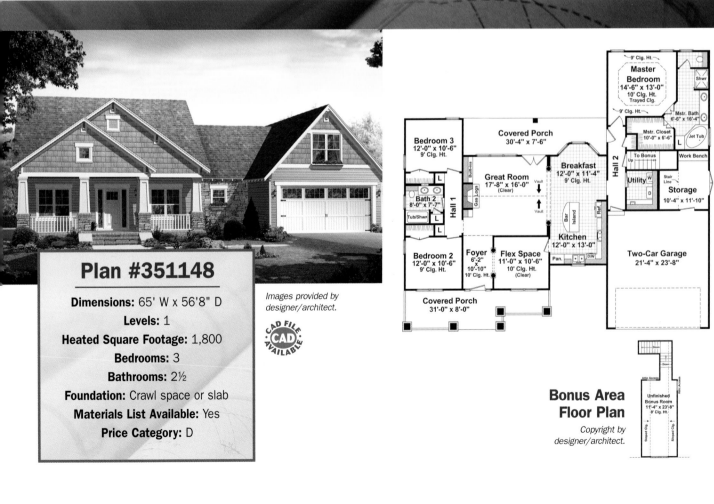

Plan #351148

Dimensions: 65' W x 56'8" D

Levels: 1

Heated Square Footage: 1,800

Bedrooms: 3

Bathrooms: 2½

Foundation: Crawl space or slab

Materials List Available: Yes

Price Category: D

Images provided by designer/architect.

CAD FILE AVAILABLE

Bedroom 3
12'-0" x 10'-6"
9' Clg. Ht.

Covered Porch
30'-4" x 7'-6"

Master Bedroom
14'-6" x 13'-0"
10' Clg. Ht.
Trayed Clg.

Mstr. Bath
6'-6" x 16'-4"

Bath 2
8'-0" x 7'-7"

Great Room
17'-8" x 16'-0"
(Clear)

Breakfast
12'-0" x 11'-4"
9' Clg. Ht.

Mstr. Closet
10'-0" x 6'-6"

Hall 2

To Bonus

Work Bench

Hall 1

Kitchen
12'-0" x 13'-0"

Utility

Storage
10'-4" x 11'-10"

Bedroom 2
12'-0" x 10'-6"
9' Clg. Ht.

Foyer
6'-2" x 10'-0"

Flex Space
11'-0" x 10'-6"
10' Clg. Ht.
(Clear)

Two-Car Garage
21'-4" x 23'-8"

Covered Porch
31'-0" x 8'-0"

Bonus Area Floor Plan

Unfinished Bonus Room
11'-4" x 23'-8"
9' Clg. Ht.

Copyright by designer/architect.

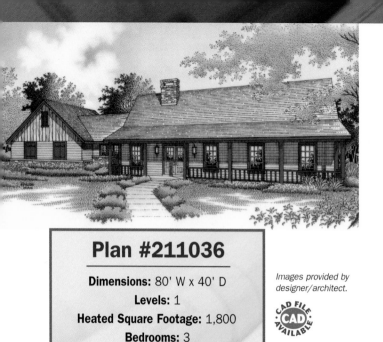

false beams

Copyright by designer/architect.

Rear View

Plan #211036

Dimensions: 80' W x 40' D

Levels: 1

Heated Square Footage: 1,800

Bedrooms: 3

Bathrooms: 2

Foundation: Slab

Materials List Available: Yes

Price Category: D

Images provided by designer/architect.

CAD FILE AVAILABLE

Plan #351040

Dimensions: 63'4" W x 53' D

Levels: 1

Heated Square Footage: 1,800

Bedrooms: 3

Bathrooms: 2½

Foundation: Crawl space, slab or basement

Materials List Available: Yes

Price Category: E

Images provided by designer/architect.

CAD FILE AVAILABLE

Copyright by designer/architect.

Plan #191003

Dimensions: 56' W x 42' D

Levels: 1

Heated Square Footage: 1,785

Bedrooms: 3

Bathrooms: 3

Foundation: Crawl space, slab, or basement

Materials List Available: No

Price Category: C

Images provided by designer/architect.

Enjoy the amenities you'll find in this gracious home, with its traditional Southern appearance.

Features:

- Great Room: This expansive room is so versatile that everyone will gather here. A built-in entertainment area with desk makes a great lounging spot, and the French doors topped by transoms open onto the lovely rear porch.

- Dining Room: An arched entry to this room helps to create the open feeling in this home.

- Kitchen: Another arched entryway leads to this fabulous kitchen, which has been designed with the cook's comfort in mind. It features a downdraft range, many cabinets, a snack bar, and a sunny breakfast area, where the family is sure to gather.

- Laundry: A sink, shower, toilet area, and cabinets galore give total convenience in this room.

- Master Suite: Enjoy the walk-in closet and bath with toilet room, tub, and shower.

Copyright by designer/architect.

56'-0" Width

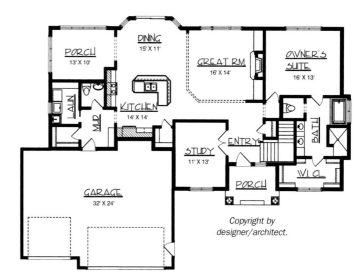

Plan #271077

Dimensions: 69'6" W x 53' D

Levels: 1

Heated Square Footage: 1,786

Bedrooms: 1

Bathrooms: 1½

Foundation: Basement or daylight basement

Materials List Available: No

Price Category: C

CAD FILE AVAILABLE

Images provided by designer/architect.

This wonderful home has an optional finished basement plan to add three more bedrooms—ideal for a growing family.

Features:

• **Great Room:** This large gathering room has a fireplace with built-in cabinets on either side.

• **Kitchen:** This island kitchen, with dinette area, is open to the great room.

• **Master Bedroom:** This luxurious room provides a view of the backyard.

• **Master Bath:** This private bathroom has a walk-in closet and double vanities.

Copyright by designer/architect.

Optional Basement Level Floor Plan

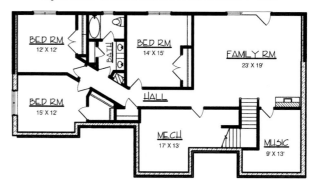

Plan #151196

Dimensions: 89' W x 49'4" D
Levels: 1
Heated Square Footage: 1,800
Bedrooms: 3
Bathrooms: 2
Foundation: Crawl space or slab; basement for fee
CompleteCost List Available: Yes
Price Category: C

Images provided by designer/architect.

This charming home, with its wide front porch, is perfect on a little piece of land or a quiet suburban street.

Features:

- Screened Porch: This screened-in porch creates extra living space where you can enjoy warm summer breezes in a bug-free atmosphere.

- Great Room: Make a "great" first impression by welcoming guests into this spacious, firelight-illuminated great room.

- Kitchen: This efficient area is surrounded on all sides by workspace and storage. A snack bar, adjacent dining room, and attached grilling porch create plenty of mealtime options.

- Master Suite: This master suite creates a stress-free environment with its, large walk-in closet, whirlpool tub, standing shower, and his and her vanities.

Copyright by designer/architect.

Plan #441005

Dimensions: 50' W x 59' D
Levels: 1
Heated Square Footage: 1,800
Bedrooms: 3
Bathrooms: 2
Foundation: Crawl space; slab or basement for fee
Materials List Available: Yes
Price Category: D

Images provided by designer/architect.

This home looks as if it's a quaint little abode—with its board-and-batten siding, cedar shingle detailing, and column-covered porch—but even a quick peek inside will prove that there is much more to this plan than meets the eye.

Features:

- Foyer: This entry area rises to a 9-ft.-high ceiling. On one side is a washer-dryer alcove with a closet across the way; on the other is another large storage area. Just down the hallway is a third closet.

- Kitchen: This kitchen features a center island, built-in desk/work center, and pantry. This area and the dining area also boast 9-ft.-high ceilings and are open to a vaulted great room with corner fireplace.

- Dining Room: Sliding doors in this area lead to a covered side porch, so you can enjoy outside dining.

- Master Suite: This suite has a vaulted ceiling. The master bath is wonderfully appointed with a separate shower, spa tub, and dual sinks.

- Bedrooms: Three bedrooms (or two plus an office) are found on the right side of the plan.

Rear Elevation

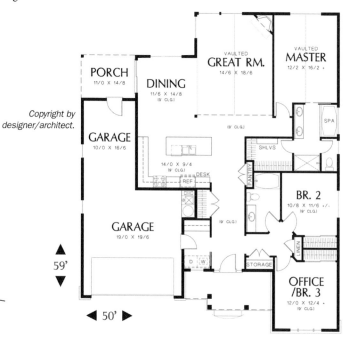

Copyright by designer/architect.

PORCH
11/0 X 14/8

DINING
11/6 X 14/8
(9' CLG.)

VAULTED
GREAT RM.
14/6 X 18/6

VAULTED
MASTER
12/2 X 16/2 +

GARAGE
10/0 X 16/6

SPA

(9' CLG.)

SHLVS

PANTRY

14/0 X 9/4
(9' CLG.)

DESK

REF

BR. 2
10/8 X 11/6 +
(9' CLG.)

GARAGE
19/0 X 19/6

(9' CLG.)

LINEN

59'

D   W

STORAGE

50'

OFFICE
/BR. 3
12/0 X 12/4
(9' CLG.)

Plan #131047

Dimensions: 69'10" W x 51'8" D

Levels: 1

Heated Square Footage: 1,793

Bedrooms: 3

Bathrooms: 2

Foundation: Crawl space, slab, or basement

Materials List Available: Yes

Price Category: D

Images provided by designer/architect.

CAD FILE AVAILABLE

Family Room

This beautiful home will be a welcome addition to any neighborhood.

Features:

- Family Room: Conveniently located at the center of the home, this spacious family room provides a wonderful space to entertain guests or relax with the family.

- Kitchen: This gourmet kitchen provides plenty of cooking and storage space for the home chef. An eating bar is a versatile spot for grabbing a quick lunch, entertaining guests, or an after-school snack.

- Den: This well-situated room can be used in a variety of ways. Depending on your family's needs, it can be an additional bedroom, a home office, or study.

- Master Suite: You'll love this large master suite with his and her sinks and walk-in closet. Direct access to the covered patio in the rear of the house is perfect for relaxing at night or waking up to see the sunrise.

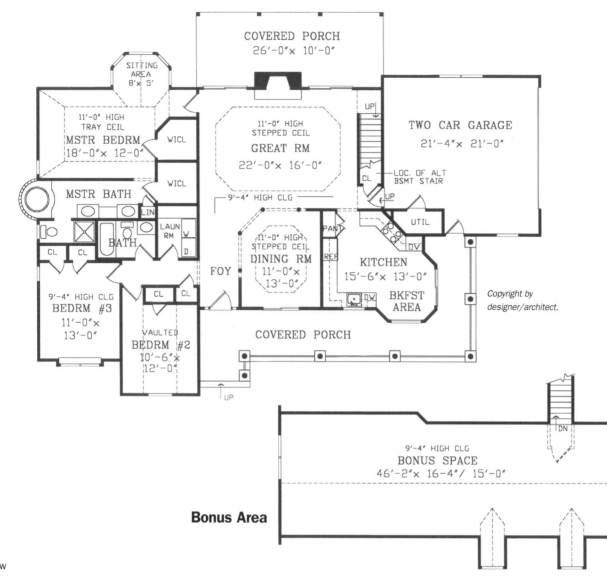

COVERED PORCH
26'-0" x 10'-0"

SITTING
AREA
8' x 5'

11'-0" HIGH
TRAY CEIL
MSTR BEDRM
18'-0" x 12'-0"

WICL

11'-0" HIGH
STEPPED CEIL
GREAT RM
22'-0" x 16'-0"

TWO CAR GARAGE
21'-4" x 21'-0"

WICL

9'-4" HIGH CLG

LOC. OF ALT
BSMT STAIR

MSTR BATH

LIN

UTIL

BATH

LAUN
RM

PANT

11'-0" HIGH
STEPPED CEIL
DINING RM
11'-0" x
13'-0"

REF

KITCHEN
15'-6" x 13'-0"

CL

CL

FOY

BKFST
AREA

9'-4" HIGH CLG
BEDRM #3
11'-0" x
13'-0"

CL

CL

VAULTED
BEDRM #2
10'-6" x
12'-0"

COVERED PORCH

UP

Copyright by designer/architect.

9'-4" HIGH CLG
BONUS SPACE
46'-2" x 16-4"/ 15'-0"

DN

Bonus Area

Rear View

Upper Level
Floor Plan

Main Level
Floor Plan

Copyright by designer/architect.

Images provided by designer/architect.

Plan #341214

Dimensions: 56'4" W x 36' D
Levels: 2
Heated Square Footage: 1,806
Main Level Sq. Ft.: 828
Upper Level Sq. Ft.: 978
Bedrooms: 3
Bathrooms: 2½
Foundation: Crawl space; slab or basement for fee
Material List Available: Yes
Price Category: D

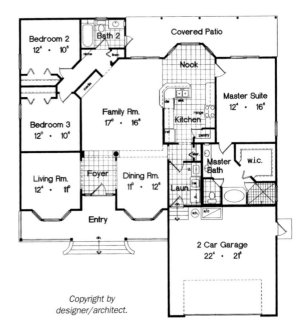

Images provided by designer/architect.

Copyright by designer/architect.

Plan #661050

Dimensions: 54' W x 63'8" D
Levels: 1
Heated Square Footage: 1,806
Bedrooms: 3
Bathrooms: 2
Foundation: Slab
Materials List Available: No
Price Category: D

**Main Level
Floor Plan**

Great Room
19' x 15'-4"

Dining
11' x 12'

Bath

Garage
20' x 21'

Ent. Cab.
Recess

Den
10' x 12'-3"

WOOD
RAIL

Kitchen
11'-4 x 14'-10"

Laun

Foyer

Porch

**Upper Level
Floor Plan**

*Copyright by
designer/architect.*

Walk In
Closet

Master
Bedroom
14'-2" x 12'-4"

Bath

Bath

Walk In
Closet

Closet

24"
LIN

Bedroom
10'-4" x 11'

WOOD
RAIL

Foyer
Below

Lin

Bedroom
11' x 10'-6"

Plan #161263

Dimensions: 60'9" W x 36'10" D

Levels: 2

Heated Square Footage: 1,808

Main Level Sq. Ft.: 1,055

Upper Level Sq. Ft.: 753

Bedrooms: 3

Bathrooms: 2½

Foundation: Basement; crawl space or walkout for fee

Materials List Available: Yes

Price Category: D

*Images provided by
designer/architect.*

CAD FILE AVAILABLE
CAD

Rear View

Plan #181724

Dimensions: 55'4"W x 58' D

Levels: 1

Heated Square Footage: 1,808

Bedrooms: 3

Bathrooms: 2

Foundation: Basement

Material List Available: Yes

Price Category: D

*Images provided by
designer/architect.*

CAD FILE AVAILABLE
CAD

14'-0" X 12'-4"
4,20 X 3,70

14'-0" X 13'-0"
4,20 X 3,90

14'-0" / 17'-8" X 14'-6"
4,20 / 5,30 X 4,35

15'-4" X 19'-0"
4,60 X 5,70

58'-0"
17,4 m

10'-0" X 11'-4"
3,00 X 3,40

20'-8" X 20'-2"
6,20 X 6,05

10'-0" X 11'-4"
3,00 X 3,40

*Copyright by
designer/architect.*

55'-4"
16,6 m

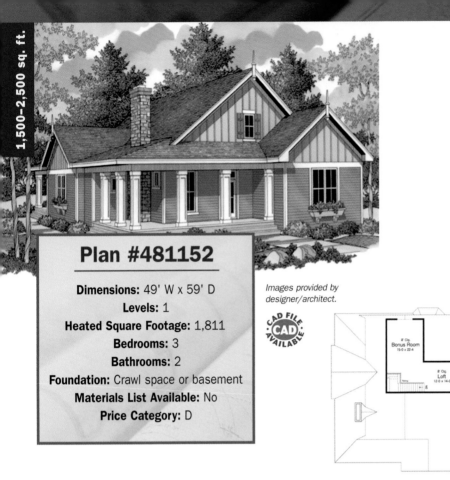

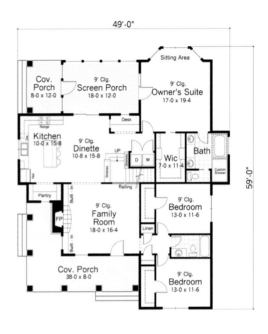

Owner's Suite 17-0 x 19-4 • 9' Clg.

Sitting Area

Cov. Porch 8-0 x 12-0

Screen Porch 18-0 x 12-0 • 9' Clg.

Desk

Kitchen 10-0 x 15-8

Range

Dinette 10-8 x 15-8 • 9' Clg.

UP

D W

Shelves

Railing

Wic 7-0 x 11-4

Bath

Custom Shower

Ref.

Pantry

Built-In

Family Room 18-0 x 16-4 • 9' Clg.

FP

Built-In

Linen

Bedroom 13-0 x 11-6 • 9' Clg.

Cov. Porch 38-0 x 8-0

Bedroom 13-0 x 11-6 • 9' Clg.

49'-0"

59'-0"

Plan #481152

Dimensions: 49' W x 59' D
Levels: 1
Heated Square Footage: 1,811
Bedrooms: 3
Bathrooms: 2
Foundation: Crawl space or basement
Materials List Available: No
Price Category: D

Images provided by designer/architect.

CAD FILE AVAILABLE

Bonus Room 15-0 x 22-4 • 8' Clg.

Loft 12-0 x 14-0 • 8' Clg.

Railing

Bonus Level Floor Plan

Copyright by designer/architect.

Master Bedroom 14-8 x 13-0 • 10' Clg. Ht. 9' Clg. Ht.

Mstr. Bath 6-6 x 16-4

Shwr.

Jet Tub

Bedroom 3 12-0 x 10-6

Closet

L

Covered Porch 30-4 x 7-6

Gas Logs

Great Room 17-8 x 16-0

VAULT

Breakfast 12-0 x 11-10 • 9' Clg. Ht.

Closet 7-8 x 6-6

C

Hall 1

Bath 2

Tub/Shwr.

L

Hall 2

Up To Unfinished Bonus

Utility 6-6 x 7-10

W D

Work Bench

Storage/ Shop 6-4 x 11-10

Closet

L

Eating Bar Island

R

Bedroom 2 12-0 x 10-6

Foyer 5-8 x 10-6

Flex Space 12-0 x 10-6 (Clear) • 10' Clg. Ht.

Breakfast 12-0 x 12-6 (Clear)

Pantry

DW

Down To Basement

Down

Two-Car Garage 21-4 x 21-8 (Clear)

Covered Porch 31-0 x 6-0

Copyright by designer/architect.

Plan #351108

Dimensions: 65' W x 60'8" D
Levels: 1
Heated Square Footage: 1,816
Bedrooms: 3
Bathrooms: 2
Foundation: Basement
Material List Available: Yes
Price Category: E

Images provided by designer/architect.

CAD FILE AVAILABLE

Rear Elevation

Bonus Area

Down

Bonus Rm. 11-4 x 25-8 • 8' Clg. Ht.

Sloped Clg.

Sloped Clg.

Sloped Clg.

Plan #161121

Dimensions: 66' W x 74' D

Levels: 1

Heated Square Footage: 1,824

Bedrooms: 3

Bathrooms: 2

Foundation: Basement

Material List Available: Yes

Price Category: D

Images provided by designer/architect.

Copyright by designer/architect.

Rear Elevation

Plan #181032

Dimensions: 49' W x 40' D

Levels: 2

Heated Square Footage: 1,826

Main Level Sq. Ft.: 910

Upper Level Sq. Ft.: 916

Bedrooms: 3

Bathrooms: 2½

Foundation: Basement; crawl space or slab for fee

Materials List Available: Yes

Price Category: D

Images provided by designer/architect.

CAD FILE AVAILABLE

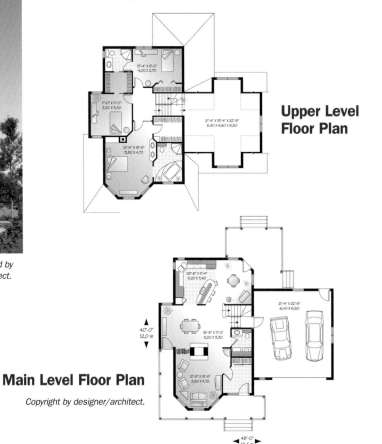

Upper Level Floor Plan

Main Level Floor Plan

Copyright by designer/architect.

Images provided by designer/architect.

Plan #351082

Dimensions: 65' W x 56'8" D

Levels: 1

Heated Square Footage: 1,800

Bedrooms: 3

Bathrooms: 2

Foundation: Crawl space, slab or basement

Material List Available: Yes

Price Category: E

CAD FILE AVAILABLE

Bonus Level Floor Plan

Copyright by designer/architect.

Unfinished Bonus Room
11-4 x 21-8
(Clear)
8-0 Clg. Ht.

Kitchen

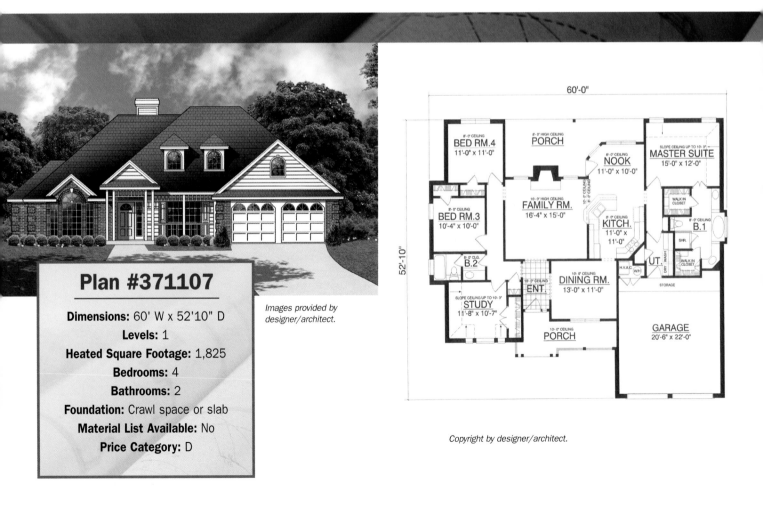

Plan #371107

Dimensions: 60' W x 52'10" D

Levels: 1

Heated Square Footage: 1,825

Bedrooms: 4

Bathrooms: 2

Foundation: Crawl space or slab

Material List Available: No

Price Category: D

Images provided by designer/architect.

Copyright by designer/architect.

Plan #351070

Dimensions: 63'4" W x 53' D

Levels: 1

Heated Square Footage: 1,818

Bedrooms: 3

Bathrooms: 3

Foundation: Basement

Materials List Available: Yes

Price Category: E

Images provided by designer/architect.

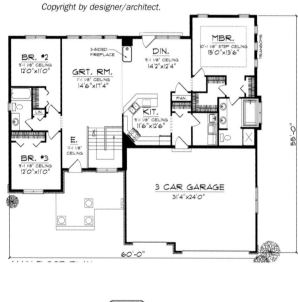

Copyright by designer/architect.

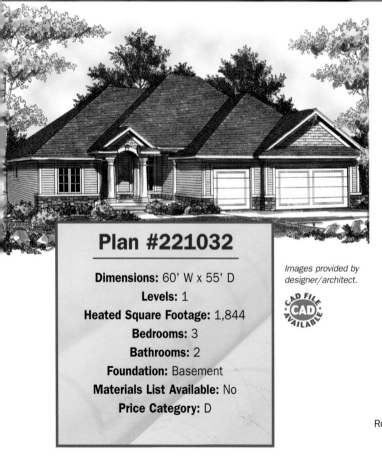

Plan #221032

Dimensions: 60' W x 55' D

Levels: 1

Heated Square Footage: 1,844

Bedrooms: 3

Bathrooms: 2

Foundation: Basement

Materials List Available: No

Price Category: D

Images provided by designer/architect.

Rear Elevation

Plan #121064

Dimensions: 44' W x 40' D
Levels: 2
Heated Square Footage: 1,846
Main Level Sq. Ft.: 919
Upper Level Sq. Ft.: 927
Bedrooms: 4
Bathrooms: 2½
Foundation: Basement; crawl space or slab for fee
Materials List Available: Yes
Price Category: D

This home, as shown in the photograph, may differ from the actual blueprints. For more detailed information, please check the floor plans carefully.

Images provided by designer/architect.

You'll love the features and design in this compact but amenity-filled home.

Features:

- Entry: A balcony overlooks this two-story entry, where a plant shelf tops the coat closet.

- Great Room: A trio of tall windows points up the large dimensions of this room, which is sure to be the hub of your home. Arrange the furniture to create a cozy space around the fireplace, or leave it open to the room.

- Kitchen: You'll love to work in this well-designed kitchen area.

- Master Suite: On the second floor, this master suite features a tiered ceiling and two walk-in closets. In the bath, you'll find a double vanity, whirlpool tub, and separate shower.

Upper Level Floor Plan

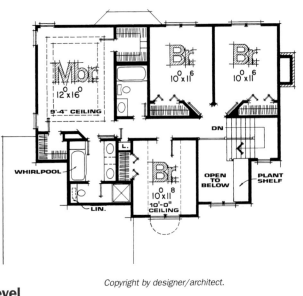

Copyright by designer/architect.

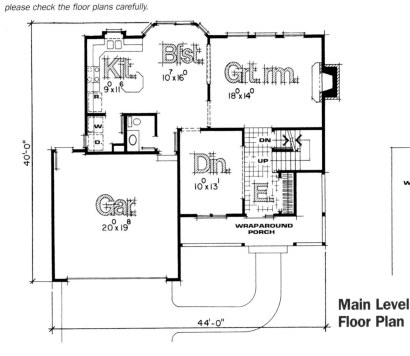

Main Level Floor Plan

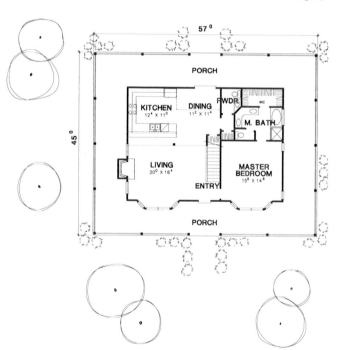

Plan #331001

Dimensions: 57' W x 45' D
Levels: 2
Heated Square Footage: 1,846
Main Level Sq. Ft.: 1,156
Upper Level Sq. Ft.: 690
Bedrooms: 3
Bathrooms: 2½
Foundation: Crawl space, slab, or basement
Materials List Available: No
Price Category: D

This home' wraparound porch provides a wonderful space to relax with friends and family.

Features:

- Porch: Surrounding the entire first floor of the home, this wraparound porch can be used for relaxing, entertaining, or dining outdoors.

- Kitchen: This U-shaped kitchen provides plenty of counter space for the home cook to prepare meals.

- Master Suite: Located on the first floor of the home, this master suite features a large bedroom space and a bathroom with two vanities, a walk-in closet, and a tub.

- Secondary Bedrooms: Upstairs, two bedrooms with a shared bathroom and loft area are perfect for children or guests.

Images provided by designer/architect.

Main Level Floor Plan

Upper Level Floor Plan

Copyright by designer/architect.

Images provided by designer/architect.

Plan #441001

Dimensions: 44' W x 68' D
Levels: 1
Heated Square Footage: 1,850
Bedrooms: 3
Bathrooms: 2
Foundation: Crawl space;
slab or basement for fee
Materials List Available: No
Price Category: D

CAD FILE AVAILABLE

With all the tantalizing elements of a cottage and the comfortable space of a family-sized home, this Arts and Crafts-style one-story design is the best of both worlds. Exterior accents such as stone wainscot, cedar shingles under the gable ends, and mission-style windows just add to the effect.

Features:

- **Great Room:** A warm hearth lights this room—right next to a built-in media center.

- **Dining Room:** This area features a sliding glass door to the rear patio for a breath of fresh air.

- **Den:** This quiet area has a window seat and a vaulted ceiling, giving the feeling of openness and letting your mind wander.

- **Kitchen:** This open corner kitchen features a 42-in. snack bar and a giant walk-in pantry.

- **Master Suite:** This suite boasts a tray ceiling and a large walk-in closet.

Rear Elevation

Plan #351004

Dimensions: 78' W x 49'6" D

Levels: 1

Heated Square Footage: 1,852

Bedrooms: 3

Bathrooms: 2½

Foundation: Crawl space, slab, or basement

Materials List Available: Yes

Price Category: E

Images provided by designer/architect.

You'll love this design if you've been looking for a one-story home large enough for both a busy family life and lots of entertaining.

Features:

- **Great Room:** A vaulted ceiling, substantial corner fireplace, and door to the rear porch give character to this sizable, airy room.

- **Dining Room:** This well-positioned room, lit by a wall of windows, can comfortably hold a crowd.

- **Kitchen:** The center island and deep pantry add efficiency to this well-planned kitchen, which also features a raised snack bar.

- **Master Suite:** Two walk-in closets and a bath with jet tub and separate shower complement the spacious bedroom here.

- **Garage Storage:** Barn doors make it easy to store yard equipment and tools here. Finish the optional area at the rear of the garage or overhead for a home office or media room.

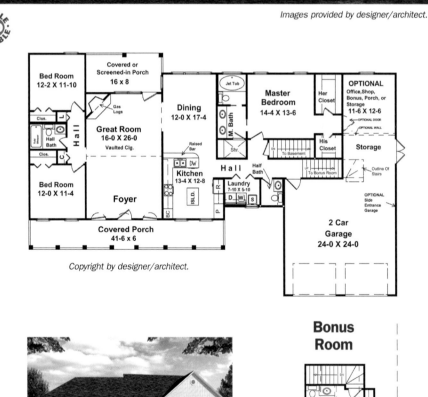

Copyright by designer/architect.

Rear Elevation

Bonus Room

Plan #151490

Dimensions: 52' W x 69'6" D

Levels: 1

Heated Square Footage: 1,869

Bedrooms: 3

Bathrooms: 2

Foundation: Crawl space or slab

CompleteCost List Available: Yes

Price Category: D

Images provided by designer/architect.

Beautiful brick and wood siding impart warmth to this French Country design.

Features:

- Open Plan: Elegance is achieved in this home by using boxed columns and 10-ft.-high ceilings. The foyer and dining room are lined with columns and adjoin the great room, all with high ceilings.

- Kitchen: This combined kitchen and breakfast room is great for entertaining and has access to the grilling porch.

- Master Suite: The split-bedroom plan features this suite, with its large walk-in closet, whirlpool tub, shower, and private area.

- Bedrooms: The two bedrooms and a large bathroom are located on the other side of the great room, giving privacy to the entire family.

Bonus Area Floor Plan

BONUS ROOM
12'-10" X 20'-4"

Copyright by designer/architect.

Plan #441002

Dimensions: 70' W x 51' D

Levels: 1

Heated Square Footage: 1,873

Bedrooms: 3

Bathrooms: 2

Foundation: Crawl space

Materials List Available: Yes

Price Category: D

Images provided by designer/architect.

Shutters flank tall windows to adorn the front of this charming home. A high roofline gives presence to the façade and allows vaulted ceilings in all the right places inside.

Features:

- **Great Room:** The entry hall overlooks this room, where a fireplace warms gatherings on chilly evenings and built-in shelves, to the right of the fireplace, add space that might be used as an entertainment center. A large three-panel window wall allows for a rear-yard view.

- **Dining Room:** This area is connected directly to the great room and features double doors to a covered porch.

- **Kitchen:** This open work area contains ample counter space with an island cooktop and large pantry.

- **Bedrooms:** The bedrooms are split, with the master suite in the back and additional bedrooms at the front.

- **Master Suite:** This suite boasts a 9-ft.-high ceiling and is graced by a luxurious bathroom and a walk-in closet.

Copyright by designer/architect.

Rear Elevation

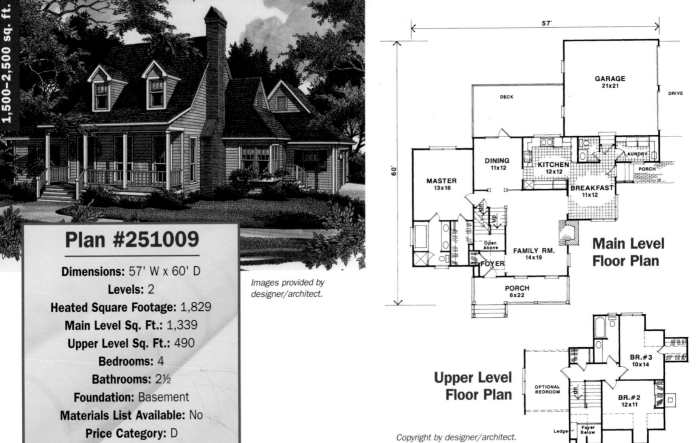

1,500–2,500 sq. ft.

GARAGE
21x21

DECK

DRIVE

57'

60'

MASTER
13x16

DINING
11x12

KITCHEN
12x12

LAUNDRY

PORCH

BREAKFAST
11x12

UP

Open
Above

FAMILY RM.
14x19

FOYER

PORCH
6x22

Main Level Floor Plan

BR.#3
10x14

Upper Level Floor Plan

OPTIONAL
BEDROOM

BR.#2
12x11

Ledge

Foyer
Below

Copyright by designer/architect.

Images provided by designer/architect.

Plan #251009

Dimensions: 57' W x 60' D
Levels: 2
Heated Square Footage: 1,829
Main Level Sq. Ft.: 1,339
Upper Level Sq. Ft.: 490
Bedrooms: 4
Bathrooms: 2½
Foundation: Basement
Materials List Available: No
Price Category: D

Plan #191004

Dimensions: 58' W x 68' D
Levels: 1
Heated Square Footage: 1,856
Bedrooms: 3
Bathrooms: 3
Foundation: Crawl space
Material List Available: No
Price Category: D

Images provided by designer/architect.

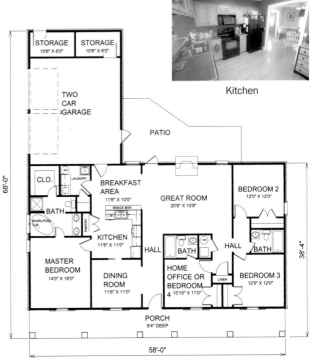

Kitchen

STORAGE
10'6" X 6'0"

STORAGE
10'6" X 6'0"

TWO
CAR
GARAGE

PATIO

68'-0"

CLO.

LAUNDRY

BREAKFAST
AREA
11'6" X 10'0"

GREAT ROOM
20'6" X 15'8"

BEDROOM 2
12'0" X 12'0"

BATH

WHIRLPOOL
TUB

SNACK BAR

KITCHEN
11'6" X 11'0"

PANTRY

HALL

BATH

HALL

BATH

MASTER
BEDROOM
14'0" X 16'0"

DINING
ROOM
11'6" X 11'0"

HOME
OFFICE OR
BEDROOM
4 10'10" X 11'0"

LINEN

BEDROOM 3
12'0" X 12'0"

38'-4"

PORCH
6'4" DEEP

58'-0"

Copyright by designer/architect.

Plan #151742

Dimensions: 42' W x 68'6" D

Levels: 1.5

Heated Square Footage: 1,875

Main Level Sq. Ft.: 1,588

Upper Level Sq. Ft.: 287

Bedrooms: 4

Bathrooms: 3

Foundation: Crawl space or slab; basement or walk out for fee

CompleteCost List Available: Yes

Price Category: D

Images provided by designer/architect.

Main Level Floor Plan

Upper Level Floor Plan

Copyright by designer/architect.

Plan #571078

Dimensions: 30' W x 32' D

Levels: 2

Heated Square Footage: 1,870

Main Level Sq. Ft.: 935

Upper Level Sq. Ft.: 935

Bedrooms: 3

Bathrooms: 2½

Foundation: Basement

Material List Available: Yes

Price Category: D

Images provided by designer/architect.

Main Level Floor Plan

Upper Level Floor Plan

Copyright by designer/architect.

Plan #351120

Dimensions: 55' W x 70' D

Levels: 1

Heated Square Footage: 1,888

Bedrooms: 3

Bathrooms: 2

Foundation: Crawl space, slab or basement

Materials List Available: Yes

Price Category: E

Images provided by designer/architect.

CAD FILE AVAILABLE

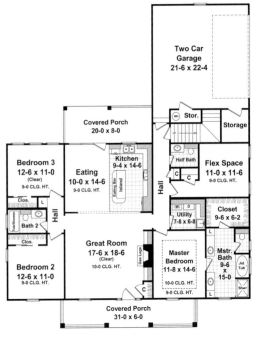

Copyright by designer/architect.

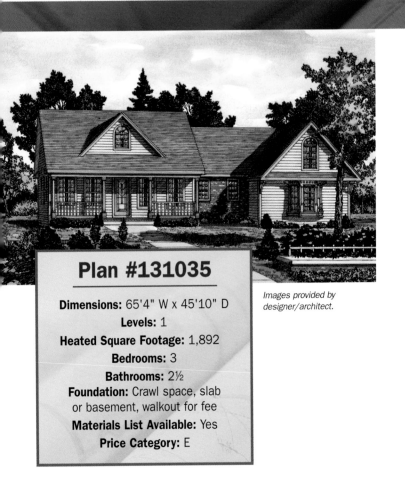

Plan #131035

Dimensions: 65'4" W x 45'10" D

Levels: 1

Heated Square Footage: 1,892

Bedrooms: 3

Bathrooms: 2½

Foundation: Crawl space, slab or basement, walkout for fee

Materials List Available: Yes

Price Category: E

Images provided by designer/architect.

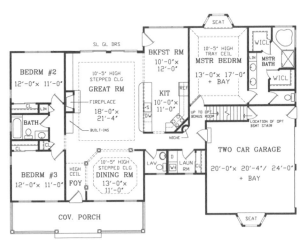

Bonus Area Floor Plan

Copyright by designer/architect.

Main Level Floor Plan

Images provided by designer/architect.

Upper Level Floor Plan

Copyright by designer/architect.

Plan #371038

Dimensions: 52'8" W x 44' D
Levels: 2
Heated Square Footage: 1,896
Main Level Sq. Ft.: 1,235
Upper Level Sq. Ft.: 661
Bedrooms: 4
Bathrooms: 2½
Foundation: Crawl space or slab
Materials List Available: No
Price Category: D

Main Level Floor Plan

Upper Level Floor Plan

Copyright by designer/architect.

Plan #441349

Dimensions: 59' W x 48' 6" D
Levels: 2
Heated Square Footage: 1,896
Main Level Sq. Ft.: 1,397
Upper Level Sq. Ft.: 499
Bedrooms: 3
Bathrooms: 2½
Foundation: Crawl space
Materials List Available: Yes
Price Category: D

Images provided by designer/architect.

Rear View

1,500-2,500 sq. ft.

www.ultimateplans.com   115

Plan #441006

Dimensions: 48' W x 64' D

Levels: 1

Heated Square Footage: 1,891

Bedrooms: 3

Bathrooms: 2

Foundation: Crawl space; slab or basement for fee

Materials List Available: Yes

Price Category: D

If you prefer the look of Craftsman homes, you'll love the details this plan includes. Wide-based columns across the front porch, Mission-style windows, and a balanced mixture of exterior materials add up to true good looks.

Features:

- **Great Room:** A built-in media center and a fireplace in this room make it distinctive.

- **Kitchen:** A huge skylight over an island eating counter brightens this kitchen. A private office space opens through double doors nearby.

- **Dining Room:** This room has sliding glass doors opening to the rear patio.

- **Bedrooms:** Two bedrooms with two bathrooms are located on the right side of the plan. One of the bedrooms is a master suite with a vaulted salon and a bath with a spa tub.

- **Garage:** You'll be able to reach this two-car garage via a service hallway that contains a laundry room, a walk-in pantry, and a closet.

Images provided by designer/architect.

Copyright by designer/architect.

CAD FILE AVAILABLE

GARAGE
19/0 X 21/6

ALT GARAGE DR LOC

MASTER
14/0 X 15/0
(9' CLG.)

HUTCH RECESS

DINING
12/0 X 16/0 +
(9' CLG.)

KITCHEN
12/8 X 13/2 +/-
(9' CLG.)

PAN

REF

NICHE

LINEN

OFFICE /BR. 3
10/0 X 10/2
(9' CLG.)

GREAT RM.
17/0 X 17/0 +
(9' CLG.)

MEDIA

BR. 2
14/0 X 12/0
(9' CLG.)

64'

PORCH

◄ 48' ►

Rear Elevation

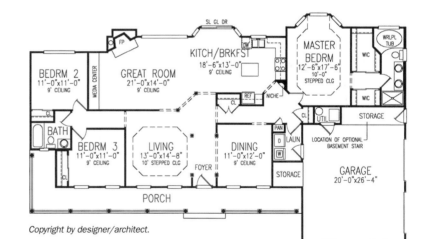

Plan #131016

Dimensions: 75' W x 45' D

Levels: 1

Heated Square Footage: 1,902

Bedrooms: 3

Bathrooms: 2

Foundation: Crawl space, slab, or basement

Materials List Available: Yes

Price Category: E

Images provided by designer/architect.

If traditional country looks appeal to you, you'll be delighted by the wraparound covered porch that forms the entryway to this comfortable home.

Features:

- Great Room: Sit by the fireplace in this room with feature walls so large that they'll suit a home theater or large media center.

- Kitchen: Overlooking the great room, this well-designed kitchen has great cabinets and ample counter space to make all your cooking and cleaning a pleasure.

- Master Suite: A large bay window makes the bedroom in this private suite sophisticated, and two walk-in closets make it practical. You'll love to relax in the master bath, whether in the whirlpool tub or the separate shower. A dual-sink vanity completes the amenities in this room.

- Garage: Find extra storage space in this two-bayed, attached garage.

Copyright by designer/architect.

Great Room

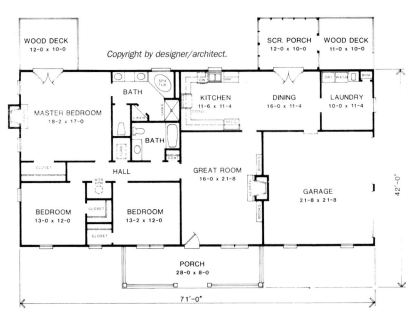

Images provided by designer/architect.

Plan #301005

Dimensions: 71' W x 42' D
Levels: 1
Heated Square Footage: 1,930
Bedrooms: 3
Bathrooms: 2
Foundation: Crawl space, slab
Materials List Available: Yes
Price Category: D

This home features an old-fashioned rocking-chair porch that enhances the streetscape.

Features:

- Ceiling Height: 8 ft.

- Dining Room: When the weather is warm, guests can step through French doors from this elegant dining room and enjoy a breeze on the rear screened porch.

- Family Room: This family room is a warm and inviting place to gather, with its handsome fireplace and built-in bookcases.

- Kitchen: This kitchen offers plenty of counter space for preparing your favorite recipes. Its U-shape creates a convenient open traffic pattern.

- Master Suite: You'll look forward to retiring at the end of the day in this truly luxurious master suite. The bedroom has a fireplace and opens through French doors to a private rear deck. The bath features a corner spa tub, a walk-in shower, double vanities, and a linen closet.

Copyright by designer/architect.

SMARTtip

Light With Shutters

For the maximum the amount of light coming through shutters, use the largest panel possible on the window. Make sure the shutters have the same number of louvers per panel so that all of the windows in the room look unified. However, don't choose a panel that is over 48 inches high, because the shutter becomes unwieldy. Also, any window that is wider than 96 inches requires extra framing to support the shutters.

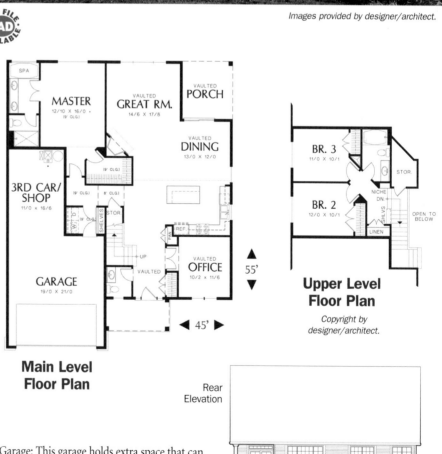

Plan #441032

Dimensions: 45' W x 55' D
Levels: 2
Heated Square Footage: 1,944
Main Level Sq. Ft.: 1,514
Upper Level Sq. Ft.: 430
Bedrooms: 3
Bathrooms: 2½
Foundation: Crawl space; slab or basement available for fee
Materials List Available: Yes
Price Category: D

Images provided by designer/architect.

It's the little things—decorative eave vents, wooden shutters, a porch column, and multiple-pane windows—that create the initial impression of this home.

Features:

- Great Design: The master suite is on the main level, while family bedrooms are upstairs, creating convenient separation and allowing full livability of the main level for empty nesters.

- Kitchen: This kitchen features an island work area and has the use of a walk-in pantry just around the corner.

- Master Suite: Don't overlook amenities in this suite: a large walk-in closet, a fully appointed bath, and a lovely wide window with views of the backyard.

- Garage: This garage holds extra space that can become a workshop, if you choose, or a place for those coveted big-boy toys.

Main Level Floor Plan

Upper Level Floor Plan

Copyright by designer/architect.

Rear Elevation

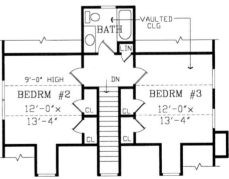

Plan #131043

Dimensions: 65'8" W x 43'10" D

Levels: 2

Heated Square Footage: 1,945

Main Level Sq. Ft.: 1,375

Upper Level Sq. Ft.: 570

Bedrooms: 3

Bathrooms: 2½

Foundation: Crawl space, slab, or basement

Materials List Available: Yes

Price Category: E

Images provided by designer/architect.

This home will delight you with its three dormers and half-round transom windows, which give a nostalgic appearance, and its amenities and conveniences that are certainly contemporary.

Features:

• **Porch:** This covered porch forms the entryway.

• **Great Room:** Enjoy the fireplace in this large, comfortable room, which is open to the dining area. A French door here leads to the covered porch at the rear of the house.

• **Kitchen:** This large, country-style kitchen has a bayed nook, and oversized breakfast bar, and pass-through to the rear porch to simplify serving and make entertaining a pleasure.

• **Master Suite:** A tray ceiling sets an elegant tone for this room, and the bay window adds to it. The large walk-in closet is convenient, and the bath is sumptuous.

• **Bedrooms:** These comfortable rooms have convenient access to a bath.

Main Level Floor Plan

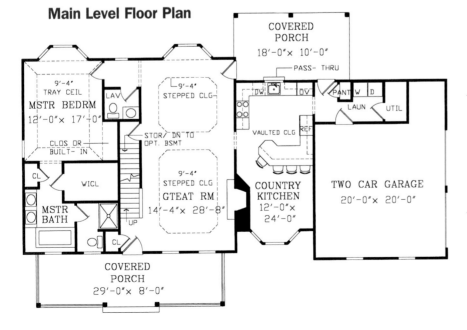

Upper Level Floor Plan

Copyright by designer/architect.

Plan #181159

Dimensions: 37' W x 31' D

Levels: 1

Heated Square Footage: 1,992

Main Level Sq. Ft.: 996

Lower Level Sq. Ft.: 996

Bedrooms: 3

Bathrooms: 2

Foundation: Walkout basement

Materials List Available: Yes

Price Category: D

Ideal for the family who loves the outdoors, this charmer features a wraparound porch that creates a covered pavilion and roofed terrace.

Features:

- Ceiling Height: 9-ft. ceilings enhance the airy feeling given by the many windows here.

- Family Rooms: These family rooms (one on each floor) allow a busy family adequate space for entertaining a crowd.

- Kitchen: Designed for efficient work patterns, this kitchen features ample work and storage space, as well as an island that can double as a

- Bedrooms: Each bedroom features a large, walk-in closet and easy access to a large, amenity-filled bathroom with a double vanity, tub, enclosed shower, and a private toilet.

- Porch: Enjoy the panoramic view from this spacious covered porch at any time of day.

Images provided by designer/architect.

Lower Level Floor Plan

Copyright by designer/architect.

Main Level Floor Plan

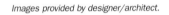

Plan #151089

Dimensions: 84" W x 55'6" D
Levels: 1
Heated Square Footage: 1,921
Bedrooms: 3
Bathrooms: 3
Foundation: Crawl space, slab, or basement
CompleteCost List Available: Yes
Price Category: D

Images provided by designer/architect.

If your family loves to combine indoor and outdoor living, this home's fabulous porches and deck space make it perfect.

Features:

- Porches: A huge wraparound front porch, sizable rear porch, and deck that joins them give you space for entertaining or simply lounging.

- Living Room: A fireplace and built-in media center could be the focal points in this large room.

- Hearth Room: Open to both the living room and kitchen, this hearth room also features a fireplace.

- Kitchen: This step-saving kitchen includes ample storage and work space, as well as an angled bar it shares with the hearth room. Atrium doors lead to the rear porch.

- Bonus Upper Level: A large game room and a full bath make this area a favorite with the children.

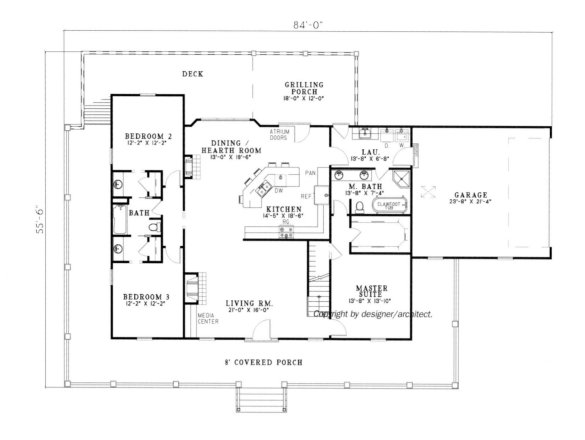

84'-0"

DECK

GRILLING PORCH
18'-0" X 12'-0"

55'-6"

BEDROOM 2
12'-2" X 12'-2"

DINING / HEARTH ROOM
13'-0" X 19'-6"

ATRIUM DOORS

LAU.
13'-8" X 6'-8"

D W

GARAGE
23'-8" X 21'-4"

BATH

PAN

KITCHEN
14'-5" X 18'-6"

DW

REF

M. BATH
13'-8" X 7'-4"

CLAWFOOT TUB

RG.

BEDROOM 3
12'-2" X 12'-2"

LIVING RM.
21'-0" X 16'-0"

MASTER SUITE
13'-8" X 13'-10"

MEDIA CENTER

Copyright by designer/architect.

8' COVERED PORCH

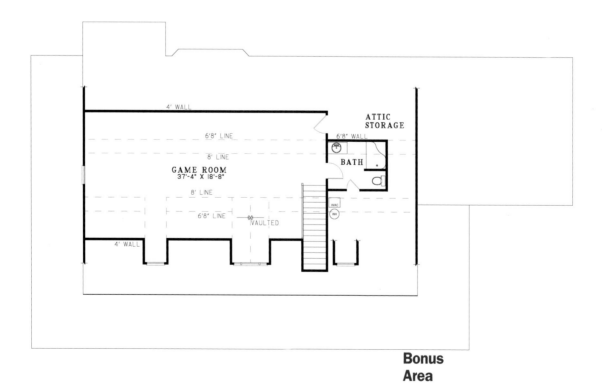

4' WALL

ATTIC STORAGE

6'8" LINE

6'8" WALL

8' LINE

BATH

GAME ROOM
37'-4" X 18'-8"

8' LINE

6'8" LINE

VAULTED

HVAC
WH

4' WALL

Bonus Area

1,500–2,500 sq. ft.

Plan #341053

Dimensions: 44'10" W x 50'6" D
Levels: 1.5
Heated Square Footage: 1,903
Main Level Sq. Ft.: 1,185
Upper Level Sq. Ft.: 718
Bedrooms: 3
Bathrooms: 2½
Foundation: Crawl space; slab or basement for fee
Materials List Available: Yes
Price Category: D

Images provided by designer/architect.

CAD FILE AVAILABLE

Upper Level Floor Plan

Main Level Floor Plan

Copyright by designer/architect.

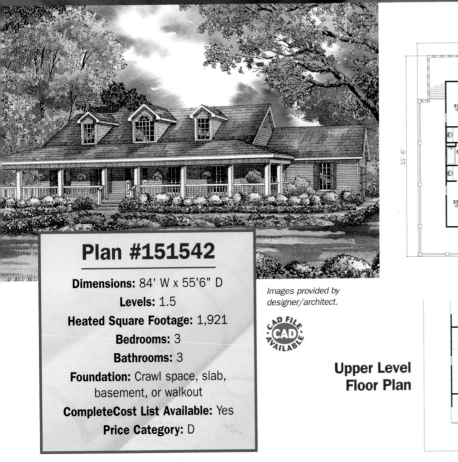

Plan #151542

Dimensions: 84' W x 55'6" D
Levels: 1.5
Heated Square Footage: 1,921
Bedrooms: 3
Bathrooms: 3
Foundation: Crawl space, slab, basement, or walkout
CompleteCost List Available: Yes
Price Category: D

Images provided by designer/architect.

CAD FILE AVAILABLE

Main Level Floor Plan

Copyright by designer/architect.

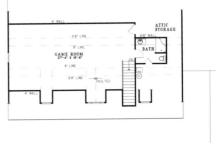

Upper Level Floor Plan

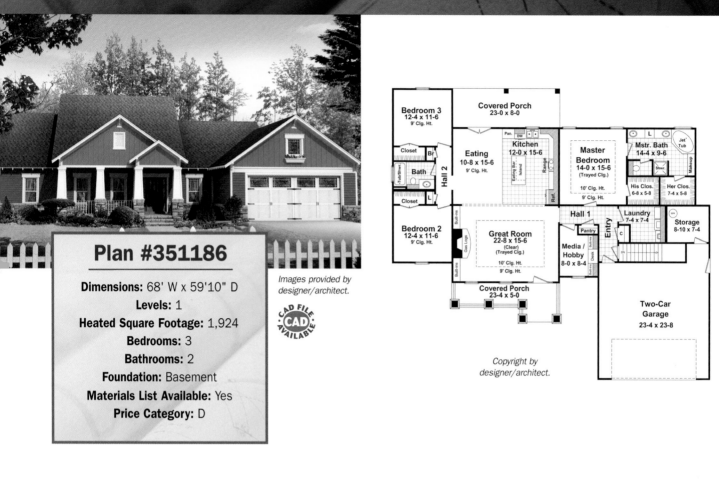

Plan #351186

Dimensions: 68' W x 59'10" D

Levels: 1

Heated Square Footage: 1,924

Bedrooms: 3

Bathrooms: 2

Foundation: Basement

Materials List Available: Yes

Price Category: D

Images provided by designer/architect.

Copyright by designer/architect.

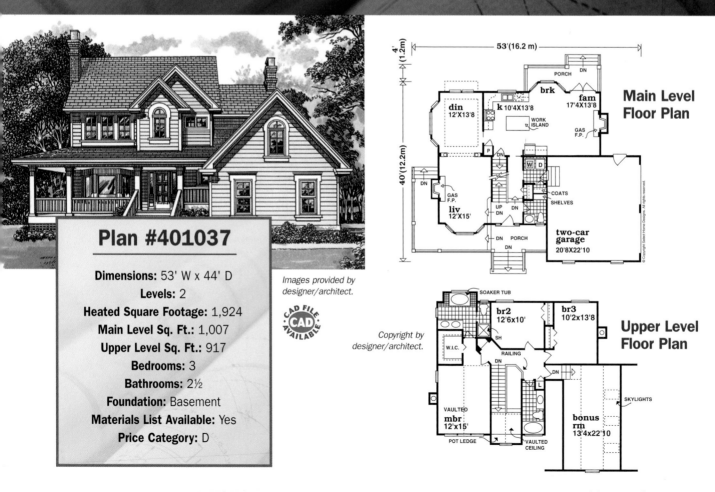

Plan #401037

Dimensions: 53' W x 44' D

Levels: 2

Heated Square Footage: 1,924

Main Level Sq. Ft.: 1,007

Upper Level Sq. Ft.: 917

Bedrooms: 3

Bathrooms: 2½

Foundation: Basement

Materials List Available: Yes

Price Category: D

Images provided by designer/architect.

Copyright by designer/architect.

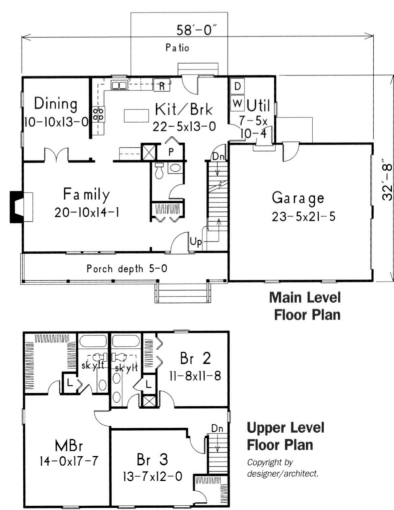

Plan #321113

Dimensions: 58' W x 32' D

Levels: 2

Heated Square Footage: 1,998

Main Level Sq. Ft.: 1,060

Upper Level Sq. Ft.: 938

Bedrooms: 3

Bathrooms: 2½

Foundation: Crawl space, slab or basement

Materials List Available: Yes

Price Category: D

This plan features outdoor living spaces at both the front and rear of the home.

Features:

- **Family Room:** Entering through the front porch, you'll step into this spacious family froom, which features a fireplace.

- **Kitchen/Breakfast Room:** You can dine inside or outside easily in this kitchen, which includes a door leading directly to the patio at the back of the home.

- **Utility Room:** Located next to the kitchen, this utility room is perfect for storage and is in a convenient spot for doing laundry.

- **Master Suite:** Upstairs, this master suite includes a walk-in closet and sky-lit bathroom.

Images provided by designer/architect.

Main Level Floor Plan

58'-0"

Patio

Dining 10-10x13-0

Kit/Brk 22-5x13-0

Util 7-5x 10-4

Family 20-10x14-1

Garage 23-5x21-5

32'-8"

Porch depth 5-0

Upper Level Floor Plan

Copyright by designer/architect.

Br 2 11-8x11-8

MBr 14-0x17-7

Br 3 13-7x12-0

sky lt sky lt

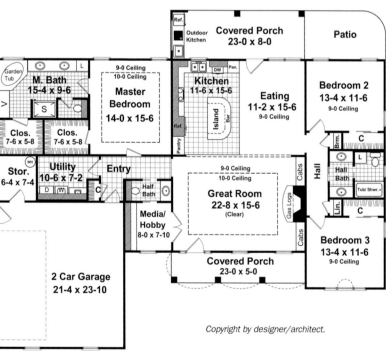

Plan #351102

Dimensions: 67' W x 56' D

Levels: 1

Heated Square Footage: 2,000

Bedrooms: 3

Bathrooms: 2½

Foundation: Crawl space, slab or basement

Materials List Available: Yes

Price Category: F

Images provided by designer/architect.

This inviting home has European country styling with upscale features.

Features:

- **Porches:** The front and rear covered porches add plenty of usable outdoor living space, and include that much-requested outdoor kitchen.

- **Great Room:** This expansive great room included a beautiful trayed ceiling and features built-in cabinets and a gas fireplace.

- **Kitchen:** The spacious kitchen features an over-sized island with a large eating bar and breakfast area.

- **Master Suite:** This room has a raised ceiling and opens into the well-equipped bath with dual lavatories, oversized corner jet tub, and large his and her walk-in closets.

Copyright by designer/architect.

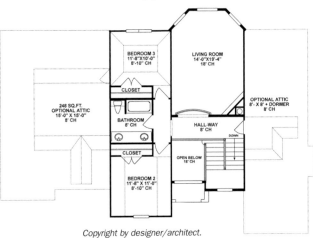

Images provided by designer/architect.

Plan #121153

Dimensions: 62' W x 42'6" D

Levels: 1.5

Heated Square Footage: 1,984

Main Level Sq. Ft.: 1,487

Upper Level Sq. Ft.: 497

Bedrooms: 3

Bathrooms: 2½

Foundation: Slab; basement for fee

Material List Available: Yes

Price Category: D

A stone and stucco exterior give this home an elegant look.

CAD FILE AVAILABLE

Features:

- **Living Room:** This two-story gathering area is available for family and friends. The fireplace adds a focal point to the room.

- **Kitchen:** This peninsula kitchen features a raised bar open to the breakfast area. The breakfast area boasts French doors that lead to the future rear deck.

- **Master Suite:** Residing on the main level is this beautiful retreat, which boasts a tray ceiling. The master bath features dual vanities, whirlpool tub, and a separate toilet area.

- **Upper Level:** Two secondary bedrooms are found on this level. A large full bathroom is centrally located for easy access.

Main Level Floor Plan

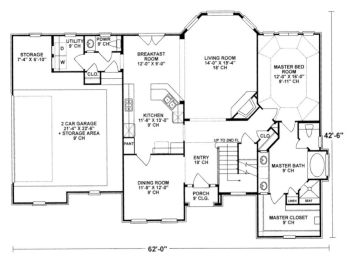

Upper Level Floor Plan

Copyright by designer/architect.

Family Room

Kitchen/Breakfast Room

Living Room

Master Bedroom

Master Bathroom

Country-Style Bathrooms

Call it pure Americana, English, Swedish, Italian, or French. The style is basic, casual, and warm—and every country has its own version. "Country" often implies a deeper connection with the outdoors and the simple life than other styles and uses an abundance of natural elements. For a Country bath, start with plain wood cabinetry stained a light maple, or add a distressed, crackled, or pickled finish. Door styles are usually framed, sometimes with a raised panel. Install a laminate countertop, and coordinate it with the tile you select for the room. Hand-painted tiles with a simple theme lend a custom touch.

For added Country charm, stencil a wall border or select a wallpaper pattern with a folk-art motif or floral prints. Checks and ticking stripes are also popular in a country-style room—on the wall, as a tile pattern, or on the shower-curtain fabric. If you feel creative, apply a painted finish to the wall. Otherwise, check out the many wallpaper designs on the market that emulate the look of sponging, ragging, combing, and other special painted effects.

Install a double-hung window in the room. (Casement windows look too contemporary in this setting.) Some window-treatment ideas include a balloon topper over miniblinds or shutters, for privacy, combined with a matching or contrasting lace café curtain. If you have a casement window in the bathroom that you do not want to change, install pop-in muntins to give the unit more of a traditional look.

A skirted pedestal sink or pine chest-turned-vanity, along with reproduction faucets, will add a nostalgic charm to a Country bathroom. Bring a playful note to this informal design with whimsical hardware fabricated in wrought iron, brushed pewter, or porcelain. Hardware and fittings that are polished look too refined for this style.

Popular Country colors include red gingham and denim blue. Choose a checkerboard floor or a mosaic of broken tiles if hardwood is not available. Or consider laminate flooring that gives you the look of real wood without the maintenance. Some styles even come with a painted-floor design.

The Country bath is the type of room that begs for baskets, old bottles, and ceramic vases filled with wildflowers. Accessorize with these items or a collection of favorite things, and you've created a very personal space.

A yellow-and-white floor, below, adds a dollop of sunshine underfoot.

A pedestal sink, opposite, is a hallmark of Country style.

A Country Bath with Efficient Style

Although the ancient Greeks and Romans, along with other prosperous early civilizations, maintained luxurious public bathhouses, it was a long road to the private, plumbed-in tub with the toilet alongside that we know today. A relatively modern convenience, the bathroom typically packs lots of essential equipment into a small space, so it's in special need of old-fashioned details to become part of a welcoming country house.

In the 1790s the French produced shoe-shaped bathtubs; Benjamin Franklin brought one back to the United States so he could enjoy soaking, reading, and relaxing for hours.

But before the late nineteenth century, for most North Americans, bathing was utilitarian. Periodically, someone filled a portable tub with hand-pumped and stove-heated water from buckets, and each family member had a turn.

By the 1870s the houses of well-to-do North Americans had flush toilets, but only the wealthiest owned a plumbed-in tub in the same room. Most folks endured the inconvenience of chamber pots, water pitchers, and washbowls in their bedrooms. Finally, nearing the twentieth century, plumbing became increasingly common, and average homeowners carved out bathroom space from a bedroom. The old-fashioned claw-foot tub not only resembled formal furniture pieces but kept the often unreliable plumbing more accessible. Into the 1920s and '30s, closed-in tubs and crisp white tile became fashionable, celebrating thoroughly modern convenience.

Today's Typical Bathroom

Though the recent trend has been toward larger bathrooms, the standard is still focused on efficient use of space. This offers the decorator an unexpected side benefit, because even minor flourishes and ornamentation go a long way toward making the Country bathroom attractive and full of character. Follow the advice below to make this sometimes sterile room charming in a Country-style way.

Design It to Suit Its Use

Not only are we spoiled with indoor plumbing, we have come to expect more than one bathroom. With bathrooms in such abundance, each may be slanted toward a different role, with different decorating demands and possibilities.

The master bath is a private retreat,

Beadboard and Shaker-style pegs, opposite, provide a Country ambiance.

This Country-style bathroom, above, features a traditional floral wall treatment and light-colored cabinetry.

deserving some luxurious amenities, such as a makeup table, television and sound system, exercise equipment, or spa features. Space permitting, the bathroom can hold a piece or two of country furniture, such as a painted bench, an armoire, a wicker chair, or an added cabinet.

A family bathroom, on the other hand, may be where everyone showers or bathes—even the dog. It requires ample storage for toys, towels, and toiletries for kids and grownups. So keep an eye out for big baskets, quaint containers, shelves, and a capacious hamper for laundry. Because space is often at a premium, seek out useful shelves, towel bars, magazine racks, storage containers, and robe hooks styled with a bit of panache, whether in ceramic, brass, hand-painted finishes, or unusual

materials. Everything should be water resistant and easy to clean, too.

Powder rooms are half-baths often located in the house's social or "public" areas. Because they're not subject to long, steamy showers or much of the morning get-up-and-go routine, durability and storage are less of an issue. Here you can indulge your decorating with delicate, eye-catching finishes, pretty collections, or displays that enhance the space.

Apply General Decorating Principles

Even if it's a small space, assess the room's strengths and weaknesses. A room's odd angles and small size can seem picturesque in lively, high-contrast finishes. Think about harmonies of scale, proportion, line, and color spiced with subtle differences. Because a bathroom tends toward slick modern surfaces, rough baskets and earthenware pots of ferns might be refreshing. Light finishes visually enlarge a small space, but wall-to-wall pastels can seem dull without a few bright notes.

Borrow Ideas from Other Rooms

Bathrooms can be too utilitarian, so have fun with unexpected elements, such as elaborate window treatments, handsome moldings, a slipper-chair, potted plants, and artwork, as long as the materials can hold up to dampness.

Fixtures

As in the kitchen, even bathrooms designed in the most authentic Country spirit can accommodate modern accoutrements. Consider a reproduction of a high-tank Victorian-style toilet, claw-foot tub, and classic gooseneck faucet with porcelain crosshandles.

Antique fixtures may be an attractive addition to your bathroom, but the inconvenience of future repairs may be a drawback.

Toilets

Many Country decorators choose standard, unobtrusive wares, often in versatile white or neutral, and concentrate their decorating efforts on elements and accessories that are easy to change, such as paint, wallpaper, linens, and rugs.

Basic two-piece toilets in white vitre-

"Brick" style ceramic tile is right at home in a Country scheme, opposite.

Use traditional fixtures, such as this crosshandle faucet set, above right, in a Country bathroom.

Period-furniture-style pieces, right, provide a distinct Country flavor.

ous china are unassuming features in a Country scheme, though more expensive, contemporary one-piece models may be your preference. New toilets feature a variety of internal mechanisms designed to meet a low-flush standard of using 1.6 gallons or less per flush. In addition to standard gravity-fed mechanisms, pressure-assisted systems use internal water pressure to compress air, which creates a more forceful flush.

Tubs and Showers

The tub and shower areas have the greatest visual weight in the room's design. Though they're most economical when combined (and a tub makes the most assuredly leakproof shower pan), the trend, especially in the master bath, is to separate the functions by creating separate fixtures for them. Tubs and shower enclosures can be found in a wide range of materials and styles. Cast-iron tubs are an attractive addition to any bathroom. However, the easier installation and lighter weight of modern plastics and ceramics make them more practical.

To keep the water contained, a clear glass shower door will do the job. A shower curtain, particularly if it consists of a waterproof liner combined with a frivolous fabric drapery, can add a soft, colorful, and easy-to-change touch amid all the hard surfaces. You can also pull it almost completely out of the way to show off any decorative tilework or handsome fittings within the tub alcove.

Sinks and Fittings

Bathroom sinks, which designers refer to as lavatories, can be made of vitreous china, cast iron, enameled steel, fiberglass, solid-surfacing material, stone, faux stone, or metal. Pedestal sinks, or wall-mounted lavatories with metal or carved-wood legs, encompass a variety of handsome vintage styles. Remember, today a beautiful fixture can stand alone as a piece of sculpture in the room.

Faucets. Faucets span a wide price range. In appearance, they can be considered as "jewelry" for the bathroom when fabricated in rich vintage styles, perhaps with china or bright crosshandles and a gooseneck spout. Brass is the traditional finish, but chrome can look at home fashioned after nostalgic styles. Single-lever controls, though undeniably modern, are convenient and easy to use.

Vanities

The vanity is often the keynote of a bathroom's country style because cabinetmaking is a venerable craft. An old but not valuable cabinet, small chest of drawers, or table can be converted into a charming vanity, though it must be carefully sealed against water. You'll also find vanities with evocative Country details made of rustic pine, smooth maple, or pickled oak, with planked or raised panel doors. Stock cabinetry often works well in standardized bathroom spaces. Custom cabinetry opens up more options and may offer accessories such as matching display shelves, moldings, or a bracket for a vase or candle.

Finishing Touches

Country bathrooms use many of the same practical finishing materials as Country kitchens. Wood instantly adds warmth and character and a "furnished" feeling. In the bath, consider softwoods such as fir, redwood, and pine or dense hardwoods like teak and maple for tongue-and-groove wainscoting, moldings, or furniture pieces.

Mirrors enhance a sense of space, albeit with a harder modern look. Downplay this by extending the mirror into a corner or framing it with molding.

Ceramic tile is a classic Country bathroom material, and it can be the decorative standout. There are some options to lend interest to a low-key background—for example, a play of different shapes, such as triangles, squares, and rectangles interlocked on a white wall. Or turn the square grid diagonally for an energetic diamond design. Try a stamped high-relief pattern or a heavy rope-molding trim to give a plain color more tactile appeal. Clay-colored tones and faux stone add a natural spirit to bare white walls and floors.

Lighting

In a room where people shave, put on makeup, remove splinters, and the like, good lighting, both natural and artificial, is essential.

Modern bathroom faucets, below left, can look like antique fixtures.

This bathroom, with its floral wallcovering and traditional faucet, below right, says "Country."

Use of a whirligig, opposite, reinforces the Country decor.

Just as in any room, windows add light and charm to a bath. Those with divided-light sash or projected bays add particular elegance. Skylights and clerestory windows can fetch sunlight with no worries about privacy.

All bathroom lighting fixtures should be suitable for damp areas. A ceiling-mounted fixture, perhaps a bowl-type pendant or a smaller chandelier, can cast a good general glow. Paired wall sconces alongside the mirror eliminate the shadows that can be cast by an overhead source.

Accessories

In limited space, every added object should be carefully chosen. Some fanciful touches with a Country sensibility might include a vintage sugar and creamer set to hold toothbrushes and cottonballs. An old teapot can be a charming planter or a place to store combs and brushes.

And don't forget the old model-home trick of displaying big fluffy towels to instantly make the room feel cozy and welcoming.

Plan #101022

Dimensions: 66'2" W x 62' D

Levels: 1

Heated Square Footage: 1,992

Bedrooms: 3

Bathrooms: 3

Foundation: Crawl space, slab, or basement

Materials List Available: Yes

Price Category: D

Images provided by designer/architect.

The exterior of this lovely home is traditional, but the unusually shaped rooms and amenities are contemporary.

Features:

- **Foyer:** This two-story foyer is open to the family room, but columns divide it from the dining room.

- **Family Room:** A gas fireplace and TV niche, flanked by doors to the covered porch, sit at the rear of this seven-sided, spacious room.

- **Breakfast Room:** Set off from the family room by columns, this area shares a snack bar with the kitchen and has windows looking over the porch.

- **Bedroom 3:** Use this room as a living room if you wish, and transform the guest room to a media room or a family bedroom.

- **Master Suite:** The bedroom features a tray ceiling, has his and her dressing areas, and opens to the porch. The bath has a large corner tub, separate shower, linen closet, and two vanities.

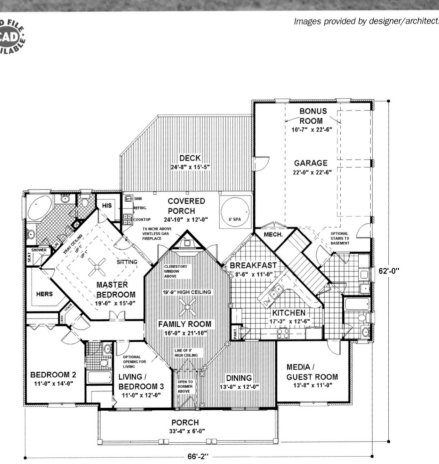

Copyright by designer/architect.

Kitchen

Great Room

Dining Room

Hearth Room

Master Bedroom

Study

Plan #441008

Dimensions: 60' W x 50' D

Levels: 1

Heated Square Footage: 2,001

Bedrooms: 3

Bathrooms: 2

Foundation: Crawl space;
slab or basement available for fee

Materials List Available: Yes

Price Category: D

A fine design for a country setting, this one-story plan offers a quaint covered porch at the entry, cedar shingles in the gables, and stonework at the foundation line.

Features:

- **Entry:** The pretty package on the outside is prelude to the fine floor plan on the inside. It begins at this entry foyer, which opens on the right to a den with a 9-ft.-high ceiling and space for a desk or closet.

- **Great Room:** This entertaining area is vaulted and contains a fireplace and optional media center. The rear windows allow a view onto the rear deck.

- **Kitchen:** Open to the dining room and great room to form one large space, this kitchen boasts a raised bar and a built-in desk.

- **Master Suite:** The vaulted ceiling in this master suite adds an elegant touch. The master bath features a dual vanities and a spa tub.

Images provided by designer/architect.

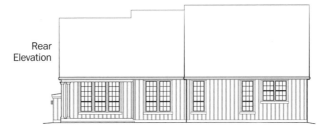

Rear Elevation

Copyright by designer/architect.

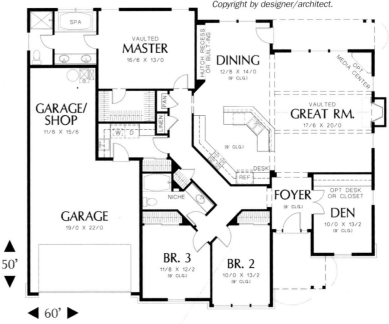

Plan #351069

Dimensions: 78' W x 49'6" D

Levels: 1

Heated Square Footage: 2,002

Bedrooms: 3

Bathrooms: 2½

Foundation: Crawl space or slab

Materials List Available: No

Price Category: F

This is a great house with a functional split-floor-plan layout.

CAD FILE AVAILABLE

Features:

- **Entertaining Areas:** A large dining area for those family get-togethers and an expansive great room with a gas log fireplace and vaulted ceiling will make entertaining easy.

- **Master Suite:** This expansive suite has a large sitting area, his and her walk-in closets, a jetted tub, and a walk-in shower.

- **Storage Areas:** The home features plenty of storage space; a large utility room will help stow away your odds and ends.

- **Expansion:** Flex space can be used as a home office/study, playroom, and/or entertainment center. There is even a bonus room above the garage.

Images provided by designer/architect.

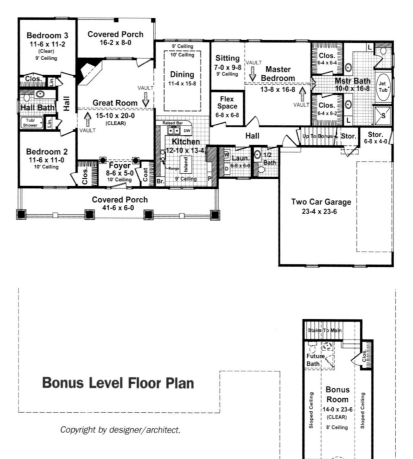

Bonus Level Floor Plan

Copyright by designer/architect.

Images provided by designer/architect.

CAD FILE AVAILABLE

Plan #321213

Dimensions: 70' W x 29' D

Levels: 1

Heated Square Footage: 1,941

Bedrooms: 5

Bathrooms: 3

Foundation: Walkout

Materials List Available: Yes

Price Category: D

Lower Level Floor Plan

Copyright by designer/architect.

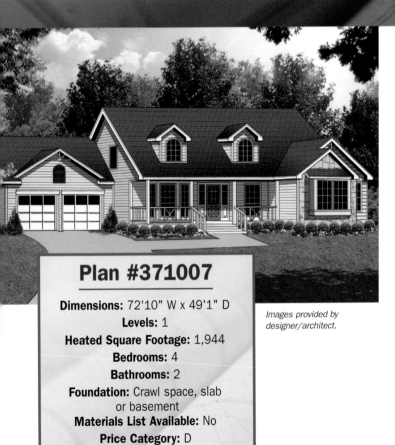

Plan #371007

Dimensions: 72'10" W x 49'1" D

Levels: 1

Heated Square Footage: 1,944

Bedrooms: 4

Bathrooms: 2

Foundation: Crawl space, slab or basement

Materials List Available: No

Price Category: D

Images provided by designer/architect.

Copyright by designer/architect.

Images provided by designer/architect.

CAD FILE AVAILABLE

Plan #661065

Dimensions: 59' W x 72'4" D

Levels: 1

Heated Square Footage: 1,993

Bedrooms: 3

Bathrooms: 2

Foundation: Slab

Materials List Available: No

Price Category: D

Copyright by designer/architect.

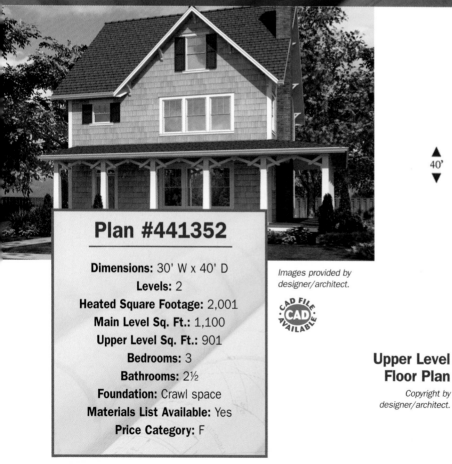

Main Level Floor Plan

Upper Level Floor Plan

Copyright by designer/architect.

Images provided by designer/architect.

CAD FILE AVAILABLE

Plan #441352

Dimensions: 30' W x 40' D

Levels: 2

Heated Square Footage: 2,001

Main Level Sq. Ft.: 1,100

Upper Level Sq. Ft.: 901

Bedrooms: 3

Bathrooms: 2½

Foundation: Crawl space

Materials List Available: Yes

Price Category: F

1,500–2,500 sq. ft.

Plan #211048

Dimensions: 66' W x 60' D

Levels: 1

Heated Square Footage: 2,002

Bedrooms: 3

Bathrooms: 2

Foundation: Crawl space; slab for fee

Materials List Available: Yes

Price Category: D

Images provided by designer/architect.

Copyright by designer/architect.

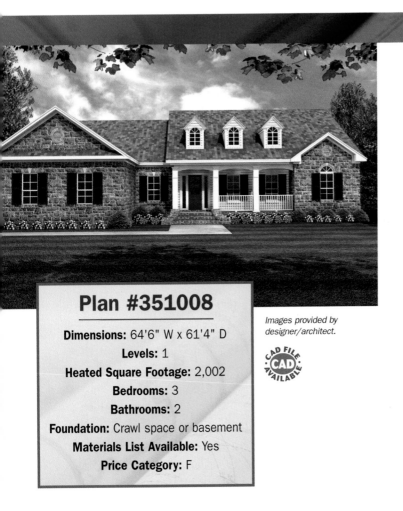

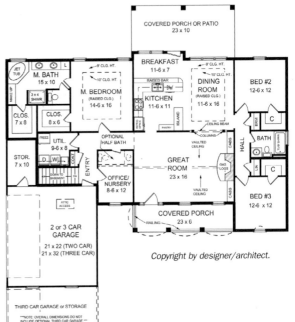

Plan #351008

Dimensions: 64'6" W x 61'4" D

Levels: 1

Heated Square Footage: 2,002

Bedrooms: 3

Bathrooms: 2

Foundation: Crawl space or basement

Materials List Available: Yes

Price Category: F

Images provided by designer/architect.

CAD FILE AVAILABLE

Copyright by designer/architect.

Images provided by designer/architect.

Copyright by designer/architect.

Plan #351141

Dimensions: 69' W x 75'10" D

Levels: 1

Heated Square Footage: 2,021

Bedrooms: 3

Bathrooms: 2½

Foundation: Crawl space, slab or basement

Material List Available: Yes

Price Category: F

Kitchen

Plan #181307

Dimensions: 46' W x 40' D

Levels: 2

Heated Square Footage: 2,028

Main Level Sq. Ft.: 971

Upper Level Sq. Ft.: 1,057

Bedrooms: 3

Bathrooms: 2½

Foundation: Basement

Materials List Available: Yes

Price Category: D

Images provided by designer/architect.

Main Level Floor Plan

Upper Level Floor Plan

Copyright by designer/architect.

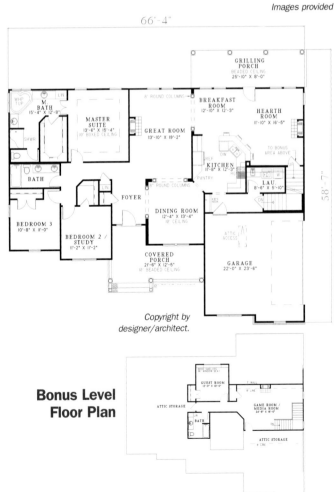

Images provided by designer/architect.

Plan #151133

Dimensions: 66'4" W x 58'7" D

Levels: 1

Heated Square Footage: 2,029

Bedrooms: 3

Bathrooms: 2½

Foundation: Crawl space, slab, or basement

CompleteCost List Available: Yes

Price Category: D

You'll love the spacious and inviting porch area this home provides.

Features:

- **Porches:** Located at the front of the home, a covered porch is a wonderful space to greet guests. A grilling porch at the back of the home is perfect for entertaining or enjoying a meal outside.

- **Great Room:** This great room, located at the heart of the home, features a beautiful fireplace.

- **Kitchen:** Preparing meals is easy in this lovely kitchen, complete with a pantry and an eating bar.

- **Master Suite:** This expansive master suite includes a large bedroom area and a bath room complete with a whirlpool tub, walk-in closet, and two separate vanities.

Copyright by designer/architect.

Bonus Level Floor Plan

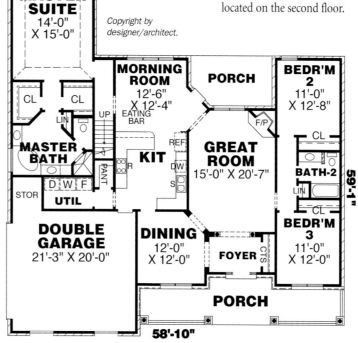

Images provided by designer/architect.

Plan #241007

Dimensions: 58'10" W x 59'1" D

Levels: 1

Heated Square Footage: 2,036

Bedrooms: 3

Bathrooms: 2

Foundation: Crawl space, slab

Materials List Available: No

Price Category: D

Enjoy summer breezes while relaxing on the large front porch of this charming country cottage.

Features:

- **Great Room:** Whether you enter from the front door or from the kitchen, you will feel welcome in this comfortable great room, which features a corner fireplace.

- **Kitchen:** This well-designed kitchen with extensive counter space offers a delightful eating bar, perfect for quick or informal meals.

- **Master Suite:** This luxurious master suite, located on the first floor for privacy, features his and her walk-in closets, separate vanities, a deluxe corner tub, a linen closet, and a walk-in shower.

- **Additional Bedrooms:** Two secondary bedrooms and an optional, large game room —well suited for a growing family—are located on the second floor.

Bonus Area Floor Plan

Copyright by designer/architect.

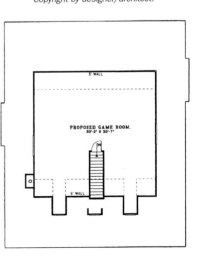

Plan #151105

Dimensions: 60'6" W x 91'4" D
Levels: 1
Heated Square Footage: 2,039
Bedrooms: 4
Bathrooms: 2
Foundation: Crawl space, slab, or optional basement
CompleteCost List Available: Yes
Price Category: D

Images provided by designer/architect.

If you've always wanted a wraparound porch with columns, this could be your dream home.

Features:

- **Great Room:** Just off the foyer, this spacious room features a handsome fireplace where friends and family are sure to gather.

- **Dining Room:** Columns set off this dining room, and the large window area allows natural lighting during the day.

- **Kitchen:** Open to the dining room, this well-planned kitchen features a large central island with a sink and a dishwasher on one side and an eating bar on the other.

- **Breakfast Room:** You'll love the unusual shape of this room and its windows overlooking the rear porch. Access to the porch is from a hallway here.

- **Master Suite:** Enjoy two walk-in closets, plus a bath with a corner whirlpool tub, glass shower, linen closet, vanity, and compartmentalized toilet.

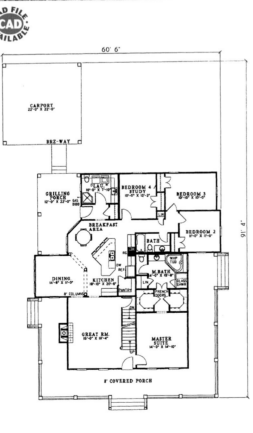

Bonus Area

Copyright by designer/architect.

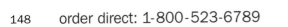

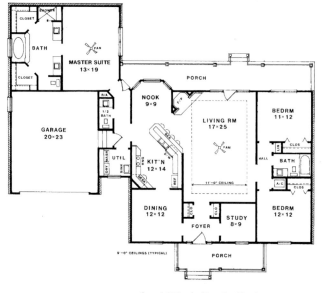

Images provided by designer/architect.

Plan #171011

Dimensions: 70' W x 58' D

Levels: 1

Heated Square Footage: 2,069

Bedrooms: 3

Bathrooms: 2½

Foundation: Crawl space, slab

Materials List Available: Yes

Price Category: D

This home combines the charm of a country cottage with all the modern amenities.

Features:

- Ceiling Height: 9 ft. unless otherwise noted.

- Front Porch: Watch the sun set, read a book, or just relax on this spacious front porch.

- Foyer: This gracious foyer has two closets and opens to the formal dining room and the study.

- Dining Room: This big dining room works just as well for family Sunday dinner as it does for entertaining guests on Saturday night.

- Family Room: This inviting family room features an 11-ft. ceiling, a paddle fan, and a corner fireplace.

- Kitchen: This smart kitchen includes lots of counter space, a built in desk, and a breakfast bar.

- Master Bedroom: This master bedroom is separate from the other bedrooms for added privacy. It includes a paddle fan.

- Master Bath: This master bath has two vanities, walk-in closets, a deluxe tub, and a walk-in shower.

SMARTtip

Types of Paintbrush Bristles

Nylon Bristles. These are most suitable for latex paint, although they can also be used with solvent-based paint.

Natural Bristles. Also called "China bristle," natural bristle brushes are preferred for use with solvent-based paints and varnishes because they tend to hold more paint and generally brush out to a smoother looking finish. Natural bristle brushes should not be used with latex paint. The water in the paint will cause the bristles to expand and ruin the brush.

Choosing Brushes. When buying a brush, check for thick, resilient bristles that are firmly held in place. Be sure, also, to get the proper type brush for the job.

Copyright by designer/architect.

Plan #191025

Dimensions: 50' W x 68' D

Levels: 1

Heated Square Footage: 2,052

Bedrooms: 3

Bathrooms: 2

Foundation: Crawl space, slab

Materials List Available: No

Price Category: D

Images provided by designer/architect.

Copyright by designer/architect.

MASTER BEDROOM 17-0 X 18-2

PORCH

PORCH 10-0 WIDE

BEDROOM 3 14-0 X 12-0

CLO.

P

REF.

GAS FIREPLACE

GREAT ROOM 23-4 X 17-0

BATH 2

KITCHEN 12-10 X 15-10

DOWNDRAFT COOKTOP

COUNTER HIGH SNACK BAR

DINING 12-10 X 10-0

SITTING AREA

BEDROOM 2 13-10 X 12-0

PORCH

68'-0"

50'-0"

Plan #351149

Dimensions: 70' W x 56' D

Levels: 1

Heated Square Footage: 2,067

Bedrooms: 3

Bathrooms: 2½

Foundation: Crawl space or slab

Materials List Available: Yes

Price Category: D

Images provided by designer/architect.

CAD FILE AVAILABLE

Rear View

Bedroom 3 12'-0" x 10'-6" 9' Clg. Ht.

Bath 2 8'-0" x 7'-7"

Hall 1

Tub/Shwr

Bedroom 2 12'-0" x 10'-6" 9' Clg. Ht.

Foyer 6'-2" x 10'-10" 10' Clg. Ht.

Covered Porch 18'-6" x 7'-8"

Gas Logs

Great Room 18'-6" x 16'-0" 11' Clg. Ht. Trayed Clg.

Flex Space 12'-0" x 10'-6" 10' Clg. Ht. (Clear)

Covered Porch 31'-6" x 8'-0"

Patio 20'-6" x 8'-10"

Breakfast 14'-0" x 13'-0" 9' Clg. Ht.

Optional Built-ins

Kitchen 14'-0" x 15'-6"

Bar

Island

Pan.

DW

Master Bedroom 14'-8" x 15'-0" 10' Clg. Ht. Trayed Clg.

To Bonus

Half Bath

Utility 6'-6" x 7'-2"

Hall 2

Sto. Under Stairs

Up

Mstr. Clos.

Mstr. Bath 8'-10" x 16'-0"

Jet Tub

Mstr. Clos. 8'-10" x 6'-0"

Storage 9'-2" x 4'-4"

Two-Car Garage 23'-10" x 22'-10"

Bonus Area Floor Plan

Copyright by designer/architect.

Down

Down

Unfinished Bonus Room 13'-10" x 22'-10" 8' Clg. Ht.

Attic Access

Main Level Floor Plan

CAD FILE AVAILABLE — CAD

Upper Level Floor Plan

Plan #371079

Dimensions: 51'4" W x 56'6" D
Levels: 2
Heated Square Footage: 2,089
Main Level Sq. Ft.: 1,441
Upper Level Sq. Ft.: 648
Bedrooms: 3
Bathrooms: 2½
Foundation: Slab
Materials List Available: No
Price Category: D

Plan #191026

Dimensions: 50' W x 62' D
Levels: 1
Heated Square Footage: 2,052
Bedrooms: 3
Bathrooms: 2
Foundation: Crawl space, slab
Materials List Available: No
Price Category: D

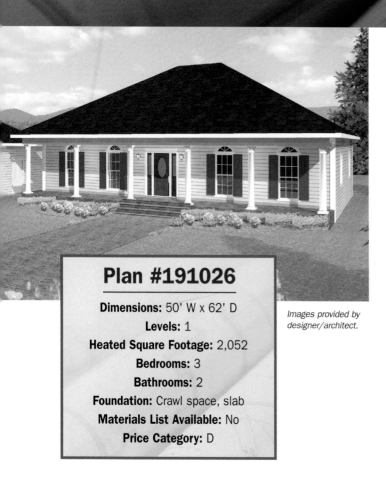

Plan #161026

Dimensions: 67'6" W x 63'6" D
Levels: 1
Heated Square Footage: 2,041
Bedrooms: 3
Bathrooms: 2
Foundation: Basement
Materials List Available: No
Price Category: D

You'll love the special features of this home, which has been designed for efficiency and comfort.

Images provided by designer/architect.

CAD FILE AVAILABLE · CAD

Features:

- Foyer: This raised foyer offers a view through the great room and beyond it to the covered deck.

- Great Room: Elegant windows allow versatility — decorate casually or more formally.

- Kitchen: You'll find ample counter space and cabinets in this spacious room, which adjoins the dining room and opens onto the rear yard.

- Library: Curl up on the window seat that wraps around the tower in this quiet spot.

- Laundry Room: A tub makes this large room practical for crafts as well as laundry.

- Master Suite: A vaulted ceiling gives grace to the sitting area, and the garden bath with a walk-in closet and whirlpool tub adds luxury.

Rear Elevation

Main Level Floor Plan

Basement Level Floor Plan

Copyright by designer/architect.

Left Side Elevation

Right Side Elevation

Front View

Living Room

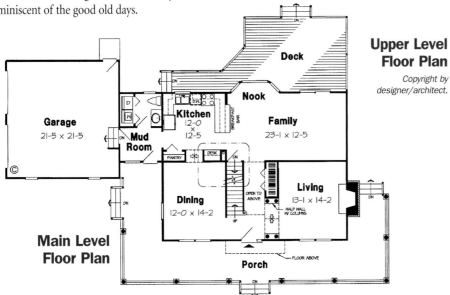

Plan #391007

Dimensions: 74' W x 41'6" D
Levels: 2
Heated Square Footage: 2,083
Main Level Sq. Ft.: 1,113
Upper Level Sq. Ft.: 970
Bedrooms: 3
Bathrooms: 2½
Foundation: Crawl space, slab, or basement
Materials List Available: Yes
Price Category: D

Images provided by designer/architect.

With a wide-wrapping porch and a pretty Palladian window peeking from a sky-high dormer, this charming home is cheerfully reminiscent of the good old days.

Features:

- Dining and Living Rooms: Over the threshold, this dining room engages one side of the staircase and the living room with fireplace occupies the other to maintain balance.

- Kitchen: One section of this functional kitchen looks out at the deck, feeds into the breakfast area, and flows into the great-sized family room while the other leads to the laundry area, half bath, mudroom, and garage.

- Master Suite: The second level delivers the master suite, with its wide walk-in closet and a full bath with separate shower and tub areas, double sinks, and a bright window.

- Bedrooms: Each of the two equally spacious secondary bedrooms with wall-length closets and large windows shares a full-size bath uniquely outfitted with double sinks so that no one has to wait to primp.

Upper Level Floor Plan

Copyright by designer/architect.

Main Level Floor Plan

Crawl Space/Slab Option

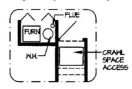

Rear View

Rear View

Loft Area

Front Porch

Master Bedroom

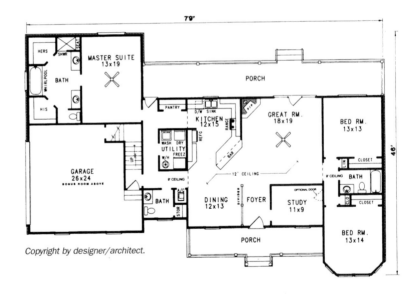

Images provided by designer/architect.

Plan #171015

Dimensions: 79' W x 46' D
Levels: 1
Heated Square Footage: 2,089
Bedrooms: 3
Bathrooms: 2½
Foundation: Crawl space or slab
Materials List Available: Yes
Price Category: D

This lovely three-bedroom country home, with a bonus room above the garage, is a perfect family home.

Features:

- Dining Room: This formal room and the great room form a large gathering space with a 12-ft.-high ceiling.

- Kitchen: The raised bar defines this kitchen and offers additional seating.

- Master Suite: This suite, located on the opposite side of the home from the secondary bedrooms, enjoys a luxurious bath with his and her walk-in closets.

- Bedrooms: Two secondary bedrooms have large closets and share a hall bathroom.

Copyright by designer/architect.

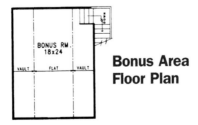

**Bonus Area
Floor Plan**

Plan #181094

Dimensions: 50' W x 39' D
Levels: 2
Heated Square Footage: 2,099
Main Level Sq. Ft.: 1,060
Upper Level Sq. Ft.: 1,039
Bedrooms: 4
Bathrooms: 2½
Foundation: Basement
Materials List Available: Yes
Price Category: D

Images provided by designer/architect.

The curved covered porch makes this is a great place to come home to.

CAD FILE AVAILABLE

Features:

- **Entry:** This air-lock entry area with closet will help keep energy costs down.

- **Family Room:** This gathering area features a fireplace and is open to the kitchen and the dining area.

- **Kitchen:** U-shaped and boasting an island and a walk-in pantry, this kitchen is open to the dining area.

- **Master Suite:** This large retreat features a fireplace and a walk-in closet. The master bath has dual vanities, a separate shower, and a large tub.

- **Bedrooms:** Located upstairs with the master suite are three additional bedrooms. They share a common bathroom, and each has a large closet.

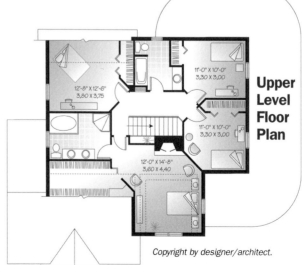

Rear View

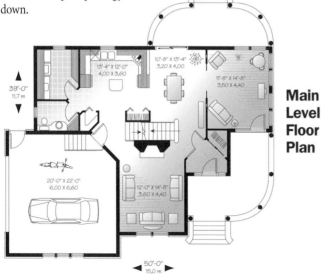

Main Level Floor Plan

39'-0"
11,7 m

13'-4" X 12'-0"
4,00 X 3,80

10'-8" X 13'-4"
3,20 X 4,00

11'-8" X 14'-8"
3,50 X 4,40

20'-0" X 22'-0"
6,00 X 6,60

12'-0" X 14'-8"
3,60 X 4,40

50'-0"
15,0 m

Upper Level Floor Plan

12'-8" X 12'-6"
3,80 X 3,75

11'-0" X 10'-0"
3,30 X 3,00

11'-0" X 10'-0"
3,30 X 3,00

12'-0" X 14'-8"
3,80 X 4,40

Copyright by designer/architect.

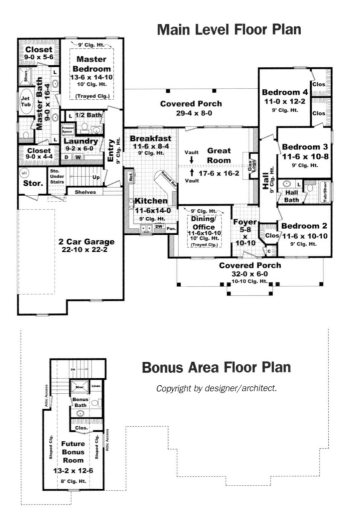

Plan #351176

Dimensions: 69' W x 59' D

Levels: 1

Heated Square Footage: 2,100

Bedrooms: 4

Bathrooms: 2½

Foundation: Crawl space, slab

Material List Available: Yes

Price Category: D

Images provided by designer/architect.

The many available features and flexibility of this home make it the perfect choice for you and your family.

Features:

- **Great Room:** This great room features vaulted ceilings, built-in cabinets, a fireplace, and direct access to the rear covered porch.

- **Kitchen:** Mornings are made easy in this kitchen, which features a raised eating bar, a breakfast area, and ample counter space.

- **Master Suite:** You'll never want to leave this beautiful master suite with its coffered ceiling, two walk-in closets, whirlpool tub, and separate vanity areas.

- **Secondary Bedrooms:** Three additional bedrooms share a separate area of the home, each with its own walk-in closet.

Main Level Floor Plan

Bonus Area Floor Plan

Copyright by designer/architect.

Plan #191012

Dimensions: 60' W x 76' D
Levels: 1
Heated Square Footage: 2,123
Bedrooms: 3
Bathrooms: 2½
Foundation: Crawl space or slab
Materials List Available: No
Price Category: D

The wraparound porch adds to the charm of this home.

Features:

- **Porches:** The front wraparound porch will be the perfect spot to greet neighbors as they stroll by. The rear porch is a private place to relax and enjoy a beautiful day.

- **Great Room:** This large gathering area features a 10-ft.-high ceiling and large windows, which offer a view of the backyard. There is even room for a formal dining table.

- **Master Suite:** Located on the opposite side of the home from the secondary bedrooms, this retreat offers a large sleeping area. The master bath will pamper you with an oversize shower, a tub, and dual vanities.

- **Secondary Bedrooms:** Two similarly sized bedrooms have ample closet space and share a full bathroom.

Images provided by designer/architect.

Kitchen

Copyright by designer/architect.

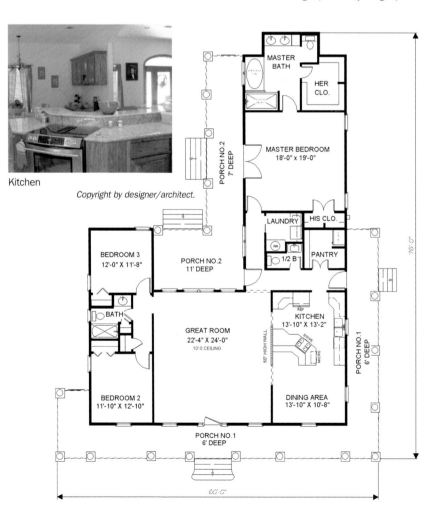

Plan #441049

Dimensions: 50' W x 47'6" D
Levels: 2
Heated Square Footage: 2,124
Main Level Sq. Ft.: 1,157
Upper Level Sq. Ft.: 967
Bedrooms: 3
Bathrooms: 2½
Foundation: Crawl space; slab or basement for fee
Materials List Available: No
Price Category: D

Take a quaint cottage design, and expand naturally with a second-floor addition over the garage-the result is a comfortable home with all the charm of bungalow style.

Features:

• Foyer: Enter the home through the covered entry porch, with Arts and Crafts columns, into this foyer brightened by sidelights and a transom at the front door. The half-bathroom and coat closet make the entry area convenient.

• Great Room: This gathering area features a vaulted ceiling and a fireplace. Tall windows allow the room to be flooded with natural light, giving a warm and airy feeling.

• Kitchen: This island kitchen boasts long counters lined with cabinetry, making it a gourmet's delight to prepare meals in the area. The raised bar is open to the great room and dining room.

• Upper Level: This upper level is devoted to sleeping space. There is the vaulted master salon with private master bath and walk-in closet, plus the two family bedrooms, which share the other full bathroom. Note the large linen closet in the upper-level hall.

Images provided by designer/architect.

Rear Elevation

Main Level Floor Plan

Upper Level Floor Plan

Copyright by designer/architect.

Plan #371081

Dimensions: 54'6" W x 41'10" D

Levels: 2

Heated Square Footage: 2,143

Main Level Sq. Ft.: 1,535

Upper Level Sq. Ft.: 608

Bedrooms: 4

Bathrooms: 3

Foundation: Slab or basement

Materials List Available: No

Price Category: D

The cozy wraparound front porch of this beautiful country home invites you to stay awhile.

CAD FILE AVAILABLE

Images provided by designer/architect.

Features:

- **Family Room:** This large gathering area features a wonderful fireplace and is open to the dining room.

- **Kitchen:** The island cabinet in this fully functional kitchen brings an open feel to this room and the adjoining dining room.

- **Master Suite:** Mom and Dad can relax downstairs in this spacious master suite, with their luxurious master bathroom, which has double walk-in closets and a marble tub.

- **Bedrooms:** The kids will enjoy these two large secondary bedrooms and the study area with bookcases upstairs.

Rear Elevation

Upper Level Floor Plan

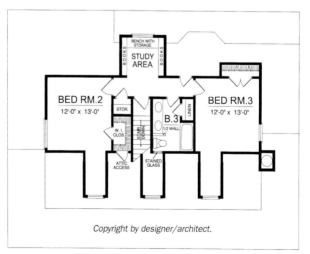

Copyright by designer/architect.

Main Level Floor Plan

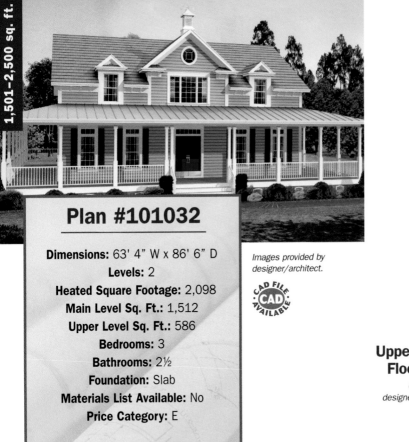

Plan #101032

Dimensions: 63' 4" W x 86' 6" D

Levels: 2

Heated Square Footage: 2,098

Main Level Sq. Ft.: 1,512

Upper Level Sq. Ft.: 586

Bedrooms: 3

Bathrooms: 2½

Foundation: Slab

Materials List Available: No

Price Category: E

Images provided by designer/architect.

CAD FILE AVAILABLE

Main Level Floor Plan

86'-6"

63'-4"

Upper Level Floor Plan

Copyright by designer/architect.

Plan #181035

Dimensions: 56' W x 38' D

Levels: 2

Heated Square Footage: 2,129

Main Level Sq. Ft.: 1,136

Upper Level Sq. Ft.: 993

Bedrooms: 3

Bathrooms: 2½

Foundation: Basement; crawl space or slab for fee

Materials List Available: Yes

Price Category: D

Images provided by designer/architect.

CAD FILE AVAILABLE

Main Level Floor Plan

38'-0"
11,4 m

56'-0"
16,8 m

Upper Level Floor Plan

Copyright by designer/architect.

Plan #151171

Dimensions: 63'10" W x 72'2" D

Levels: 1

Heated Square Footage: 2,131

Bedrooms: 3

Bathrooms: 2½

Foundation: Crawl space, slab; basement or daylight basement for fee

CompleteCost List Available: Yes

Price Category: D

Images provided by designer/architect.

CAD FILE AVAILABLE

Copyright by designer/architect.

Plan #161109

Dimensions: 50' W x 50'2" D

Levels: 1.5

Heated Square Footage: 2,132

Main Level Sq. Ft.: 1,337

Upper Level Sq. Ft.: 795

Bedrooms: 4

Bathrooms: 2½

Foundation: Basement; crawl space, slab or walk out for fee

Materials List Available: Yes

Price Category: D

Images provided by designer/architect.

Main Level Floor Plan

Upper Level Floor Plan

Copyright by designer/architect.

Plan #351206

Dimensions: 71' W x 77' D

Levels: 1

Heated Square Footage: 2,140

Bedrooms: 4

Bathrooms: 2½

Foundation: Crawl space, slab or basement

Materials List Available: Yes

Price Category: D

Images provided by designer/architect.

CAD FILE AVAILABLE

Copyright by designer/architect.

Bonus Area Floor Plan

Plan #121176

Dimensions: 67' W x 52' D

Levels: 1

Heated Square Footage: 2,144

Bedrooms: 4

Bathrooms: 2

Foundation: Slab; basement for fee

Materials List Available: Yes

Price Category: D

Images provided by designer/architect.

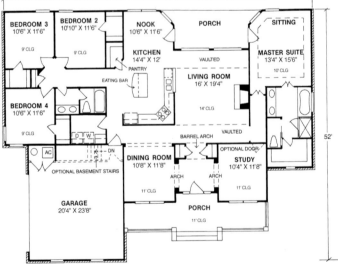

Copyright by designer/architect.

Images provided by designer/architect.

Copyright by designer/architect.

Plan #151076

Dimensions: 58' W x 66'6" D
Levels: 1
Heated Square Footage: 2,187
Bedrooms: 4
Bathrooms: 2
Foundation: Crawl space or slab; basement for fee
CompleteCost List Available: Yes
Price Category: D

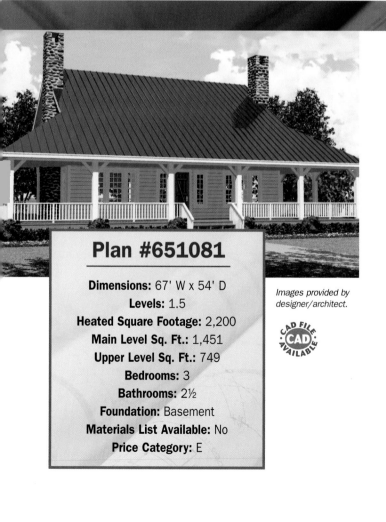

Plan #651081

Dimensions: 67' W x 54' D
Levels: 1.5
Heated Square Footage: 2,200
Main Level Sq. Ft.: 1,451
Upper Level Sq. Ft.: 749
Bedrooms: 3
Bathrooms: 2½
Foundation: Basement
Materials List Available: No
Price Category: E

Images provided by designer/architect.

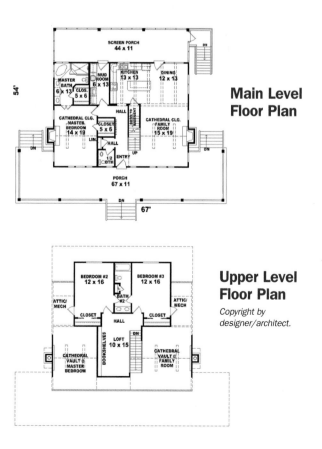

Main Level Floor Plan

Upper Level Floor Plan

Copyright by designer/architect.

Plan #181085

Dimensions: 56'4" W x 44' D
Levels: 2
Heated Square Footage: 2,183
Main Level Sq. Ft.: 1,232
Second Level Sq. Ft.: 951
Bedrooms: 3
Bathrooms: 2½
Foundation: Basement
Materials List Available: Yes
Price Category: D

This country home features an inviting front porch and a layout designed for modern living.

Images provided by designer/architect.

Features:

- Ceiling Height: 8 ft.
- Solarium: Sunlight streams through the windows of this solarium at the front of the house.
- Living Room: Walk through French doors, and you will enter this inviting living room. Family and friends will be drawn to the corner fireplace.
- Formal Dining Room: Usher your guests directly from the living room into this formal dining room. The kitchen is located on the other side of the dining room for convenient service.
- Kitchen: This generously sized kitchen is a delight, it offers a center island, separate eat-in area, and access to the back deck.
- Bonus Room: This room just off the entry hall can become a family room, a bedroom, or an office.
- Master Suite: Curl up by the corner fireplace in this master retreat, with its walk-in closet and lavish bath with separate shower and tub.

Main Level Floor Plan

Upper Level Floor Plan

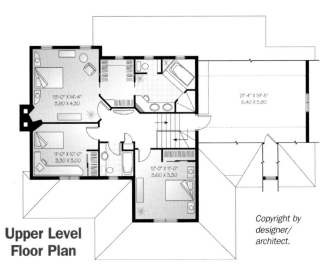

Plan #151113

Dimensions: 62'10" W x 91'4" D

Levels: 1

Heated Square Footage: 2,186

Bedrooms: 4

Bathrooms: 3

Foundation: Crawl space, slab, or basement

CompleteCost List Available: Yes

Price Category: D

The porch on this four-bedroom ranch welcomes you home.

Features:

- **Great Room:** You'll find this large room just off the foyer.

- **Dining Room:** This room, with a view of the side yard, is located adjacent to the kitchen and the great room.

- **Kitchen:** This island kitchen, with a built-in pantry, is open to the breakfast area.

- **Master Suite:** This suite features his and her walk-in closets and a private bathroom with double vanities and whirlpool tub.

- **Bedrooms:** Three secondary bedrooms have large closets and share a hall bathroom.

Images provided by designer/architect.

CAD FILE AVAILABLE

Copyright by designer/architect.

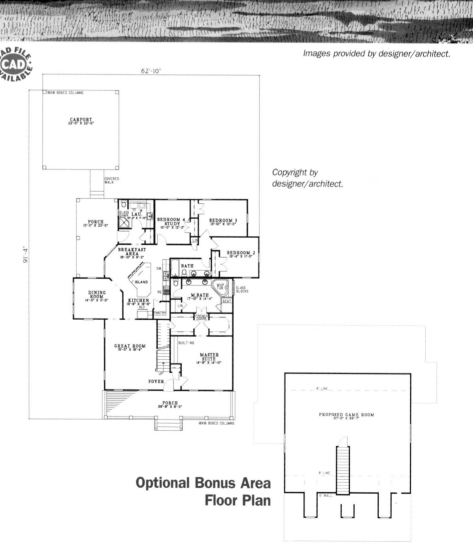

Optional Bonus Area Floor Plan

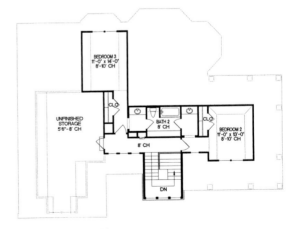

Plan #121160

Dimensions: 66'4½" W x 49'9½" D
Levels: 1.5
Heated Square Footage: 2,188
Main Level Sq. Ft.: 1,531
Upper Level Sq. Ft.: 657
Bedrooms: 3
Bathrooms: 2½
Foundation: Slab; basement for fee
Materials List Available: Yes
Price Category: D

The standing-seam roof on the wraparound porch gives this home a charming country look.

Images provided by designer/architect.

Features:

- **Family Room:** The open design that leads to the adjoining breakfast area makes this space airy and welcoming. The room also features a tray ceiling. The fireplace adds to the comfortable feel of the space.

- **Dining Room / Sunroom:** Featuring three exterior walls with windows, this space can either be your formal dining room or your casual sunroom.

- **Kitchen:** This peninsula kitchen boasts a raised bar open to the breakfast room. The walk-in pantry is always a welcome feature.

- **Master Suite:** Located on the main level, this retreat features a bay window with a view of the backyard. The master bath features a large walk-in closet and dual vanities.

Front View

Main Level Floor Plan

Upper Level Floor Plan

Copyright by designer/architect.

Plan #341295

Dimensions: 46' W x 58'8" D

Levels: 2

Heated Square Footage: 2,188

Main Level Sq. Ft.: 1,569

Upper Level Sq. Ft: 619

Bedrooms: 3

Bathrooms: 2½

Foundation: Crawl space; slab or basement for fee

Materials List Available: Yes

Price Category: D

This traditional two-story home includes a covered entry and plenty of space and features for the modern family.

Features:

- **Foyer:** A dramatic entry, the quaint covered porch welcomes guests into this two-story foyer, which includes closet space and a half bathroom.

- **Kitchen:** This L-shaped kitchen features an island and a large pantry. The busy room sits close to the dining room, family room, and breakfast room, providing many choices for mealtime.

- **Deck:** Through the breakfast area is this back deck for barbecues or meals outside.

- **Master Suite:** The vaulted ceilings, walk-in closet, and full master bath with a garden tub make this area the perfect retreat from everyday life.

- **Second Floor:** Both secondary bedrooms feature a large closet and share the second full bathroom. The second floor is open to the first over the foyer and family room, giving the house an attractive sense of freedom.

Main Level Floor Plan

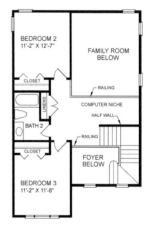

Upper Level Floor Plan

Copyright by designer/architect.

Plan #351067

Dimensions: 78' W x 58'6" D
Levels: 1
Heated Square Footage: 2,200
Bedrooms: 3
Bathrooms: 3½
Foundation: Crawl space or slab
Material List Available: Yes
Price Category: F

Images provided by designer/architect.

The whole family will love this country home's classically designed exterior and flexibly designed interior.

CAD FILE AVAILABLE

Features:

• **Porches:** A covered porch is great for welcoming guests or sitting out with neighbors. A door from the great room opens onto the back covered porch, perfect for outdoor meals or relaxing afternoons enjoying the unfettered breeze. This leads down onto the back patio, with plenty of room for barbecuing and soaking up the sun.

• **Kitchen:** Featuring an L-shaped design with an island, this kitchen has plenty of work space and storage and is separated from the dining area only by a raised bar.

• **Master Bedroom:** This room plays two roles: preparing you for everyday life while giving you an escape from it when needed. Vaulted ceilings and a sitting area give you the space you need to relax. The master bath features his and her closets and sinks, as well as linen cabinets, a standing shower, a jetted tub, and a compartmentalized toilet.

• **Secondary Bedrooms:** In a wing of their own, the other two bedrooms each feature a large closet and private full bathroom. Between the two is a media room with built-in entertainment space.

• **Bonus Area:** Above the garage is this flexible space, which can easily be used as a spare bedroom.

Copyright by designer/architect.

Bonus Area Floor Plan

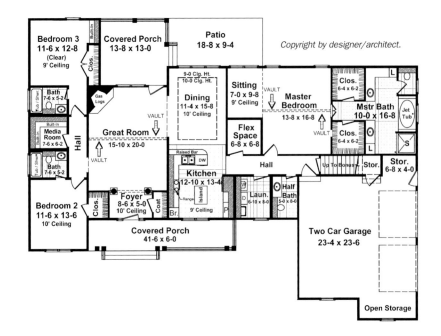

Images provided by designer/architect.

Plan #401028

Dimensions: 25'6" W x 54'9" D

Levels: 2

Heated Square Footage: 2,219

Main Level Sq. Ft.: 1,136

Upper Level Sq. Ft.: 1,083

Bedrooms: 4

Bathrooms: 2½

Foundation: Basement

Materials List Available: Yes

Price Category: E

This inviting narrow-lot design borrows classic details from a bygone era–a covered verandah in the front, a gabled roof, and fish-scale detailing.

Features:

- Porches: At the front of the home is a beautiful covered verandah, wonderful for greeting and relaxing with guests. At the back of the home is another porch, which opens out from the breakfast nook, perfect for dining outside.

- Living Room: This beautiful formal living room is open to the dining room and includes a gas fireplace.

- Kitchen: Toward the rear of the home, this kitchen overlooks a breakfast nook and the family room

- Master Suite: Upstairs, this master suite includes a walk-in closet and a private bath that includes a separate tub and shower and double vanities.

**Optinonal
Main Level Floor Plan**

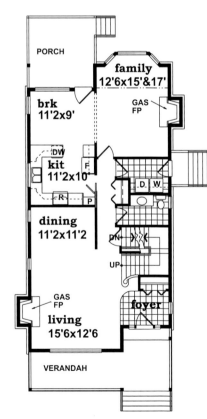

Main Level Floor Plan

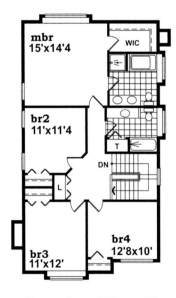

Upper Level Floor Plan

Copyright by designer/architect.

1,501-2,500 sq. ft.

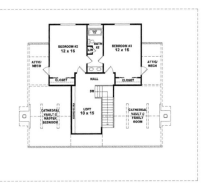

Main Level Floor Plan

Plan #651079

Dimensions: 67' W x 54' D

Levels: 1.5

Heated Square Footage: 2,207

Main Level Sq. Ft.: 1,466

Upper Level Sq. Ft.: 741

Bedrooms: 3

Bathrooms: 2½

Foundation: Crawl space or basement

Material List Available: No

Price Category: E

Images provided by designer/architect.

CAD FILE AVAILABLE

Upper Level Floor Plan

Copyright by designer/architect.

Main Level Floor Plan

Plan #181243

Dimensions: 67' W x 40' D

Levels: 2

Heated Square Footage: 2,219

Main Level Sq. Ft.: 1,232

Upper Level Sq. Ft.: 987

Bedrooms: 3

Bathrooms: 3½

Foundation: Basement, or walkout

Materials List Available: Yes

Price Category: E

Images provided by designer/architect.

CAD FILE AVAILABLE

Copyright by designer/architect.

Upper Level Floor Plan

BATH 1

SEE THRU FIREPLACE

3 CAR GARAGE
21'-0" x 31'-0"

STEP UP CLG.

MASTER SUITE
14'-0" x 17'-0"

PORCH

BED RM.2
12'-0" x 11'-0"

WORK BENCH

GLASS SHR.

B.3

UTIL.

11'-0" HIGH CLG.

LIVING RM.
20'-0" x 16'-0"

B.2

STAIR WOOD RAIL

BOOKS

LIN

STOR

BED RM.3
12'-0" x 11'-0"

DESK

PANT.

NOOK
8'-0" x 8'-0"

KITCH.
12'-0" x 10'-0"

11'-0" HIGH CLG.

DINING RM.
11'-0" x 15'-0"

WOOD COLUMN

ENT

10'-0" HIGH CLG.

BED RM.4
11'-8" x 10'-0"

CLG. SLOPES

P.

CLG. SLOPES

CLG. SLOPES

BONUS RM.
21'-4" x 14'-0"

WOOD RAIL

STAIR DOWN

CLG. SLOPES

Bonus Area

Copyright by designer/architect.

Images provided by designer/architect.

CAD FILE AVAILABLE

Plan #371059

Dimensions: 77'8" W x 56'6" D

Levels: 1

Heated Square Footage: 2,240

Bedrooms: 4

Bathrooms: 2½

Foundation: Slab; crawl space for fee

Materials List Available: No

Price Category: E

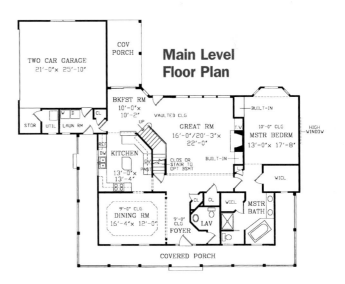

TWO CAR GARAGE
21'-0" x 25'-10"

COV PORCH

Main Level Floor Plan

STOR

UTIL

LAUN RM

CL

W D

BKFST RM
10'-0" x 10'-2"

VAULTED CLG

UP

GREAT RM
16'-0"/20'-3" x 22'-0"

BUILT-IN

10'-0" CLG

MSTR BEDRM
13'-0" x 17'-8"

HIGH WINDOW

REF

DW

KITCHEN
13'-0" x 13'-4"

OV

PANT

CLOS OR STAIR TO OPT BSMT

BUILT-IN

T V

WICL

9'-0" CLG

DINING RM
16'-4" x 12'-0"

9'-0" CLG

CL

CL

WICL

MSTR BATH

LAV

FOYER

COVERED PORCH

Upper Level Floor Plan

Copyright by designer/architect.

BEDRM #2
13'-0" x 11'-0"

WICL

UPPER GREAT RM

RAIL

DN

BALCONY

STOR
FUTURE SPACE

VAULTED

BATH #2

LIN

BEDRM #3
12'-0" x 10'-0"

WICL

Images provided by designer/architect.

Plan #131046

Dimensions: 68' W x 57'6" D

Levels: 1.5

Heated Square Footage: 2,245

Main Level Sq. Ft.: 1,720

Upper Level Sq. Ft.: 525

Bedrooms: 3

Bathrooms: 2½

Foundation: Crawl space, slab, or basement

Materials List Available: Yes

Price Category: F

Main Level Floor Plan

Upper Level Floor Plan

Copyright by designer/architect.

1,501–2,500 sq. ft.

Plan #181256

Dimensions: 50'4" W x 45'4" D

Levels: 2

Heated Square Footage: 2,245

Main Level Sq. Ft.: 1,229

Upper Level Sq. Ft.: 1,016

Bedrooms: 3

Bathrooms: 2½

Foundation: Basement

Materials List Available: Yes

Price Category: E

Images provided by designer/architect.

CAD FILE AVAILABLE · CAD

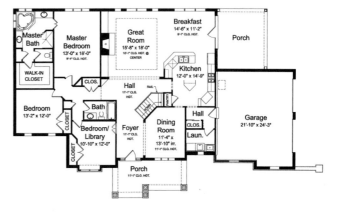

Copyright by designer/architect.

Plan #161249

Dimensions: 80'2" W x 51'8" D

Levels: 1

Heated Square Footage: 2,246

Bedrooms: 3

Bathrooms: 2

Foundation: Basement; crawl space, slab or walkout for fee

Materials List Available: Yes

Price Category: E

Images provided by designer/architect.

CAD FILE AVAILABLE · CAD

Main Level Floor Plan

Upper Level Floor Plan

Copyright by designer/architect.

Plan #551052

Dimensions: 62' W x 41' D

Levels: 2

Heated Square Footage: 2,250

Main Level Sq. Ft.: 1,230

Upper Level Sq. Ft.: 1,020

Bedrooms: 3

Bathrooms: 2½

Foundation: Crawl space or basement

Materials List Available: No

Price Category: E

Images provided by designer/architect.

Plan #151045

Dimensions: 68'6" W x 65' D

Levels: 1

Heated Square Footage: 2,250

Bedrooms: 4

Bathrooms: 2

Foundation: Crawl space, slab; basement for fee

CompleteCost List Available: Yes

Price Category: E

Images provided by designer/architect.

CAD FILE AVAILABLE

Copyright by designer/architect.

Main Level Floor Plan

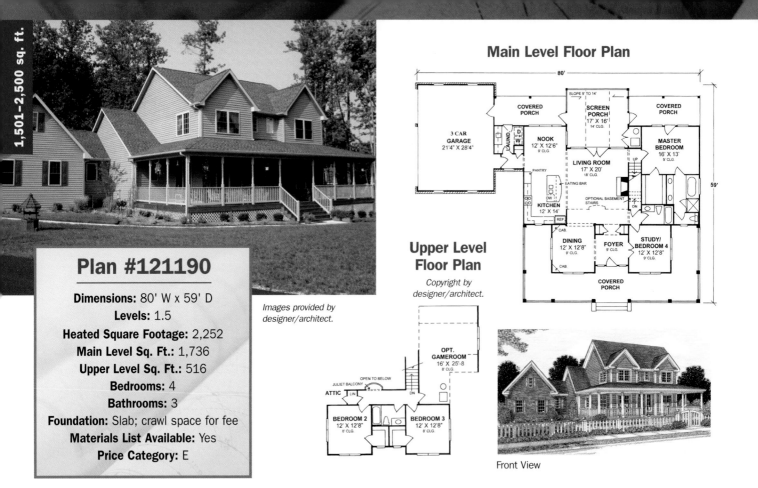

Images provided by designer/architect.

Upper Level Floor Plan

Copyright by designer/architect.

Front View

Plan #121190

Dimensions: 80' W x 59' D
Levels: 1.5
Heated Square Footage: 2,252
Main Level Sq. Ft.: 1,736
Upper Level Sq. Ft.: 516
Bedrooms: 4
Bathrooms: 3
Foundation: Slab; crawl space for fee
Materials List Available: Yes
Price Category: E

Plan #151028

Dimensions: 36' W X 69' D
Levels: 2
Heated Square Footage: 2,252
Main Level Sq. Ft.: 1,694
Upper Level Sq. Ft.: 558
Bedrooms: 3
Bathrooms: 3
Foundation: Crawl space, slab; basement for fee
CompleteCost List Available: Yes
Price Category: E

Images provided by designer/architect.

CAD FILE AVAILABLE

Main Level Floor Plan

Upper Level Floor Plan

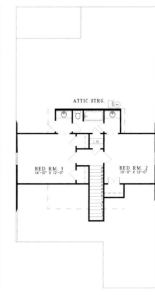

Copyright by designer/architect.

Plan #421011

Dimensions: 64'6" W x 47'7" D
Levels: 2
Heated Square Footage: 2,266
Main Level Sq. Ft.: 1,216
Upper Level Sq. Ft.: 1,050
Bedrooms: 4
Bathrooms: 2½
Foundation: Crawl space, slab, or basement
Materials List Available: Yes
Price Category: E

Images provided by designer/architect.

CAD FILE AVAILABLE

Alternate Upper Level Bath/Laundry

Upper Level Floor Plan

Plan #121123

Dimensions: 54' W x 52' D
Levels: 1.5
Heated Square Footage: 2,277
Main Level Sq. Ft.: 1,570
Upper Level Sq. Ft.: 707
Bedrooms: 4
Bathrooms: 2½
Foundation: Basement; crawl space for fee
Material List Available: Yes
Price Category: E

Images provided by designer/architect.

Upper Level Floor Plan

Main Level Floor Plan

Copyright by designer/architect.

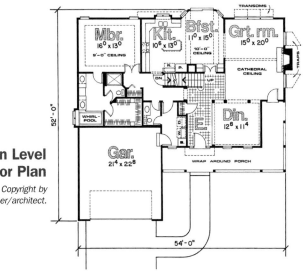

Plan #161115

Dimensions: 79'8" W x 44'2" D

Levels: 1

Heated Square Footage: 2,253

Bedrooms: 4

Bathrooms: 3

Foundation: Walkout basement

Material List Available: Yes

Price Category: E

This one-level home offers a beautiful exterior of brick and stone with shake siding.

Images provided by designer/architect.

Features:

• Great Room: This open gathering area features an 11-foot-high ceiling and access to the rear yard. Turn on the corner gas fireplace, and fill the room with warmth and charm.

• Kitchen: This peninsula kitchen with built-in pantry and counter seating offers easy access to both formal and informal dining. The laundry facilities and the garage are just a few steps away. A magnificent bay window decorates the breakfast room and brings natural light into the area.

• Master Suite: This retreat offers a furniture alcove in the sleeping area and a walk-in closet. The private bath features a double-bowl vanity and a whirlpool tub.

• Guest Suite: This private bedroom suite is located behind the three-car garage and offers a welcoming environment for your overnight guests.

• Basement: This full walkout basement expands the living space of the delightful home.

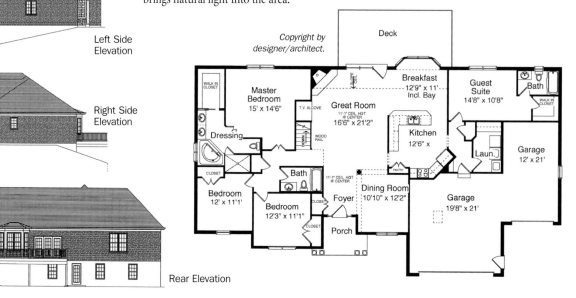

Left Side Elevation

Right Side Elevation

Rear Elevation

Copyright by designer/architect.

Plan #441044

Dimensions: 54' W x 47' D
Levels: 2
Heated Square Footage: 2,277
Main Level Sq. Ft.: 1,563
Upper Level Sq. Ft.: 714
Bedrooms: 5
Bathrooms: 2½
Foundation: Crawl space;
slab or basement available for fee
Materials List Available: Yes
Price Category: E

This handsome design takes its initial cues from the American farmhouse style, but it blends in a wonderful mixture of exterior materials to enliven the look. Cedar battens, lap siding, and stone accents work together for an out-of-the-ordinary facade.

Features:

• **Open Living:** The floor plan is thoughtfully created and holds just the right amount of space for exceptional livability. An open living area, comprising a vaulted great room, dining room, and large kitchen, lies to the rear of the main level and can take advantage of backyard views and a patio.

• **Den:** This room, which is located at the front of the main level, may also become an additional bedroom if you need the space.

Images provided by designer/architect.

• **Master Suite:** This suite is located on the main level. It features a salon with a vaulted ceiling and a bath with a spa tub, separate shower, and compartmented toilet.

• **Bonus Space:** This space on the upper level complements two family bedrooms and a shared full bathroom.

Main Level Floor Plan

Upper Level Floor Plan

Copyright by designer/architect.

Rear Elevation

Stone and Water Features

Combining water and stone in landscape design has been popular for millennia. The sight and sound of water imparts feelings of calm, luxury, and rejuvenation no matter how modest or grand your water feature may be. Deciding on the installation that best suits your needs depends upon your local climate, your budget, and your overall landscape design plan. Ultimately, whether you select a simple stone bowl or a formal fountain, a stone and water feature is guaranteed to enhance your outdoor enjoyment.

Water Features

Small water features are relatively inexpensive and easy to install, yet they can have a big impact on the landscape. You can install water bowls and low-flow, gravity-fed fountains and other features virtually anywhere. Water features that rely on pumps also provide an environment for water-loving plants that would otherwise be impossible to maintain.

Circulating pump kits available at home and garden centers make the installation of water features such as streams, ponds, and waterfalls relatively straightforward. Some kits offer the option to combine features, such as a pond with a fountain or a waterfall with a stream.

Carving a Water Bowl

A stone water bowl provides a sculptural feature adaptable to any type of garden. You can use it as a prominent focal point or tuck one in an unexpected place for surprise, texture, or as part of a smaller composition within a larger design. Whether it is polished or rough, geometric or freeform, a bowl of water entices the viewer with a natural show created by the play of light, shadow, depth, and reflection.

Carving a water bowl need not take a lot of time. There is no need to buy expensive specialized equipment—though renting certain professional-grade tools will make the work go along more quickly.

If you want to create a polished surface on the bowl, you will need sophisticated equipment. For this look, consider carving out the bowl yourself and having a stone sculptor polish it.

To create a quick garden accessory, fill an old birdbath with rounded river stones, top.

Use large stones to secure the liner of a man-made pond or to enhance a natural pond or stream, above.

Find Your Stone

Some types of stone are easier to carve than others. A stone with distinct layers is not recommended for carving because it tends to split and break up too easily. Sandstone and limestone are softer and require less muscle to carve than metamorphic rock, such as marble. A more homogeneous stone presents fewer carving challenges in terms of predictability, hence the popularity of marble for carving.

Natural Indentations. Natural or blasted rock that already has an indentation will reduce the amount of time it will take to carve out a basin shape. If you have a circular saw with a masonry blade, a right-angle grinder, and a few good chisels (and your arms are up to the task), you can carve out a 12-inch-diameter by 5-inch-deep basin in an afternoon.

Examine the Stone

Examine your stone for fractures, and note their location in relation to where you will carve out the basin. To check for fractures, thoroughly wet the stone and let it air dry. Fractures will show up as wet lines after the overall surface of the stone has dried. The presence of fractures does mean an increased risk of having the stone break apart while you are working on it. But you can still use it. For best results, carve out small pieces of stone, and calculate the direction and impact as you carve to minimize stress on a fracture line.

Even if your stone has no obvious fractures on the outer surface, it may have some hidden ones. Frequently examine the area where you are working for cracks. An attentive work habit will more likely result in a finished bowl instead of a pile of rubble.

Carving the Bowl

1. Cut pie-shaped wedges using a circular saw with masonry blade, or hammer and chisel.

2. Use the hammer and chisel to remove small sections of stone. Work on small sections to maintain control.

3. You have the option of leaving the surface rough or using a grinder to achieve a smoother surface.

Choosing a Chisel and Hammer

Use a pointed chisel if the stone is soft. For working hard stone, a 1-inch blunt or flat chisel is a good all-purpose size. If your chisel does not have a carbide edge, sharpen it often as you work. If you are unsure about the hardness of your stone and the type of chisel to use, experiment with both. After a little practice, it will become obvious which one is best.

A 2- or 2½-pound sledgehammer is a typical size for this kind of carving. Hammer technology has changed significantly in the last 10 years, so it may make sense to shop for a new one for your carving project. In general, any tool that works for concrete will work well on soft stone.

Rough-out the Bowl

Outline the shape for the top rim of the basin with a nail, graphite, chalk, or a felt tip marker. Holding the chisel at about a 45-degree angle, make a ¼- to ½-inch-deep groove along the outline.

Cut in Sections. Cut pie-shaped sections no more than every 1½ inches using a circular saw with a masonry blade or a chisel and hammer. The smaller you make the pie sections, the easier it is to even out the surface of the basin. Also, the larger the piece you try to remove, the less control you have.

Starting at the rim of the bowl, place your chisel in one of the cuts and hit the opposite end of the chisel with the hammer to remove pieces of stone. Work your way around the rim of the basin; then gradually work toward the center. After you have removed all the stone to the depth of the cuts, again divide the area to be carved into pie-shaped sections and carve out (pitch) the stone you want to remove. Continue in this manner until the bowl is roughly the depth and shape you want.

Finishing the Bowl

After the bowl is roughed out, continue to remove stone in smaller pieces to smooth out the surface. At some point, you will have to decide how smooth you want the surface to be, and what kind of lip or edge you want the bowl to have. The bowl shown in the photos on the opposite page has a crisp edge determined by the original layout. You can round this edge to varying degrees by working it down with your chisel and hammer. You can tool and finish the surface of your bowl in a number of ways, from rough to highly polished. The tools you have available to you and the type of stone with which you're working will determine in part how you finish the bowl.

To achieve a softer, less angular finish, smooth out the surface with a low-grit grinding wheel attachment on a right-angle grinder. (Consider renting a heavy duty professional-grade grinder for large projects.) Soft stone can be worked dry, or wet, which keeps the stone dust to a minimum.

Maintaining the Water Bowl

Because the water in a bowl is stagnant, you will need to change it occasionally. If unwanted moss or lichen grow on the bowl, remove it with a brush. No soap is needed. Use a soft-bristled brush on soft stone.

In climates with below-freezing temperatures, empty water bowls in the fall to reduce the risk of fracturing the stone from freezing water. Tip the bowl upside down; cover it with a tarp; or cover the basin with a piece of plywood to keep out snow and rain.

This carved water bowl serves as a destination in this backyard garden, top.

Carved water bowls are filled with water that can become stagnant after a period of time. Change the water regularly, and clean the stone with a soft-bristle brush, above.

Constructing a Fountain

Fountains are popular additions to sitting areas, and for centuries they have been installed near house entrances in hot, dry climates. Stone fountains come in all sizes, from a dinner-plate-size basin to a prominent garden feature 4 feet or more across. You can install these fountains in a lawn, in a flower bed, or on a terrace or courtyard.

Fountain Types. Because the reservoir is buried, a recirculating water feature that resembles a bubbling spring is a good choice for households with small children. A boulder or pebble fountain is easy to assemble and is adaptable to any landscape aesthetic. They can contribute both moisture and a cooling effect in the area immediately surrounding the fountain. If you have access to electricity, you can install this type of fountain wherever you can excavate a hole large enough for a 5-gallon pail. You can also create the reservoir from a broader, shallower container with a similar volume or form a basin made of flexible pond liner material.

Stone for the Fountain

Stone yards often stock large, predrilled boulders for fountains, or they will custom drill to your specifications. There are many variations of the boulder fountain, including boulders with a basin carved out, a stone bowl, or a basin with a hole drilled in it. An old millstone or an arrangement of stones can also be used with the hardware for a boulder fountain. Smooth, worn stones, sometimes called river stone, are typically used for pebble fountains.

SMARTtip

If you opt to work with an electric grinder on wet stone, plug the tool into a ground-fault circuit-interrupter (GFCI) outlet. All outdoor outlets are required to be equipped with GFCI protection. These types of outlets can cut power to the circuit if there is a grounding fault. You can also use an adapter for a regular electrical outlet.

Create a custom garden fountain by having specimen stones drilled to hold pipes. The pumps are buried in the base, above.

Strive for a natural look when creating a water feature, right. Note how the top piece pushes the water away from the wall.

Assembling a Pump

Vertical gusher spouts or bubblers are usually used with fountain-style water features. They can be adjusted from 3 to 24 inches or higher depending on the size pump you use. If you have questions about matching the size of the pump to the fountain, discuss the project with the fountain supplier. As with any fountain, you need to have easy access to an electrical outlet with GFCI protection.

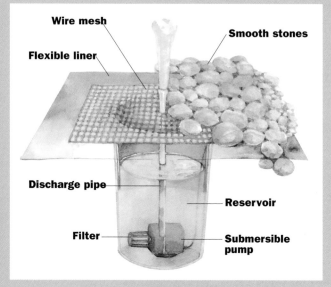

Installing the Pump

Begin the installation by digging a hole slightly larger than your reservoir. (See illustration at right.) A 5-gallon plastic pail works well as a reservoir. Place the reservoir into the hole, and check to make sure it is plumb. Backfill the hole with soil, and contour the soil at grade level to create a basin that will funnel the water back to the reservoir.

Set the fountain assembly in the reservoir, and drill a hole in the side of the pail near the top for the electrical cord. Place a rectangle of flexible liner material (pond liner or heavy plastic sheeting) over the reservoir, pushing the material down slightly into the pail. The liner material should extend beyond the edge of the reservoir to serve as the catch area to return the water to the reservoir. Use scissors to cut an 8- to 10-inch X-shaped hole in the liner centered over the reservoir.

Place a piece of wire mesh (at least 10 inches larger than the diameter of the reservoir) over the liner. Cut a hole in the mesh large enough for the vertical pipe that connects to the fountain pump. For pebble fountains, trim the pipe if needed so that the stones will hide it. Test the assembly by filling the reservoir with water and following the instructions in the fountain kit to adjust the flow rate of the water.

Fountain Maintenance

The amount of water your fountain will lose to evaporation will depend on how often you run the fountain and the ambient temperature. Using a stick, check the level of the reservoir frequently until you can establish a refilling schedule.

Algae. You can remove algae that builds up on the fountain stones by scrubbing them with a soft-bristled brush.

Freezing. Empty the reservoir before freezing temperatures can turn the water to ice. Check the reservoir if you have a midwinter thaw or rain. Remove any water that accumulates from groundwater runoff.

Here's a new slant on a traditional fire pit. Rather than a flame at the center of the seating area, consider a fountain as the focal point.

Dry Streambeds

A dry streambed is a wonderful garden feature that provides visual interest and often serves more than one function. It can create space to display favorite plants, provide a solution to a difficult grade change, disguise a drainage channel, and of course, create the illusion of water where it is impractical to install a water feature.

Design

A dry streambed mimics nature, so let nature be your guide in designing one. Notice how rocks in or adjacent to a stream are dispersed when the water moves at different speeds, and when the terrain is steep or level. Experiment with stones of different sizes and shapes and their placement. Although some trial and error is inevitable, place your stones and plants with both nature and your design goals in mind to achieve the most naturalistic results.

Vary the width and the types of stones used to add interest to your dry streambed.

Installation

Stone in a dry streambed has three uses: it forms the edge or bank of the stream; it takes the place of water; or it makes the streambed itself. Usually, stone for a dry streambed is used 'as is' and is less expensive than wall or patio stone.

Any changes you make after the initial installation can usually be done with hand tools. In fact, you can install many dry streambeds with a shovel, pry bar, and wheelbarrow. Low-tech installation and inexpensive materials make this an ideal project for a homeowner with little do-it-yourself experience.

SMARTtip

Bends in the River

Use bends in a streambed to draw the eye to other garden features, such as a specimen plant or a viewing spot with seating.

CONSTRUCTIONtip

Installation Savvy

- **Use hose or a rope** to lay out the shape of the streambed you desire.
- **Use a plastic barrier** under the streambed for weed control.
- **Set large boulders** and rocks first.
- **Cover any areas** that are not planted at the time of construction with plastic and mulch until you are ready to plant. This will reduce erosion and control weeds.

The Natural Look

The following design guidelines will help you construct a natural-looking dry streambed:

- **Choose a layout** that fits the topography and natural drainage patterns of the site.
- **Change the character** of the streambed if it goes through different parts of the garden. For example, use larger angular stones on a steep grade to indicate a falls.
- **Vary the width** of the bed. Add a beach or dry pond for visual interest.
- **Vary the depth** and steepness of the banks for visual interest and to enhance plantings.
- **Make islands** of vegetation or stone.
- **Place stepping-stones** or a bridge across the streambed.
- **Use shadows** from nearby foliage plants to mimic rippling water.

Dry streambeds can help lead the eye from one landscape feature to another, unifying the design, top right.

Flank a planting bed with a flowing river of stones to separate one area from another, bottom right.

Images provided by designer/architect.

Plan #181151

Dimensions: 50' W x 46' D
Levels: 2
Heated Square Footage: 2,283
Main Level Sq. Ft.: 1,274
Second Level Sq. Ft.: 1,009
Bedrooms: 3
Bathrooms: 2½
Foundation: Basement
Materials List Available: Yes
Price Category: E

Multiple porches, stately columns, and arched multi-paned windows adorn this country home.

CAD FILE **CAD** AVAILABLE

Features:

- Ceiling Height: 8 ft. unless otherwise noted.
- Great Room: The second-floor mezzanine overlooks this great room. With its soaring ceiling, this dramatic room is the centerpiece of a spacious and flowing design that is just as suited to entertaining as it is to family life.
- Dining Area: Guests will naturally flow into this dining area when it is time to eat. After dinner they can step directly out onto the porch to enjoy coffee and dessert when the weather is fair.

- Kitchen: This efficient and well-designed kitchen has double sinks and offers a separate eating area for those impromptu family meals.
- Master Suite: This master retreat has a walk-in closet and its own sumptuous bath.

- Home Office: Whether you work at home or just need a place for the family computer and keeping track of family finances, this home office fills the bill.

Front View

Main Level Floor Plan

21'-0" X 20'-8"
6,30 X 6,20

46'-0"
13,8 m

17'-0" X 11'-8"
5,10 X 3,50

9'-8" X 8'-8"
2,90 X 2,60

9'-0" X 10'-0"
2,70 X 3,00

10'-0" X 12'-0"
3,00 X 3,60

9'-8" X 9'-4"
2,90 X 2,80

12'-0" X 20'-8"
3,60 X 6,20

50'-0"
15,0 m

Upper Level Floor Plan

13'-4" X 10'-0"
4,00 X 3,00

17'-0" X 13'-0"
5,10 X 3,90

14'-0" X 10'-0"
4,20 X 3,00

Copyright by designer/architect.

SMARTtip

Coping Chair Rails

If the teeth of your rasp tend to break out thin edges of the cope, try wrapping the rasp with sandpaper to make fine adjustments.

Dining Room

Living Room

Master Bath

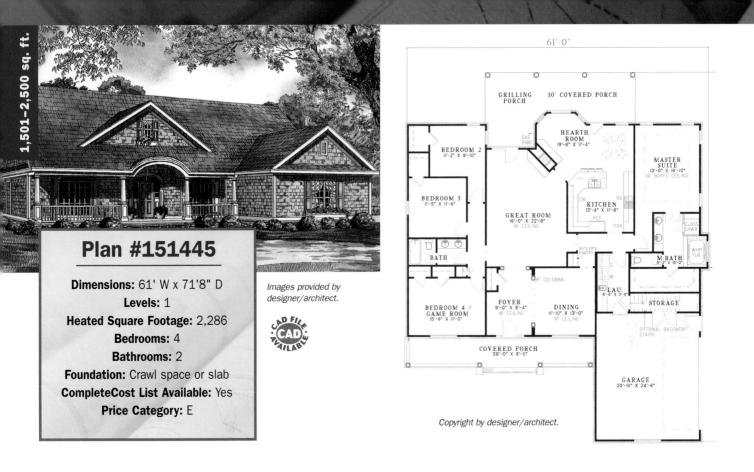

Plan #151445

Dimensions: 61' W x 71'8" D
Levels: 1
Heated Square Footage: 2,286
Bedrooms: 4
Bathrooms: 2
Foundation: Crawl space or slab
CompleteCost List Available: Yes
Price Category: E

Images provided by designer/architect.

CAD FILE AVAILABLE

Copyright by designer/architect.

Floor plan rooms: GRILLING PORCH, 10' COVERED PORCH, HEARTH ROOM 19'-8" X 11'-4", MASTER SUITE 13'-4" X 16'-10" 10' BOXED CEILING, BEDROOM 2 11'-2" X 9'-10", KITCHEN 13'-4" X 11'-8", BEDROOM 3 11'-8" X 11'-6", GREAT ROOM 16'-0" X 22'-8" 10' CEILING, BATH, M.BATH 9'-2" X 15'-2", WHP TUB, GLASS SHWR, BEDROOM 4 / GAME ROOM 15'-6" X 11'-0", FOYER 9'-0" X 8'-4" 10' CEILING, DINING 11'-10" X 13'-0" 10' CEILING, LAU. 6'-4" X 11'-4", STORAGE, 8" COLUMNS, OPTIONAL BASEMENT STAIRS, COVERED PORCH 38'-0" X 6'-0", GARAGE 20'-10" X 24'-6"

Plan #101146

Dimensions: 40' W x 68' D
Levels: 2
Heated Square Footage: 2,296
Main Level Sq. Ft.: 1,636
Upper Level Sq. Ft.: 660
Bedrooms: 3
Bathrooms: 3½
Foundation: Crawl space
Materials List Available: No
Price Category: E

Images provided by designer/architect.

CAD FILE AVAILABLE

Main Level Floor Plan

Floor plan rooms: MASTER BDRM 21'-6" X 16'-4" TRAY CEILING, SITTING AREA, SCREENED PORCH 17'-8" X 9'-0", CLOSET, FAMILY 17'-8" X 23'-0", NOOK 9'-1" X 9'-11", KITCHEN 12'-0" X 12'-0", LAUNDRY, STORAGE 7'-8" X 6'-0", DINING 13'-3" X 12'-6", GARAGE 21'-4" X 20'-6", ENTRY 9'-4" X 9'-0", PORCH 17'-9" X 5'-9", 68'-0", 40'-0"

Upper Level Floor Plan

Copyright by designer/architect.

Floor plan rooms: SUITE 3 13'-5" X 11'-4", CLOSET, BOOK NOOK 12'-0" X 13'-1", OPEN BELOW, BALCONY, SUITE 2 13'-0" X 11'-0", CLOSET, ELEVATOR, OPEN BELOW

Main Level Floor Plan

GARAGE 20⁰x20⁰
STO
STO
SEAT
SPA
DECK
SEAT
1/2 B
MUD RM
COVERED PORCH
BBQ
M BATH
KITCHEN 12⁰x10⁰
UP
GREAT ROOM 16⁶x17⁴
DN
M BEDROOM 16⁶x14⁶
MORNING 13⁰x10⁰
DINING 12⁴x11⁴
ENTRY 6⁶x9⁰
STUDY 12⁴x11⁴
COVERED PORCH

Upper Level Floor Plan

Copyright by designer/architect.

STO
BEDRM 2 11³x14²
BATH 2
DN
AC
STORAGE
BEDRM 3 10¹⁰x16¹⁰
STO
PLAYROOM 16⁰x9⁴

Plan #331002

Dimensions: 62'2" W x 66'8" D

Levels: 2

Heated Square Footage: 2,299

Main Level Sq. Ft.: 1,517

Upper Level Sq. Ft.: 782

Bedrooms: 3

Bathrooms: 2½

Foundation: Crawl space, slab, or basement

Materials List Available: No

Price Category: E

Images provided by designer/architect.

Main Level Floor Plan

SHWR TILE
JACC
MASTER BATH (9' CLG)
W.I.C.
STEPS
COVERED PORCH
48" DIAM
SHOP/STORAGE 9'-2"x15'-6"
LNDRY
KITCHEN 15'-6"x11'-8" (9' CLG)
ISLAND
GREAT ROOM 21'-5"x15'-1" (9' CLG)
MASTER BDRM 14'-0"x18'-0" (10' TRAY CLG)
PWDR
FRENCH DOORS
FORMAL DINING 10'-8"x11'-0" (9' CLG)
COATS
OFFICE/GUEST ROOM 10'-8"x11'-0" (9' CLG)
FOYER (9' CLG)
2 BAY GARAGE 22'-0"x23'-0"
COVERED PORCH
STEPS

Upper Level Floor Plan

BONUS ROOM 21'-5"x18'-0" (FUTURE)
HOME ENTERTAINMENT AREA
FAMILY ROOM 10'-8"x24'-5" (VAULTED)
BATH
BEDROOM #2 11'-0"x10'-8"
8' CLG
COMPUTER AREA
BEDROOM #3 10'-8"x11'-0"
STORAGE
OPEN TO BELOW (VAULTED)
OPEN RAILING

Copyright by designer/architect.

Plan #421044

Dimensions: 70'8" W x 53' D

Levels: 2

Heated Square Footage: 2,302

Main Level Sq. Ft.: 1,570

Upper Level Sq. Ft.: 732

Bedrooms: 4

Bathrooms: 2½

Foundation: Crawl space, slab or basement

Material List Available: Yes

Price Category: E

Images provided by designer/architect.

Plan #321041

Dimensions: 64' W x 34' D
Levels: 2
Heated Square Footage: 2,286
Main Level Sq. Ft.: 1,283
Upper Level Sq. Ft.: 1,003
Bedrooms: 4
Bathrooms: 2½
Foundation: Crawl space, slab, or basement
Materials List Available: No
Price Category: E

If you love the way these gorgeous windows look from the outside, you'll be thrilled with the equally gracious interior of this home.

Features:

- Entryway: This two-story entryway shows off the fine woodworking on the railing and balustrades.

- Living Room: The large front windows form a glamorous background in this spacious room.

- Family Room: A handsome fireplace and a sliding glass door to the backyard enhance the open design of this room.

- Breakfast Room: Large enough for a crowd, this room makes a perfect dining area.

- Kitchen: The angled bar and separate pantry are highlights in this step-saving design.

- Master Suite: Enjoy this suite's huge walk-in closet, vaulted ceiling, and private bath, which features a double vanity, tub, and shower stall.

Images provided by designer/architect.

Main Level Floor Plan

64'-0"

Family 18-6x14-0
Bar
Brk 10-0x11-10
Kit 11-10x10-6
Living 12-8x16-0
Up
Entry
Dn
Dining 11-0x13-0
Garage 19-4x23-4
W D
Porch depth 4-0
34'-0"

Upper Level Floor Plan

Br 4 10-2x10-8
Br 3 11-7x10-8
MBr 12-8x15-11 vaulted
Dn
open to below
Br 2 12-4x10-8

Front View

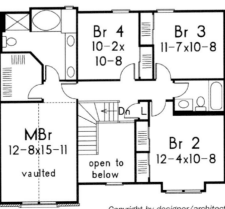

Copyright by designer/architect.

Plan #151027

Dimensions: 37' W x 73' D

Levels: 2

Heated Square Footage: 2,323

Main Level Sq. Ft.: 1,713

Upper Level Sq. Ft.: 610

Bedrooms: 3

Bathrooms: 3

Foundation: Crawl space, slab; basement option for fee

CompleteCost List Available: Yes

Price Category: E

A traditional design with a covered front porch and high ceilings in many rooms gives this home all the space and comfort you'll ever need.

Features:

- Foyer: A formal foyer with 8-in. wood columns will lead you to an elegant dining area.

- Great Room: This wonderful gathering room has 10-ft. boxed ceilings, a built-in media center, and an atrium door leading to a rear grilling porch.

- Kitchen: Functional yet cozy, this kitchen opens to the breakfast area with built-in computer desk and is open to the great room as well.

- Master Suite: Pamper yourself in this luxurious bedroom with 10-ft. boxed ceilings, large walk-in closets, and a bath area with a whirlpool tub, shower, and double vanity.

- Second Level: A game room and two bedrooms with walk-thru baths make this floor special.

Images provided by designer/architect.

Main Level Floor Plan

Upper Level Floor Plan

Copyright by designer/architect.

Plan #181078

Dimensions: 58' W x 42'2" D
Levels: 2
Heated Square Footage: 2,336
Main Level Sq. Ft.: 1,266
Upper Level Sq. Ft.: 1,070
Bedrooms: 3
Bathrooms: 2½
Foundation: Full basement
Materials List Available: Yes
Price Category: E

This two-story home will be a fine addition to any neighborhood.

Features:

- Living Room: This gathering area is open to the kitchen and will warm you with its cozy fireplace.

- Kitchen: This island kitchen has a raised bar that looks into the living room, and it provides access to the rear porch.

- Master Suite: This private area has a cozy fireplace in the sleeping area. The master bath features dual vanities, a walk-in closet, and a large tub.

- Bedrooms: The two additional bedrooms are located upstairs with the master suite and share the Jack-and-Jill bathroom.

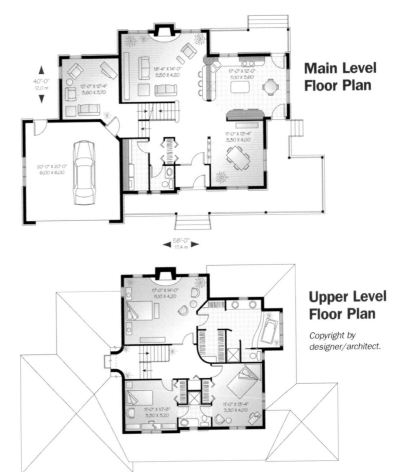

CAD FILE AVAILABLE

Images provided by designer/architect.

This home, as shown in the photograph, may differ from the actual blueprints. For more detailed information, please check the floor plans carefully.

Main Level Floor Plan

Upper Level Floor Plan

Copyright by designer/architect.

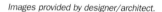

Plan #181081

Dimensions: 58' W x 33' D
Levels: 2
Square Footage: 2,350
Main Level Sq. Ft.: 1,107
Second Level Sq. Ft.: 1,243
Bedrooms: 3
Bathrooms: 2½
Foundation: Basement
Materials List Available: Yes
Price Category: F

Images provided by designer/architect.

This traditional country home features a wrap-around porch and a second-floor balcony.

Features:

- Ceiling Height: 8 ft. unless otherwise noted.

- Family Room: Double French doors and a fireplace in this inviting front room enhance the beauty and warmth of the home's open floor plan.

- Kitchen: You'll love working in this bright and convenient kitchen. The breakfast bar is the perfect place to gather for informal meals.

- Master Suite: You'll look forward to retiring to this elegant upstairs suite at the end of a busy day. The suite features a private bath with separate shower and tub, as well as dual vanities.

- Secondary Bedrooms: Two family bedrooms share a full bath with a third room that opens onto the balcony.

- Basement: An unfinished full basement provides plenty of storage and the potential to add additional finished living space.

CAD FILE AVAILABLE

Main Level Floor Plan

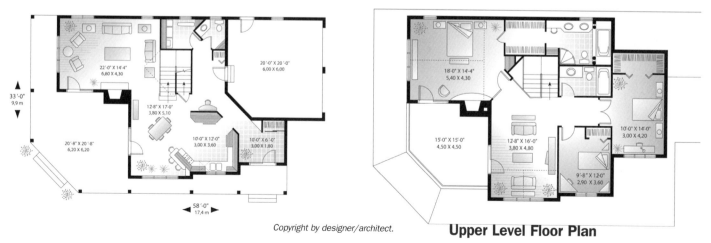

Copyright by designer/architect.

Upper Level Floor Plan

Plan #101146

Dimensions: 40' W x 68' D
Levels: 2
Heated Square Footage: 2,296
Main Level Sq. Ft.: 1,636
Upper Level Sq. Ft.: 660
Bedrooms: 3
Bathrooms: 3½
Foundation: Crawl space
Materials List Available: No
Price Category: E

Images provided by designer/architect.

CAD FILE AVAILABLE

Main Level Floor Plan

Upper Level Floor Plan

Copyright by designer/architect.

Plan #121164

Dimensions: 74'11" W x 68'9½" D
Levels: 1
Square Footage: 2,331
Bedrooms: 3
Bathrooms: 2½
Foundation: Slab; basement for fee
Material List Available: Yes
Price Category: E

Images provided by designer/architect.

CAD FILE AVAILABLE

Copyright by designer/architect.

Plan #351208

Dimensions: 72'8" W x 73'10" D
Levels: 1
Heated Square Footage: 2,336
Bedrooms: 4
Bathrooms: 2½
Foundation: Crawl space or slab
Materials List Available: Yes
Price Category: E

Images provided by designer/architect.

CAD FILE AVAILABLE

Bonus Area Floor Plan

Copyright by designer/architect.

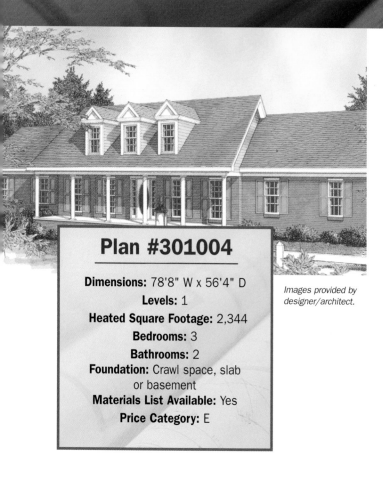

Plan #301004

Dimensions: 78'8" W x 56'4" D
Levels: 1
Heated Square Footage: 2,344
Bedrooms: 3
Bathrooms: 2
Foundation: Crawl space, slab or basement
Materials List Available: Yes
Price Category: E

Images provided by designer/architect.

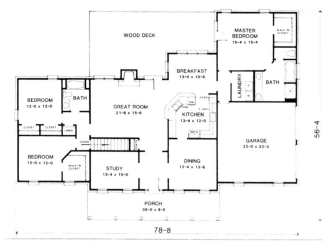

Copyright by designer/architect.

Plan #181137

Dimensions: 68' W x 34' D

Levels: 2

Heated Square Footage: 2,353

Main Level Sq. Ft.: 1,281

Upper Level Sq. Ft.: 1,072

Bedrooms: 3

Bathrooms: 2½

Foundation: Basement; crawl space or slab for fee

Materials List Available: Yes

Price Category: E

CAD FILE AVAILABLE

Images provided by designer/architect.

Family Room

Kitchen

Quaint brick and stone, plus deeply pitched rooflines, create the storybook aura folks fall for when they see this home, but it's the serenely versatile interior layout that captures their hearts.

Features:

- Family Room: The floor plan is configured to bring a panoramic view to nearly every room, beginning with this room, with its fireplace and towering cathedral ceiling.

- Kitchen: This kitchen, with its crowd-pleasing island, has an eye on the outdoors. It also has all the counter and storage space a cook would want, plus a lunch counter with comfy seats and multiple windows to bring in the breeze.

- Bedrooms: Downstairs, you'll find the master bedroom, with its adjoining master bath. Upstairs, three uniquely shaped bedrooms, styled with clever nooks and windows to dream by, easily share a large bathroom.

- Mezzanine: This sweeping mezzanine overlooks the open living and dining rooms.

13'-0"x 13'-8"
3,90 x 4,10

12'-4"x 11'-4"
3,70 x 3,40

12'-0"x 14'-4"
3,60 x 4,30

20'-4"x 24'-8"
6,10 x 7,40

34'-0"
10,2 m

7'-8"x 15'-0"
2,30 x 4,50

17'-0"x 16'-0"
5,10 x 4,80

8'-0"x 9'-0"
2,40 x 2,70

68'-0"
20,4 m

10'-8"x 11'-4"
3,20 x 3,40

17'-0"x 14'-0"
5,10 x 4,20

11'-0"x 13'-0"
3,30 x 3,90

10'-0"x 13'-0"
3,00 x 3,90

Upper Level
Floor Plan

*Copyright by
designer/architect.*

Front View

Plan #181053

Dimensions: 56' W x 53'2" D

Levels: 2

Heated Square Footage: 2,353

Main Level Sq. Ft.: 1,606

Upper Level Sq. Ft.: 747

Bedrooms: 4

Bathrooms: 2½

Foundation: Crawl space or basement, slab for fee

Material List Available: Yes

Price Category: E

Images provided by designer/architect.

CAD FILE AVAILABLE

Rear View

Main Level Floor Plan

Upper Level Floor Plan

Copyright by designer/architect.

Plan #191027

Dimensions: 62' W x 42' D

Levels: 1

Heated Square Footage: 2,354

Bedrooms: 4

Bathrooms: 2½

Foundation: Crawl space or slab

Materials List Available: No

Price Category: E

Images provided by designer/architect.

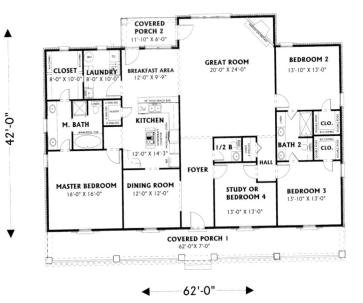

COVERED PORCH 2
11'-10" X 6'-0"

CLOSET
8'-0" X 10'-0"

LAUNDRY
8'-0" X 10'-0"

BREAKFAST AREA
12'-0" X 9'-9"

GREAT ROOM
20'-0" X 24'-0"

BEDROOM 2
13'-10" X 13'-0"

M. BATH

KITCHEN
12'-0" X 14'-3"

1/2 B

BATH 2

CLO.

FOYER

HALL

CLO.

MASTER BEDROOM
16'-0" X 16'-0"

DINING ROOM
12'-0" X 12'-0"

STUDY OR
BEDROOM 4
13'-0" X 13'-0"

BEDROOM 3
13'-10" X 13'-0"

COVERED PORCH 1
62'-0" X 7'-0"

42'-0"

62'-0"

Copyright by designer/architect.

Images provided by designer/architect.

Copyright by designer/architect.

Plan #521017

Dimensions: 94'11" W x 94'10" D

Levels: 1

Heated Square Footage: 2,359

Bedrooms: 3

Bathrooms: 3

Foundation: Slab

Material List Available: No

Price Category: E

CAD FILE AVAILABLE

Rear View

Plan #151204

Dimensions: 76'10" W x 53'4" D

Levels: 1.5

Heated Square Footage: 2,373

Bedrooms: 4

Bathrooms: 3

Foundation: Crawl space or slab

CompleteCost List Available: Yes

Price Category: E

Images provided by designer/architect.

CAD FILE AVAILABLE

Main Level Floor Plan

Upper Level Floor Plan

Copyright by designer/architect.

Plan #561006

Dimensions: 61'4" W x 72'8" D

Levels: 1

Heated Square Footage: 2,408

Bedrooms: 3

Bathrooms: 2½

Foundation: Basement

Material List Available: Yes

Price Category: E

This magnificent farmhouse design, with its traditional front porch and rear screened-in porch, is more than just a home.

CAD FILE AVAILABLE

Features:

• Great Room: Gather by the glowing fire on cold nights, or expand your entertaining space any other time. This great room is at the center of everything and has plenty of space for friends, family, and anyone else you can think to invite.

• Kitchen: A built-in pantry and ample counter space make a great work area for the family cook and the aspiring chef alike. An open transition to the breakfast area simplifies morning chaos, while a defined separation formalizes the dining room.

• Master Suite: This area is a welcome retreat where you can shut out the frenzied world and simply relax. The attached master bath includes dual walk-in closets, his and her

sinks, a standing shower, and a separate tub — perfect for busy mornings and romantic evenings.

• Secondary Bedrooms: These bedrooms boast ample closet space and equal distance to a full bathroom. They're also off the beaten path, creating a calmer space for study and sleep.

Images provided by designer/architect.

Rear Elevation

Copyright by designer/architect.

Plan #131051

Dimensions: 64'4" W x 53'4" D

Levels: 2

Heated Square Footage: 2,431

Main Level Sq. Ft.: 1,293

Upper Level Sq. Ft.: 1,138

Bedrooms: 4

Bathrooms: 2½

Foundation: Crawl space, slab, or basement

Materials List Available: Yes

Price Category: F

Gracious and charming with a wrap-around front porch and a backyard terrace, this home also has a ready-to-finish third floor all-purpose room and a full bath.

Features:

- Main Level Ceiling Height: 8 ft.

- Family Room: A comfortable space for the entire family to gather, this delightful room can be warmed by a heat-circulating fireplace.

- Dining Room: A cozy dinette boasts a sliding glass door with access to a gorgeous backyard terrace with an optional calm reflecting pool.

- Kitchen: Adjoining the dining area, the kitchen offers plenty of storage and counter space. The laundry room and half-bath are nearby for convenience.

- Garage: The garage is tucked way back to keep it from intruding into the traditional facade.

CAD FILE AVAILABLE

Main Level Floor Plan

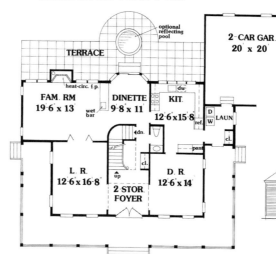

Images provided by designer/architect.

This home, as shown in the photograph, may differ from the actual blueprints. For more detailed information, please check the floor plans carefully.

Rear Elevation

Upper Level Floor Plan

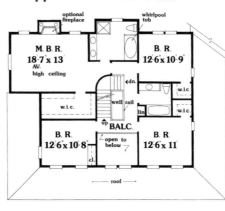

Optional 3rd Level Floor Plan

Copyright by designer/architect.

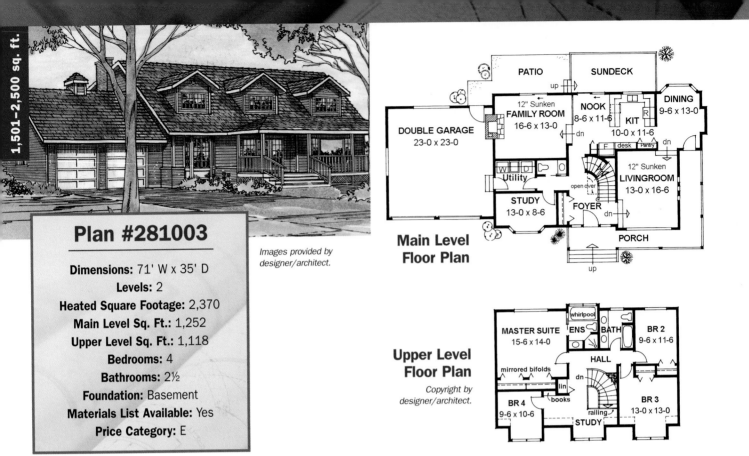

Main Level Floor Plan

PATIO SUNDECK

DOUBLE GARAGE
23-0 x 23-0

12" Sunken
FAMILY ROOM
16-6 x 13-0

NOOK
8-6 x 11-6

KIT
10-0 x 11-6

DINING
9-6 x 13-0

up

dn

desk pantry dn

Utility

W/D

12" Sunken
LIVINGROOM
13-0 x 16-6

open over

STUDY
13-0 x 8-6

FOYER

dn

PORCH

up

Images provided by designer/architect.

Upper Level Floor Plan

MASTER SUITE
15-6 x 14-0

whirlpool

ENS BATH

BR 2
9-6 x 11-6

mirrored bifolds

HALL

lin

BR 4
9-6 x 10-6

dn

books

railing

BR 3
13-0 x 13-0

STUDY

Copyright by designer/architect.

Plan #281003

Dimensions: 71' W x 35' D

Levels: 2

Heated Square Footage: 2,370

Main Level Sq. Ft.: 1,252

Upper Level Sq. Ft.: 1,118

Bedrooms: 4

Bathrooms: 2½

Foundation: Basement

Materials List Available: Yes

Price Category: E

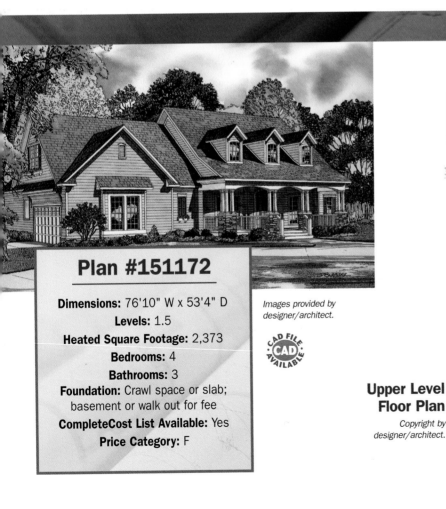

Plan #151172

Dimensions: 76'10" W x 53'4" D

Levels: 1.5

Heated Square Footage: 2,373

Bedrooms: 4

Bathrooms: 3

Foundation: Crawl space or slab; basement or walk out for fee

CompleteCost List Available: Yes

Price Category: F

Images provided by designer/architect.

CAD FILE AVAILABLE

Main Level Floor Plan

MASTER SUITE

GRILLING PORCH

BEDROOM 4

M.BATH LAUNDRY

BREAKFAST ROOM

GREAT ROOM

BATH

GARAGE

KITCHEN

BEDROOM 3

STORAGE

DINING

FOYER

BEDROOM 2/STUDY

BATH

COVERED PORCH

Upper Level Floor Plan

BONUS ROOM

STORAGE

BONUS ROOM 1

BONUS ROOM 2

ATTIC STORAGE

Copyright by designer/architect.

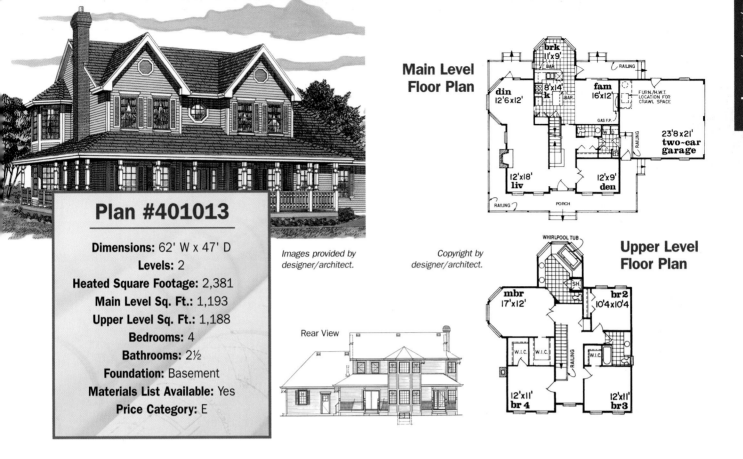

**Main Level
Floor Plan**

*Images provided by
designer/architect.*

*Copyright by
designer/architect.*

Plan #401013

Dimensions: 62' W x 47' D

Levels: 2

Heated Square Footage: 2,381

Main Level Sq. Ft.: 1,193

Upper Level Sq. Ft.: 1,188

Bedrooms: 4

Bathrooms: 2½

Foundation: Basement

Materials List Available: Yes

Price Category: E

Rear View

**Upper Level
Floor Plan**

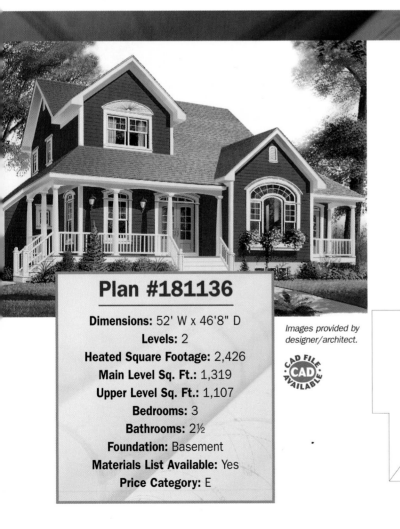

Plan #181136

Dimensions: 52' W x 46'8" D

Levels: 2

Heated Square Footage: 2,426

Main Level Sq. Ft.: 1,319

Upper Level Sq. Ft.: 1,107

Bedrooms: 3

Bathrooms: 2½

Foundation: Basement

Materials List Available: Yes

Price Category: E

*Images provided by
designer/architect.*

CAD FILE AVAILABLE

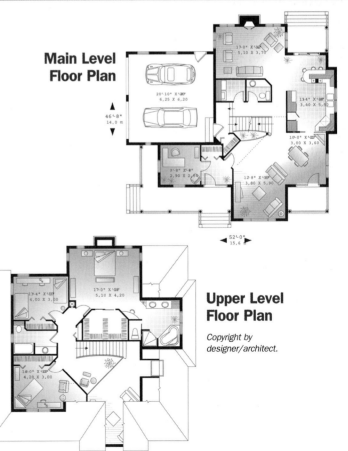

**Main Level
Floor Plan**

**Upper Level
Floor Plan**

*Copyright by
designer/architect.*

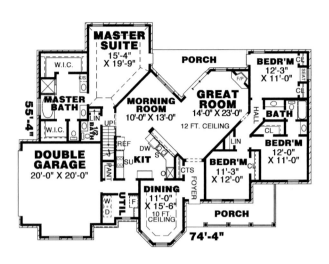

Plan #241017

Dimensions: 74'4" W x 55'4" D

Levels: 1

Heated Square Footage: 2,431

Bedrooms: 4

Bathrooms: 2½

Foundation: Slab; crawl space for fee

Materials List Available: No

Price Category: E

Images provided by designer/architect.

MASTER SUITE 15'-4" X 19'-9"

PORCH

BEDR'M 12'-3" X 11'-0"

W.I.C.

MASTER BATH

W.I.C.

MORNING ROOM 10'-0" X 13'-0"

GREAT ROOM 14'-0" X 23'-0"
12 FT. CEILING

BATH

BEDR'M 12'-0" X 11'-0"

DOUBLE GARAGE 20'-0" X 20'-0"

KIT

BEDR'M 11'-3" X 12'-0"

DINING 11'-0" X 15'-6"
10 FT. CEILING

UTIL

FOYER

PORCH

55'-4"

74'-4"

Bonus Area Floor Plan

PLAYROOM 16'-10" X 14'-3"

DN

Copyright by designer/architect.

Plan #151181

Dimensions: 76'10" W x 59'2" D

Levels: 1.5

Heated Square Footage: 2,373

Bedrooms: 4

Bathrooms: 3

Foundation: Crawl space or slab; basement or walk out for fee

CompleteCost List Available: Yes

Price Category: E

Images provided by designer/architect.

CAD FILE AVAILABLE

76'-10"

MASTER SUITE

GRILLING PORCH

BEDROOM 4

M. BATH

LAUNDRY

BREAKFAST ROOM

MEDIA CENTER

BATH

GARAGE

KITCHEN

GREAT ROOM

BEDROOM 3

STORAGE

DINING

FOYER

BEDROOM 2 STUDY

COVERED PORCH

59'-2"

Bonus Area Floor Plan

Copyright by designer/architect.

BONUS ROOM

STORAGE

ATTIC STORAGE

BONUS ROOM 1

BONUS ROOM 2

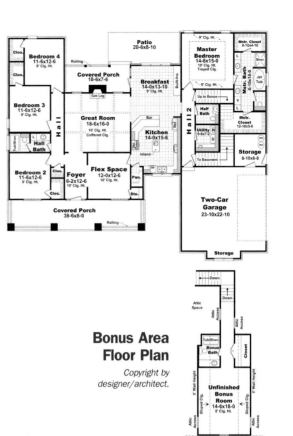

Images provided by designer/architect.

Plan #351203

Dimensions: 73'6" W x 62' D

Levels: 1

Heated Square Footage: 2,447

Bedrooms: 4

Bathrooms: 2½

Foundation: Basement

Materials List Available: Yes

Price Category: E

Bonus Area Floor Plan

Copyright by designer/architect.

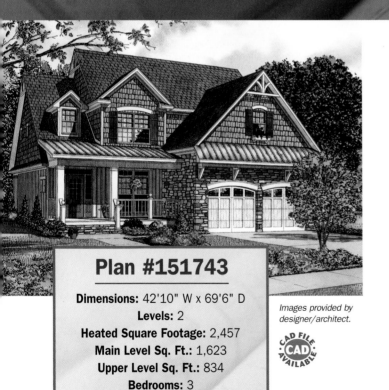

Main Level Floor Plan

Upper Level Floor Plan

Copyright by designer/architect.

Plan #151743

Dimensions: 42'10" W x 69'6" D

Levels: 2

Heated Square Footage: 2,457

Main Level Sq. Ft.: 1,623

Upper Level Sq. Ft.: 834

Bedrooms: 3

Bathrooms: 2½

Foundation: Crawl space or slab

CompleteCost List Available: Yes

Price Category: E

Images provided by designer/architect.

Main Level Floor Plan

Upper Level Floor Plan

Copyright by designer/architect.

Images provided by designer/architect.

Plan #151176

Dimensions: 60' W x 77'6" D

Levels: 1.5

Heated Square Footage: 2,445

Main Level Sq. Ft.: 2,129

Upper Level Sq. Ft.: 316

Bedrooms: 4

Bathrooms: 3½

Foundation: Crawl space or slab; basement or walk out for fee

CompleteCost List Available: Yes

Price Category: E

Main Level Floor Plan

Upper Level Floor Plan

Copyright by designer/architect.

Images provided by designer/architect.

Plan #401039

Dimensions: 69'8" W x 46' D

Levels: 2

Heated Square Footage: 2,462

Main Level Sq. Ft.: 1,333

Upper Level Sq. Ft.: 1,129

Bedrooms: 4

Bathrooms: 2½

Foundation: Basement

Materials List Available: Yes

Price Category: E

Plan #441023

Dimensions: 60' W x 42' D
Levels: 2
Heated Square Footage: 2,500
Main Level Sq. Ft.: 1,319
Upper Level Sq. Ft: 1,181
Bedrooms: 4
Bathrooms: 2½
Foundation: Crawl space;
slab or basement for fee
Materials List Available: Yes
Price Category: E

Images provided by designer/architect.

CAD FILE AVAILABLE

Main Level Floor Plan

Upper Level Floor Plan

Copyright by designer/architect.

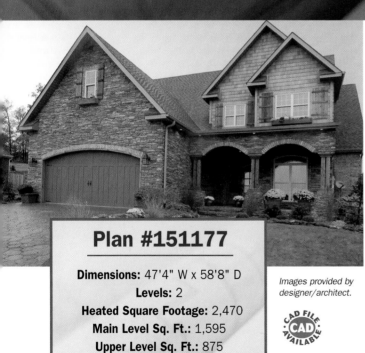

Plan #151177

Dimensions: 47'4" W x 58'8" D
Levels: 2
Heated Square Footage: 2,470
Main Level Sq. Ft.: 1,595
Upper Level Sq. Ft.: 875
Bedrooms: 4
Bathrooms: 2½
Foundation: Crawl space or slab
CompleteCost List Available: Yes
Price Category: E

Images provided by designer/architect.

CAD FILE AVAILABLE

Main Level Floor Plan

Upper Level Floor Plan

Copyright by designer/architect.

Plan #131030

Dimensions: 51' W x 41'10" D
Levels: 2
Heated Square Footage: 2,470
Main Level Sq. Ft.: 1,290
Upper Level Sq. Ft.: 1,180
Bedrooms: 4
Bathrooms: 2½
Foundation: Crawl space, slab, basement, or walkout
Materials List Available: Yes
Price Category: F

Images provided by designer/architect.

This home, as shown in the photograph, may differ from the actual blueprints. For more detailed information, please check the floor plans carefully.

Master Bedroom

Master Bathroom

Entry

If high ceilings and spacious rooms make you happy, you'll love this gorgeous home.

Features:

- **Family Room:** An 18-ft. vaulted ceiling that's open to the balcony above, a corner fireplace, and a wall of windows make this room feel special.

- **Dining Room:** This formal room, which flows into the living room, also opens to the front porch and optional backyard deck.

- **Kitchen:** A bright breakfast room joins with this kitchen and opens to the backyard deck.

- **Master Suite:** You'll smile when you see the 11-ft. vaulted ceiling, stunning arched window, and two walk-in closets in the bedroom. A skylight lets natural light into the private bath, with its spa tub, separate shower, and dual-sink vanity.

- **Bedrooms:** To reach these three charming bedrooms, you'll admire the view into the family room below as you walk along the balcony hall.

Main Level Floor Plan

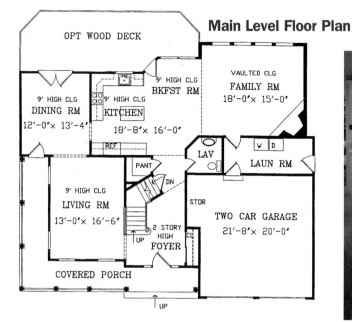

- OPT WOOD DECK
- 9' HIGH CLG — BKFST RM
- VAULTED CLG — FAMILY RM 18'-0" x 15'-0"
- 9' HIGH CLG — DINING RM 12'-0" x 13'-4"
- 9' HIGH CLG — KITCHEN 18'-8" x 16'-0"
- REF
- LAV
- W D — LAUN RM
- PANT
- 9' HIGH CLG — LIVING RM 13'-0" x 16'-6"
- DN
- STOR
- 2 STORY HIGH FOYER
- UP
- TWO CAR GARAGE 21'-8" x 20'-0"
- COVERED PORCH
- UP

Upper Level Floor Plan

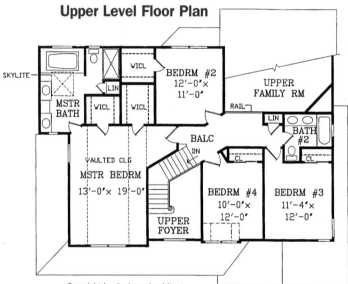

- SKYLITE
- MSTR BATH
- WICL
- LIN
- WICL
- WICL
- BEDRM #2 12'-0" x 11'-0"
- UPPER FAMILY RM
- RAIL
- LIN
- BALC
- BATH #2
- VAULTED CLG — MSTR BEDRM 13'-0" x 19'-0"
- DN
- CL
- CL
- CL
- UPPER FOYER
- BEDRM #4 10'-0" x 12'-0"
- BEDRM #3 11'-4" x 12'-0"

Copyright by designer/architect.

Kitchen/Breakfast Area

Dining Room

Living Room

Kitchen/Breakfast Area

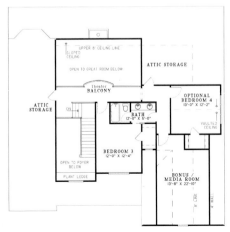

Plan #151237

Dimensions: 57'4" W x 55'10" D
Levels: 2
Heated Square Footage: 2,481
Main Level Sq. Ft.: 2,084
Upper Level Sq. Ft.: 397
Bedrooms: 4
Bathrooms: 3
Foundation: Crawl space, slab; basement or walkout for fee
CompleteCost List Available: Yes
Price Category: E

This beautiful home includes all of the features you may need.

CAD FILE AVAILABLE — CAD

Images provided by designer/architect.

Features:

- Porches: Two porches, one at the front and one at the back of the house, provide space for relaxing or having a barbecue with friends.

- Great Room: This two-story great room, overlooked by a balcony above, features a fireplace and French doors that open out to the grilling porch.

- Kitchen: Connected to a breakfast room, this kitchen includes a pantry, an eating bar, and an island.

- Master Suite: End your day relaxing in this master suite, which is home to a whirlpool tub, a walk-in closet, a glass shower, and a dual-sink vanity.

Upper Level Floor Plan

Copyright by designer/architect.

Main Level Floor Plan

Plan #351088

Dimensions: 66'8" W x 73'2" D
Levels: 1
Heated Square Footage: 2,500
Bedrooms: 4
Bathrooms: 3
Foundation: Crawl space or slab
Material List Available: Yes
Price Category: G

Images provided by designer/architect.

The dashing contemporary-country style of brick and siding with attractive architectural details, like a string of dormers, makes this home's exterior as lovely as its interior.

CAD FILE AVAILABLE CAD

Features:

• **Great Room:** Opening onto the rear covered porch for the overflow of relaxing warm-weather gatherings and enjoyment of the outdoor kitchen, this great room also features a fireplace and built-in storage for when you'd rather stay comfortably inside. Vaulted ceilings give the an even greater amount of freedom.

• **Kitchen:** This efficiently designed space features an L-shaped work area, a pantry, and an island with a raised eating bar.

Opening into the formal dining room, fireplace-warmed breakfast room, and large great room gives mealtime plenty of possibilities.

• **Master Suite:** In a space of its own, this retreat exudes relaxation and privacy. A hallway leads to the expansive space, which features an extensive master bath with dual sinks, an oversized jetted tub, a stall shower, and his and her walk-in closets.

• **Secondary Bedrooms:** The other bedrooms have hallways of their own and are all just steps away from full bathrooms.

• **Flex Space:** A small room adjacent to the master suite is in perfect proximity for use as a home office, a nursery, or extra storage space. Above the garage is an unfinished bonus space that can be used however you like.

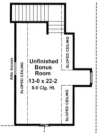

Bonus Room Floor Plan

Copyright by designer/architect.

Unfinished Bonus Room
13-0 x 22-2
8-0 Clg. Ht.

Attic Access
SLOPED CEILING

Rear Elevation

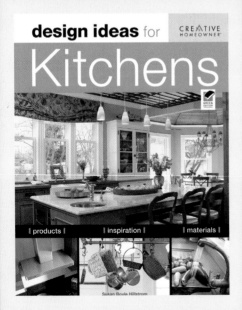

design ideas for CREATIVE HOMEOWNER

Kitchens

| products | | inspiration | | materials |

Susan Boyle Hillstrom

Choosing Your Sink

Today's kitchen sinks and faucets are making a bold design statement. While stainless steel endures as the most popular sink finish, there are more options to consider—bigger sizes, deeper bowls, new configurations, and colors and materials galore. There are also great new faucets with multiple spray features and accessories ranging from soap dispensers to water purification systems. Despite their glamour, sinks and faucets are still the workhorses of the kitchen, so make sure your choices look good and work hard.

Here's a helpful rule of thumb for choosing a kitchen sink—identify your practical needs first; then go for good looks. With so many choices you won't have to sacrifice one for the other. Another pointer comes from the National Kitchen & Bath Association (NKBA), an industry trade group: a standard 22 x 24-inch single-bowl sink is sufficient for kitchens that measure 150 square feet or less; for kitchens that are over that size, a larger single-bowl design or a double- or triple-bowl model are better choices.

If you haven't bought a kitchen sink for a while you'll be dazzled by your choices. You may also be surprised that many kitchens, even relatively modest ones, sport two or even three sinks. There's the primary one, located at the heart of the work area near the dishwasher and devoted to cleanup. There may also be a small prep sink, often located away from the busiest area and intended for a second cook or for a helpful dinner guest who may be washing or chopping vegetables or fruit. This secondary sink, a nice amenity for any household, is practically a necessity for a two-cook kitchen. If you have a large family or entertain often, you may want to install a bar sink that allows people to help themselves to beverages without getting in the cooks' way. If this auxiliary sink is accompanied by an undercounter refrigerator and enough counter space for a coffeemaker, you've got a beverage center.

Unless you select unusual shapes, super sizes, or deluxe materials such as natural stone, concrete, copper, brass, fire clay, or handmade ceramics, kitchen sinks are not especially big-ticket items. An investment of a couple of hundred dollars will get you a high-quality single- or double-bowl model in porcelain, stainless steel, or a composite material. The price could go up several hundred more for color, multiple bowls, or solid surfacing. You'll also pay a premium for an apron-front farmhouse sink of any material.

In this unusual melding of form with function, an antique pot of hammered copper works beautifully as a kitchen sink, opposite.

This integrated stainless-steel double sink, top, contrasts with the butcher-block counter material.

This shallow prep sink, above, with a self-draining bottom grid is ideal for rinsing fruits and vegetables.

Popular Materials

When it's time to choose a kitchen sink, you can go for the glamour, selecting a material such as stone, hand-painted china, or even glass. But if you want to make a more conventional choice, there are some solid options for your consideration.

The familiar look of glossy white porcelain over cast iron has great appeal for many people, and this durable material is also available in myriad colors. Stains that may develop over time are generally easy to remove. A perfect match for trendy pro-style appliances, **stainless steel** is affordable, easy-care, and long lasting; 18- or 20-gauge steel promises durability and strength, and a satin finish disguises most water spots and scratches. Other metals, such as **copper** and **brass**, look great but require lots of care and polishing. Used alone or molded into a counter-top, **solid surfacing** comes in many colors and stone-looks. It's pricey but requires little maintenance; the occasional scratch, dent, or stain can be successfully repaired. Often used for trendy farmhouse sinks, **concrete** and **soapstone** are costly but practically indestructible. Soapstone comes in several earthy colors, and concrete can be tinted any shade you like.

This brushed stainless-steel sink, top, features a sculptural shape, elegant corners, and generous dimensions.

A polyester-acrylic double sink, above, in bright blue provides a bold pop of color at a reasonable price.

Three Main Composite Materials

Ever since plastic laminate was cooked up in a laboratory early in the last century, product engineers have been working to create materials that supply the look and durability of stone but cost less. One case in point: composites, which are available in three basic types.

- **Polyester/acrylic** is the least expensive and least durable of the big three. It's somewhat soft, so it scratches and stains easily. Still, if your budget is tight, you'll like its price, glossy surface, and bright colors.

- **Quartz composite**, a mixture of crushed quartz and resin fillers, is durable and resistant to most stains and scratches. Its moderate price and earthy or bright colors—including a brilliant blue and zippy yellow—make it appealing.

- **Granite composite**, a mixture of crushed granite and resin fillers, is the most expensive—and most durable—of the composites, offering high resistance to chips, stains, scratches, and burns. It's available in a number of colors and in several neutrals.

In this traditional-style kitchen, above, the exposed-apron sink matches the warm metallic of the faucet.

A 90-deg.—or "zero radius"—sink looks especially cutting edge mounted under a bright solid-surface countertop, below left.

Because the color goes all the way through, this retro-pattern composite countertop, below right, is unlikely to fade over time.

Installation Styles

- **Self-rimming (drop-in) sinks** are the least costly and most common. Available in any material, they are set into the counter with the edges overlapping. The downside: crumbs, water splashes, other debris, and germs can collect along the seam of the rim.

- **Undermounted sinks** attach below the countertop. With no visible edges, they make a smooth transition between sink and counter. To avoid warping or buckling, choose a water-resistant counter material.

- **Integral sinks**, made of the same material as the counter, look seamless and sleek and provide no crevices where food can lodge. They can be fabricated of any moldable material, such as stainless steel, solid surfacing, composites, and concrete.

- **Exposed-apron sinks** are undermounted but reveal the sink's front panel. They can be made from most types of sink materials.

This under-mounted single-bowl kitchen sink, top, is deep enough to accommodate whatever can fit in the oven.

The clean look of this contemporary kitchen, left, is enhanced by the integral double sinks made of pure white solid-surfacing material.

This humble farmhouse-style sink, above, gets a sophisticated makeover in sleek black.

This tiny marble vessel was cleverly installed in an antique dry sink, left.

Bar sinks are so small that you can afford to splurge a little with a fancy faucet set or a gleaming hammered-copper finish, below.

Prep and Bar Sinks

In addition to the primary sink, prep and bar sinks are becoming standard equipment.

You'll welcome a prep sink if your kitchen is large, if two cooks often work together in it, or if you entertain frequently. Especially useful when two cooks are working simultaneously or when a dinner guest is pressed into service to scrub some vegetables or make a salad, prep sinks are placed away from the work zone. Typically drop-in or undermount models, they are small, ranging in size from 9-inch. rounds to 18-inch. squares, although some are smaller. Because such a diminutive sink doesn't represent a major investment or get hard use, you can splurge a little bit on sexy materials that wouldn't hold up well in the primary work area—gleaming copper or brass, or a hand-painted ceramic or glass bowl, for example.

The popularity of bar sinks is a direct result of the kitchen's current status as a living center. With one cook busy at the main sink and a helper using the prep sink, a third sink where hot or cold drinks can be served is useful.

A swan-neck spout is both graceful and practical—it allows plenty of clearance for tall pots, right.

This integral, zero-radius sink, below, is a kitchen star thanks to its unusual size, shape, color, and material.

Standard Sizes

Sink Type	Width	Front to Rear	Basin Depth
Single-bowl	25	21–22	8–9
Double-bowl	33, 36	21–22	8–9
Side-disposal	33	21–22	8–9, 7
Triple-bowl	43	21–22	8, 6, 10
Corner (each way)	17–18	21–11	8–9
Bar	15–25	15	5½–6

Note: Sink dimensions (in inches)

How To Choose a Kitchen Sink

It's tempting to put looks first, but give some thought to your day-to-day practical needs, too. If you have a dishwasher, a large single-bowl sink may be sufficient; add a prep sink if yours is a two-cook household—but only if you have space for it. No dishwasher? You'll need a double-bowl design with equal-size basins. Other double-bowl options include one large and one medium or one small bowl. A triple-bowl sink with two deep basins for washing and rinsing and a small basin is a good choice for a kitchen with no dishwasher and no space for a separate prep sink. If you entertain, a bar sink is a bonus.

Match the sink with the decor, too. Stainless steel, for example, looks good in a contemporary room, but it's also at home in any style kitchen, as are solid-surface and composite-stone designs. Copper sinks, or porcelain sinks in white or a pretty color, blend beautifully with traditional or country decors. Concrete or soapstone designs have a handsome, sturdy quality. Depending on the other elements in the kitchen, they can look rustic or refined.

A single-hole faucet with a swivel spout can easily service a two-bowl sink.

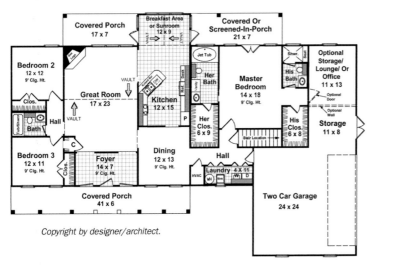

Plan #351089

Dimensions: 79'4" W x 53'6" D
Levels: 1
Heated Square Footage: 2,505
Bedrooms: 3
Bathrooms: 3
Foundation: Crawl space or slab
Material List Available: Yes
Price Category: G

CAD FILE AVAILABLE

Images provided by designer/architect.

Rear View

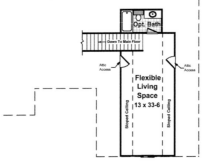

This colonial farmhouse has beautiful architectural features and a unique interior design, a combination that you'll love to come home to.

Features:

- Porches: Columns and arched windows add a graceful touch to the front porch, which opens into a large, inviting foyer. The breakfast area opens on either side to porches, one covered and one you can choose to be covered or screened. Either way, you'll be able to relax over breakfast on the porch.

- Great Room: Vaulted ceilings, windows opening to the covered porch, and a gas fireplace provide a warm welcome for guests and make this a great space for gatherings.

- Kitchen: Working from the concept of the kitchen as the heart of the home, this design centralizes it between the breakfast room/sunroom, dining room, and great room for easy transitions between preparing and serving. It features plenty of workspace, a raised bar, and a desk area for organizing mail, grocery lists, and the family calendar.

- Master Suite: This suite has a unique design, with his and her bathrooms and closets. "Her bath" features a vanity and jetted tub, while "his" has a stall shower with seat and sink. But there's no harm in sharing.

- Garage: This attached garage has enough space for two cars, as well as room for his "toys" and a workshop.

Bonus Area Floor Plan

Copyright by designer/architect.

Plan #441042

Dimensions: 52' W x 45' D
Levels: 2
Heated Square Footage: 2,538
Main Level Sq. Ft.: 1,342
Upper Level Sq. Ft.: 1,196
Bedrooms: 3
Bathrooms: 2½
Foundation: Crawl space;
slab or basement available for fee
Materials List Available: Yes
Price Category: E

Images provided by designer/architect.

Features:

- **Foyer:** This entry soars up two stories with a view to the open hallway above.

- **Family Room:** This large informal gathering area has large windows with a view to the backyard. It also has a two-sided fireplace, which it shares with the den.

- **Kitchen:** This fully equipped island kitchen has a built-in pantry and desk. The nook and family room are open to it.

- **Master Suite:** This private retreat includes a sitting area in the master bedroom that

provides ample space for a comfortable lounge in front of its fireplace. The master bath features a compartmentalized lavatory, spa tub, large shower, and his and her vanities.

- **Bedrooms:** The two additional bedrooms are located on the upper level with the master suite. Both rooms have large closets and share a common bathroom.

It's never too late to have a happy childhood—or the exact home you want.

CAD FILE AVAILABLE

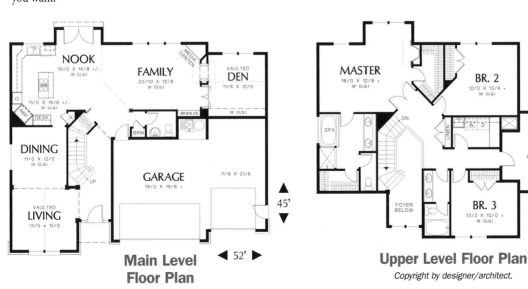

Rear Elevation

Main Level Floor Plan

◀ 52' ▶

Upper Level Floor Plan

Copyright by designer/architect.

Plan #321055

Dimensions: 70' W x 40' D

Levels: 2

Heated Square Footage: 2,505

Main Level Sq. Ft.: 1,436

Upper Level Sq. Ft.: 1,069

Bedrooms: 3

Bathrooms: 2½

Foundation: Basement

Materials List Available: Yes

Price Category: E

Images provided by designer/architect.

CAD FILE AVAILABLE CAD

Main Level Floor Plan

Upper Level Floor Plan

Copyright by designer/architect.

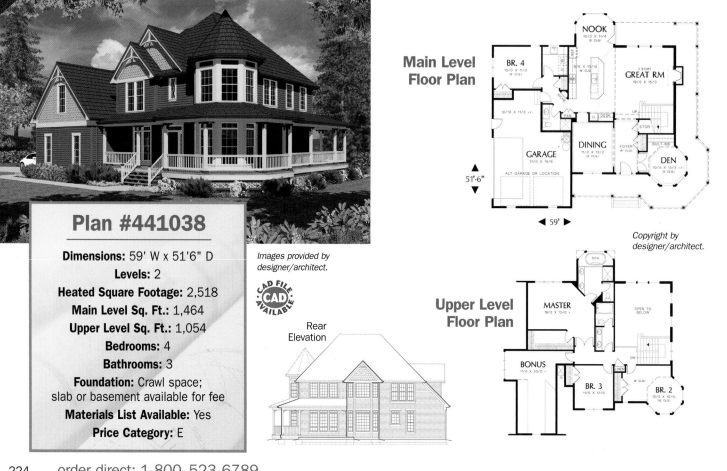

Plan #441038

Dimensions: 59' W x 51'6" D

Levels: 2

Heated Square Footage: 2,518

Main Level Sq. Ft.: 1,464

Upper Level Sq. Ft.: 1,054

Bedrooms: 4

Bathrooms: 3

Foundation: Crawl space; slab or basement available for fee

Materials List Available: Yes

Price Category: E

Images provided by designer/architect.

CAD FILE AVAILABLE CAD

Main Level Floor Plan

Rear Elevation

Upper Level Floor Plan

Copyright by designer/architect.

Main Level Floor Plan

Dining 11'-0" x 12'-0" 8'-0" CLG. HGT.
PORCH
Great Room 27'-4" x 16'-4" IRR. 8'-1" CLG. HGT.
Kitchen 16'-4" x 10'-0"
CLOSET
STORAGE 6'-0" x 6'-0"
POWDER
DOWN UP
RAIL
Study/Parlor 10'-6" x 12'-6" 8'-0" CLG. HGT.
FOYER
Garage 21'-0" x 22'-0"
PORCH

Alternate Floor Plan

MASTER BATH
WALK-IN CLOSET
ALTERNATE MASTER BATH

Upper Level Floor Plan

MASTER BATH
WALK-IN CLOSET
Master Bedroom 17'-2" x 14'-0" 8'-11" CLG. HGT.
Bedroom 14'-0" x 12'-2" IRR. 8'-1" CLG. HGT.
DOWN
CLOSET
BATH
BALCONY
Bedroom 10'-8" x 12'-6" 8'-1" CLG. HGT.
Bedroom 11'-0" x 16'-0"
LAUNDRY

Copyright by designer/architect.

Plan #161182

Dimensions: 38'8" W x 57'10" D
Levels: 2
Heated Square Footage: 2,549
Main Level Sq. Ft.: 1,192
Upper Level Sq. Ft.: 1,357
Bedrooms: 4
Bathrooms: 2½
Foundation: Basement
Materials List Available: Yes
Price Category: E

Images provided by designer/architect.

Main Level Floor Plan

84'
STORAGE
CARPORT 22x22
BREEZEWAY
PORCH
UTILITY FOLDING
WASH SINK DRY
FREEZ
CLOSET
DINING 13x11 9' CEILINGS
KITCHEN 16x11
PANTRY
BREAKFAST 11x11
MORNING PORCH
REFG
RANGE
BUFFET
BATH
CLOSET
MASTER BATH
PORCH
GREAT ROOM 17x23 2 STORY CEIL.
MASTER SUITE 14x18
FOYER
PORCH
54'
PORCH
PORCH

Upper Level Floor Plan

GAME RM./ BEDRM. 17x13
CLOSET
STORAGE
BEDRM. 14x17
1/2 WALL 36" HIGH
LANDING
BATH
OPEN TO GREAT RM.
DOWN
LINEN
CLOSET
BEDRM. 14x13
VAULT FLAT VAULT

Copyright by designer/architect.

Plan #171017

Dimensions: 84' W x 54' D
Levels: 2
Heated Square Footage: 2,558
Main Level Sq. Ft.: 1,577
Upper Level Sq. Ft.: 981
Bedrooms: 4
Bathrooms: 2½
Foundation: Crawl space or slab
Materials List Available: Yes
Price Category: E

Images provided by designer/architect.

Plan #131027

Dimensions: 62'4" W x 53'6" D
Levels: 1.5
Heated Square Footage: 2,567
Main Level Sq. Ft.: 2,017
Upper Level Sq. Ft.: 550
Bedrooms: 4
Bathrooms: 3
Foundation: Crawl space, slab, or basement
Materials List Available: Yes
Price Category: F

This home, as shown in the photograph, may differ from the actual blueprints. For more detailed information, please check the floor plans carefully.

Images provided by designer/architect.

The features of this home are so good that you may have trouble imagining all of them at once.

Features:

- **Great Room:** Imagine a stepped ceiling, corner fireplace, built-media center, and wall of windows with a glass door to the backyard—in one room.

- **Dining Room:** A stepped ceiling and server with a sink add to the elegance of this formal room.

- **Breakfast Room:** Eat at the bar this room shares with the island kitchen, and admire the 12-ft. cathedral ceiling and bayed group of 8- and 9-ft. windows. Or go through the sliding glass door to the covered side porch.

- **Master Suite:** The bedroom has a tray ceiling and cozy sitting area, and a whirlpool tub, shower, and walk-in closet are in the skylighted bath.

- **Optional Study:** The private bath in bedroom 2 makes it ideal for a study or home office.

Breakfast Nook

Rear View

SMARTtip

Painting Tips

As with any skill, there is a right and a wrong way to paint. There is a right way to hold a brush, a right way to maneuver a roller, a right way to spray a wall, etc. Follow these basic professional tips:

Brushing vs. Rolling. Some painters insist that only a brush-painted job looks right. However, most painters will "cut in" the edges with a brush, and then finish the main body of a wall or ceiling using a roller. Brushing alone can be time-consuming, and it is typically reserved for architectural woodwork.

Using the Right Brush. Use the largest brush with which you are comfortable. Professional painters seldom pick up anything smaller than a 4-inch brush. Most homeowners will achieve good results using a 4-inch brush for "cutting in" and for large surfaces, and an angled 2½- to 3-inch sash brush for trim around windows and doors. Be sure, also, to use brushes that are appropriate for the type of paint being applied. Oil-based paints require a natural bristle (also called "China bristles"), while water-based paints are applied with a synthetic bristle brush.

Handling a Brush. Many people grip a paintbrush as if they were shaking someone's hand. It is better to grip a brush more like a pencil, with the fingers and thumb wrapped around the metal ferrule. This grip provides the hand and wrist with a wider range of motion and therefore greater speed and precision. If your hand cramps, switch hands or switch temporarily to the handshake grip.

Wiping Rags. Before you begin painting, put a dust rag in your pocket. This is helpful for clearing away cobwebs and dust before painting. It is also handy for wiping off paint drips before they have a chance to dry.

Paint Hooks. When working on a ladder, use a good-quality paint hook to secure the paint bucket to your ladder. Avoid makeshift hooks made with wire or coat hangers. Paint hooks are inexpensive and available at virtually all paint and hardware stores.

Great Room

Main Level Floor Plan

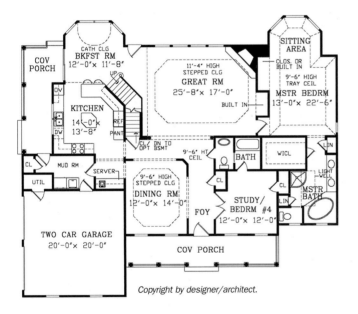

Copyright by designer/architect.

Upper Level Floor Plan

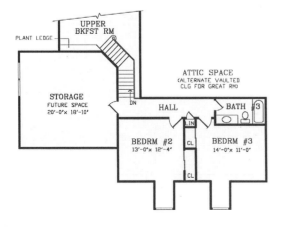

2,501–3,000 sq. ft.

Plan #421023

Dimensions: 72' W x 52'4" D
Levels: 2
Heated Square Footage: 2,579
Main Level Sq. Ft.: 1,399
Upper Level Sq. Ft.: 1,180
Bedrooms: 4
Bathrooms: 2½
Foundation: Crawl space, slab or basement
Material List Available: Yes
Price Category: E

Images provided by designer/architect.

Main Level Floor Plan

Upper Level Floor Plan

Copyright by designer/architect.

Plan #121208

Dimensions: 68' W x 65' D
Levels: 1
Heated Square Footage: 2,598
Bedrooms: 3
Bathrooms: 2½
Foundation: Slab; basement for fee
Material List Available: Yes
Price Category: E

Images provided by designer/architect.

Optional Dining Room

Optional Stairs

Bonus Area Floor Plan

Optional Basement Level Floor Plan

Copyright by designer/architect.

Main Level Floor Plan

Plan #421026

Dimensions: 71'8" W x 57' D

Levels: 2

Heated Square Footage: 2,599

Main Level Sq. Ft.: 1,602

Upper Level Sq. Ft.: 997

Bedrooms: 5

Bathrooms: 2½

Foundation: Crawl space, slab or basement

Materials List Available: Yes

Price Category: E

Images provided by designer/architect.

Upper Level Floor Plan

Copyright by designer/architect.

Plan #121028

Dimensions: 58' W x 45' D

Levels: 2

Heated Square Footage: 2,644

Main Level Sq. Ft.: 1,366

Upper Level Sq. Ft.: 1,278

Bedrooms: 4

Bathrooms: 2½

Foundation: Basement

Materials List Available: Yes

Price Category: F

Images provided by designer/architect.

Main Level Floor Plan

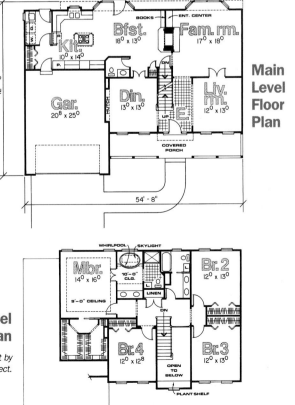

Upper Level Floor Plan

Copyright by designer/architect.

Plan #121016

Dimensions: 56' W x 48' D

Levels: 2

Heated Square Footage: 2,594

Main Level Sq. Ft.: 1,322

Upper Level Sq. Ft.: 1,272

Bedrooms: 4

Bathrooms: 3

Foundation: Basement

Materials List Available: Yes

Price Category: E

Images provided by designer/architect.

A huge wraparound porch gives this home warmth and charm.

Features:

- Ceiling Height: 8 ft. except as noted.
- Family Room: This informal sunken room's beamed ceiling and fireplace flanked by windows makes it the perfect place for family gatherings.
- Formal Dining Room: Guests will enjoy gathering in this large elegant room.

- Master Suite: The second-floor master bedroom features its own luxurious bathroom.
- Compartmented Full Bath: This large bathroom serves the three secondary bedrooms on the second floor.
- Optional Play Area: This special space, included in one of the bedrooms, features a cathedral ceiling.
- Kitchen: A large island is the centerpiece of this modern kitchen's well-designed food-preparation area.

CAD FILE AVAILABLE

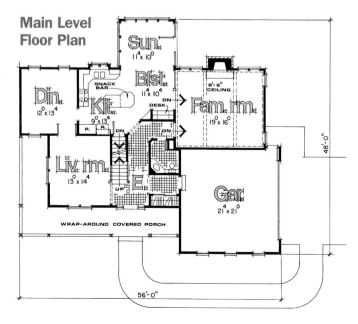

Main Level Floor Plan

Upper Level Floor Plan

Copyright by designer/architect.

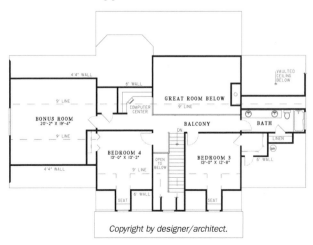

Plan #151537

Dimensions: 70'2" W x 53'4" D
Levels: 2
Heated Square Footage: 2,603
Main Level Sq. Ft.: 1,813
Upper Level Sq. Ft.: 790
Bedrooms: 4
Bathrooms: 2½
Foundation: Crawl space or slab
CompleteCost List Available: Yes
Price Category: F

Images provided by designer/architect.

Eye-catching covered porches and columns are used on both the front and rear of this traditional home.

Features:

• Great Room: A vaulted ceiling, balcony, and built-in media center enhance this great room, which is open to the kitchen and breakfast room.

• Kitchen: This large kitchen, with a raised bar, has an abundance of cabinets and a walk-in pantry.

• Master Suite: This suite and an additional bedroom or study are located on the main level for privacy and convenience.

• Upper Level: The upstairs has a balcony overlooking the great room. In addition, it has two bedrooms, a full bathroom, a built-in computer nook, and a large bonus room.

Main Level Floor Plan

Upper Level Floor Plan

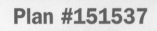

Copyright by designer/architect.

Plan #371087

Dimensions: 88'2" W x 62'10" D

Levels: 1

Heated Square Footage: 2,643

Bedrooms: 3

Bathrooms: 2½

Foundation: Crawl space, slab, or basement

Materials List Available: No

Price Category: F

This beautiful country home has a warm look that is all its own.

CAD FILE CAD AVAILABLE

Images provided by designer/architect.

Features:

• Dining Room: Once inside you will find a tiled entry that leads into this elegant room, with its 11-ft.-high ceiling.

• Living Room: This large gathering area has a 10-ft.-high ceiling, built-in bookcases, and a country fireplace.

• Kitchen: This island kitchen, with a raised bar, is open to the breakfast nook and meets the garage entrance.

• Master Suite: This suite, located in the rear of the home, features a private bathroom, large walk-in closet, marble tub, and double vanities.

• Bedrooms: Two secondary bedrooms have large closets and share a hall bathroom.

Copyright by designer/architect.

Rear Elevation

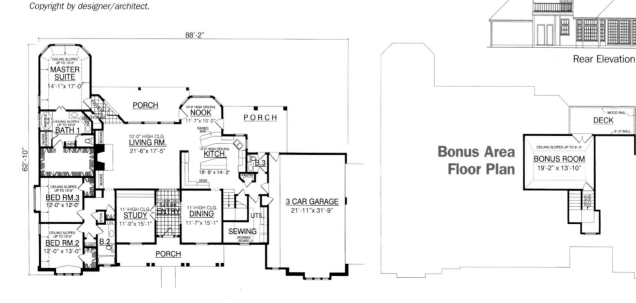

Bonus Area Floor Plan

Plan #641009

Dimensions: 61' W x 37'6" D
Levels: 2
Heated Square Footage: 2,648
Main Level Sq. Ft.: 1,373
Upper Level Sq. Ft.: 1,275
Bedrooms: 4
Bathrooms: 2½
Foundation: Basement; crawl space, slab or walkout for fee
Materials List Available: No
Price Category: F

Images provided by designer/architect.

This home features a beautiful exterior and large, open rooms inside.

Features:

- **Living Room:** Located next to the spacious entry, this living room features a large fireplace, making it the perfect place to entertain guests.

- **Dining Room:** You'll love having this conveniently located dining room near both the kitchen and living room.

- **Kitchen:** This expansive kitchen has plenty of space for helping hands.

- **Master Suite:** Located near the secondary bedrooms, this mater suite features two walk-in closets, two vanities, and a tub.

Main Level Floor Plan

Upper Level Floor Plan

Copyright by designer/architect.

Plan #391056

Dimensions: 73'10" W x 53'4" D
Levels: 2
Heated Square Footage: 2,607
Main Level Sq. Ft.: 1,429
Upper Level Sq. Ft.: 1,178
Bedrooms: 3
Bathrooms: 2½
Foundation: Basement
Materials List Available: No
Price Category: F

The spectacular pavilion front with Palladian window creates a dramatic picture indoors and out.

Images provided by designer/architect.

Features:

• Walk up the steps, onto the porch, and then through the front door with sidelights, this entry opens into a two-story space and feels light and airy. The nearby coat closet is a convenient asset.

• Living Room: This "sunken" room features a cozy fireplace flanked by two doors, allowing access to the wraparound deck. The dining room is open to the area, creating a nice flow between the two spaces.

• Family Room: This casual relaxing area is one step down from the kitchen; it boasts another fireplace and access to the large wraparound deck.

• Kitchen: This island kitchen features plenty of cabinet and counter space and is waiting for the chef in the family to take control. The breakfast area with bay window is the perfect place to start the day.

• Upper Level: This area is dedicated to the master suite with full master bath and two family bedrooms. Enjoy the dramatic view as you look down into the entry.

Copyright by designer/architect.

Main Level Floor Plan

Upper Level Floor Plan

Rear View

Kitchen

Living Room

Master Bath

Master Bedroom

Bedroom

Plan #441009

Dimensions: 94' W x 53' D
Levels: 1
Heated Square Footage: 2,650
Bedrooms: 4
Bathrooms: 2½
Foundation: Crawl space; slab or basement available for fee
Materials List Available: Yes
Price Category: F

You'll love to call this plan home. It's large enough for the whole family and has a façade that will make you the envy of the neighborhood.

CAD FILE AVAILABLE

Features:

- **Foyer:** The covered porch protects the entry, which has a transom and sidelights to brighten this space.

- **Great Room:** To the left of the foyer, beyond decorative columns, lies this vaulted room, with its fireplace and media center. Additional columns separate the room from the vaulted formal dining room.

Images provided by designer/architect.
This home, as shown in the photograph, may differ from the actual blueprints. For more information, please check the floor plans carefully.

- **Kitchen:** A casual nook and this island work center are just around the corner from the great room. The second covered porch can be reached via a door in the nook.

- **Master Suite:** This luxurious space boasts a vaulted salon, a private niche that could be a small study, and a view of the front yard. The master bath features a spa tub, separate shower, compartmented toilet, huge walk-in closet, and access to the laundry room.

- **Bedrooms:** The two additional bedrooms are located at the back of the plan and share the Jack-and-Jill bathroom.

Copyright by designer/architect.

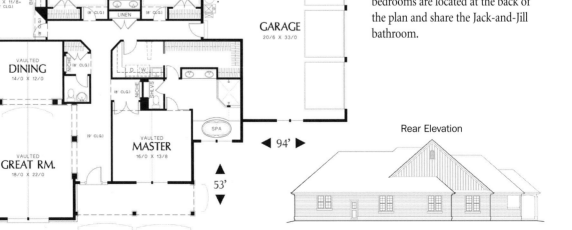

Rear Elevation

Plan #641002

Dimensions: 75'6" W x 52' D
Levels: 2
Heated Square Footage: 2,655
Main Level Sq. Ft.: 1,512
Upper Level Sq. Ft.: 1,143
Bedrooms: 3
Bathrooms: 3
Foundation: Basement; crawl space, slab or walkout for fee
Materials List Available: No
Price Category: F

This home's front porch and rear deck are wonderful for relaxing with family or friends.

Features:

- **Entry:** You'll love stepping inside of this airy two-story entry to the home.

- **Kitchen:** This kitchen is conveniently located next to the laundry area and a breakfast nook, which is open to the upper level.

- **Master Suite:** Upstairs, this master suite is filled with amenities such as a fireplace, walk-in closet, and dual-sink vanity.

- **Bonus Room:** Located above the garage, this bonus room can be used as a home office, playroom, or extra bedroom.

Images provided by designer/architect.

Main Level Floor Plan

Upper Level Floor Plan

Copyright by designer/architect.

Plan #371008

Dimensions: 86'4" W x 45'4" D

Levels: 2

Heated Square Footage: 2,656

Main Level Sq. Ft: 1,969

Upper Level Sq. Ft.: 687

Bedrooms: 4

Bathrooms: 3

Foundation: Crawl space, slab, or basement

Materials List Available: No

Price Category: F

This lovely farmhouse-style home would be the perfect place to come home to.

Features:

- **Entry:** Dramatic, and with easy access to all areas of the home, this two-story entry welcomes you home in style.

- **Master Suite:** This large secluded area has a 10-ft.-high ceiling in the sleeping area. The luxurious private bath has his and her walk-in closets.

- **Living Room:** The voluminous two-story space, beautiful fireplace, and windows that provide a view of the backyard add up to gracious drama in this room.

- **Kitchen:** This large U-shaped kitchen with built-in pantry is open to the breakfast nook.

- **Bedrooms:** Bedroom 2 is located on the main level, while the other two remaining bedrooms are on the second level.

Images provided by designer/architect.

- **Loft:** This peaceful area has a view down into the living room on one side and down to the entry on the other.

Rear Elevation

Upper Level Floor Plan

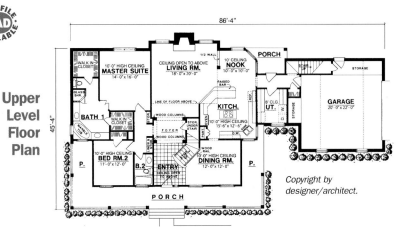

Copyright by designer/architect.

Main Level Floor Plan

Plan #641005

Dimensions: 50' W x 38' D

Levels: 2

Heated Square Footage: 2,669

Main Level Sq. Ft.: 1,017

Upper Level Sq. Ft.: 1,652

Bedrooms: 3

Bathrooms: 2½

Foundation: Crawl space; slab, basement or walkout for fee

Materials List Available: No

Price Category: F

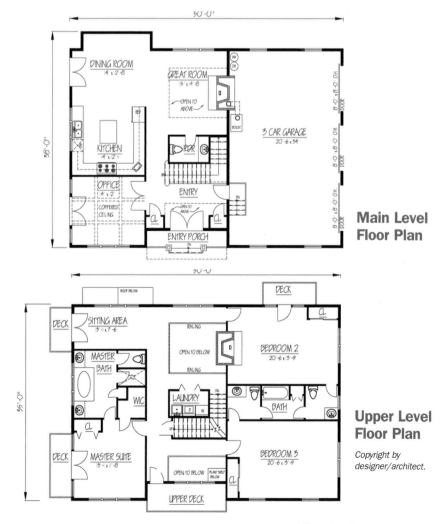

Images provided by designer/architect.

This beautiful home was designed using the ancient principles of Feng Shui to incorporate positive energy into this home.

Features:

- Great Room: This spacious great room is open to the second floor, making it well-lit and airy.

- Kitchen: You'll never run out of counter space in this U-shaped kitchen, with its generous workspace and center island.

- Master Suite: Upstairs, this master suite is complete with a private deck, two separate vanities, and a large tub.

- Secondary Bedrooms: Two additional bedrooms are also located upstairs, with a shared Jack-and-Jill bathroom. One of the bedrooms features a fireplace and private deck.

Main Level Floor Plan

Upper Level Floor Plan

Copyright by designer/architect.

2,501-3,000 sq. ft.

Plan #211062

Dimensions: 96'6" W x 43' D
Levels: 1
Heated Square Footage: 2,682
Bedrooms: 4
Bathrooms: 2½
Foundation: Slab
Materials List Available: Yes
Price Category: F

Images provided by designer/architect.

If you're looking for a beautiful home that combines luxurious amenities with a separate, professional office space, this could be the one.

Features:

- Living Room: Enjoy an 11-ft. ceiling, brick fireplace, and built-in shelving in this room.

- Dining Room: A 2-story ceiling gives presence to this room.

- Kitchen: A breakfast bar here is open to the breakfast room beyond for ease of serving.

- Breakfast Room: A built-in corner china closet adds to the practicality you'll find here.

- Office: A separate entrance makes it possible to run a professional business from this home.

- Master Suite: Separated for privacy, this suite includes two vanities and a walk-in closet.

- Porch: The rear screened porch opens to a courtyard where you'll love to entertain.

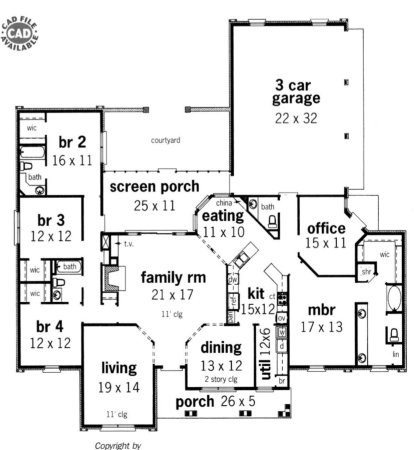

Copyright by designer/architect.

Plan #151014

Dimensions: 70'2" W x 51'4" D
Levels: 1.5
Heated Square Footage: 2,698
Main Level Sq. Ft.: 1,813
Upper Level Sq. Ft.: 885
Bedrooms: 5
Bathrooms: 3
Foundation: Crawl space, slab; basement for fee
CompleteCost List Available: Yes
Price Category: F

Images provided by designer/architect.

A comfortable front porch welcomes you into this home that features a balcony over the great room, a study, and a kitchen designed for gourmet cooks.

CAD FILE AVAILABLE

Features:

- Ceiling Height: 9 ft.
- Front Porch: Stately 12-in.-wide pillars form the entryway.
- Foyer: Open to upper story.
- Great Room: A fireplace, vaulted 9-ft. ceiling, and balcony from the second floor add character to this lovely room.
- Dining Room: Open to the kitchen for convenience.
- Kitchen: A large walk-in pantry, well-designed work areas, and eat-in bar make this room a treasure.

- Breakfast Room: Enjoy this spot that opens to both the kitchen and a large covered porch at the rear of the house.
- Study: This quiet room has French doors leading to the yard.
- Master Suite: This spacious area has cozy window seats as well as his and her walk-in closets. The master bathroom is fitted with a whirlpool tub, a glass shower, and his and her sinks.

Upper Level Floor Plan

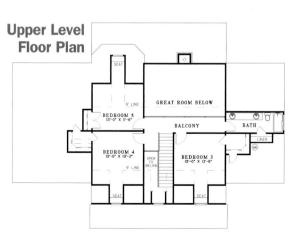

Main Level Floor Plan

Copyright by designer/architect.

Plan #271090

Dimensions: 78' W x 49' D
Levels: 2
Heated Square Footage: 2,708
Main Level Sq. Ft.: 1,430
Upper Level Sq. Ft.: 1,278
Bedrooms: 3
Bathrooms: 2½
Foundation: Daylight basement
Materials List Available: No
Price Category: F

This home blends an updated exterior with a contemporary interior design.

Images provided by designer/architect.

Features:

- Great Room: The first thing your guests will see upon entering the house in the evening is glowing light from the fireplace competing with streaming moonlight from the flanking windows. Look deeply enough into the flames and you'll see the study on the other side of the through-the-wall fireplace.

- Kitchen: The open design of this kitchen allows for multiple cooks to work comfortably together.

- Master Suite: Great for hectic mornings or relaxing evenings, this spacious master suite includes his and her walk-in closets and a compartmentalized master bath with dual vanities, a standing shower, and a separate tub. The room also includes a private entrance to the balcony.

- Secondary Bedrooms: Both of these rooms enjoy walk-in closets and access to a compartentalized bathroom with dual sinks, which makes it easier for two people to get ready in the morning.

Main Level Floor Plan

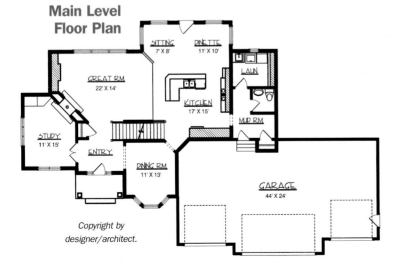

Copyright by designer/architect.

Upper Level Floor Plan

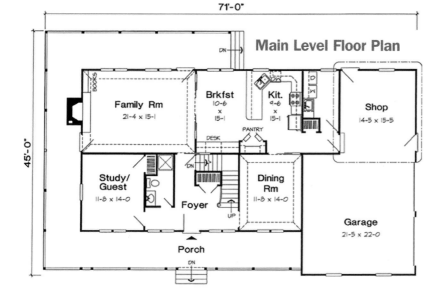

Plan #391024

Dimensions: 71' W x 45' D
Levels: 1.5
Square Footage: 2,647
Main Level Sq. Ft.: 1,378
Upper Level Sq. Ft.: 1,269
Bedrooms: 3
Bathrooms: 3
Foundation: Crawl space, slab, or basement
Materials List Available: Yes
Price Category: F

Images provided by designer/architect.

The large wraparound porch adds a touch of country to this fine home.

Features:

- Foyer: Enter through the decorative front door, and you'll find this large foyer, with its attractive staircase to the second floor.

- Family Room: This room is expansive and includes a massive fireplace with built-in bookshelves.

- Kitchen: Built-in features continue in this kitchen, with its built-in pantry, and the breakfast room, with its built-in planning desk. The peninsula counter/eating bar separates the two rooms. Ample counter and storage space add to the kitchen's efficiency.

- Master Bedroom: This master bedroom is crowned by a cathedral ceiling and includes a lavish private bathroom with a walk-in closet.

- Study/Guest Room: To the left of the foyer is this dual-purpose room, which has convenient access to a full bathroom.

Optional Upper Level Floor Plan

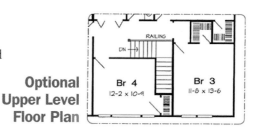

Upper Level Floor Plan

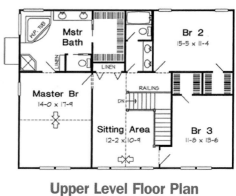

Copyright by designer/architect.

Main Level Floor Plan

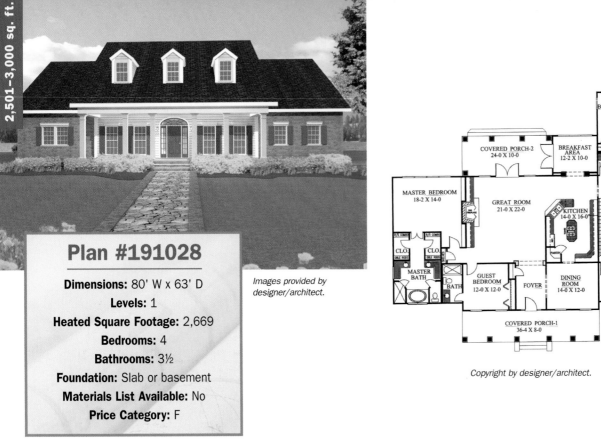

Images provided by designer/architect.

Copyright by designer/architect.

Plan #191028

Dimensions: 80' W x 63' D

Levels: 1

Heated Square Footage: 2,669

Bedrooms: 4

Bathrooms: 3½

Foundation: Slab or basement

Materials List Available: No

Price Category: F

Images provided by designer/architect.

Main Level Floor Plan

Upper Level Floor Plan

Copyright by designer/architect.

Plan #181034

Dimensions: 60' W x 44' D

Levels: 2

Heated Square Footage: 2,687

Main Level Sq. Ft.: 1,297

Upper Level Sq. Ft.: 1,390

Bedrooms: 3

Bathrooms: 2½

Foundation: Full basement

Materials List Available: Yes

Price Category: F

CAD FILE AVAILABLE

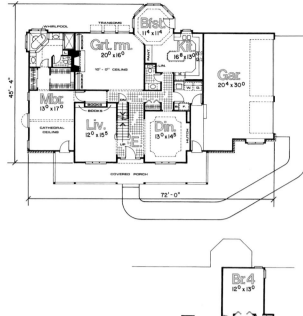

Plan #121083

Dimensions: 72' W x 45'4" D
Levels: 2
Heated Square Footage: 2,695
Main Level Sq. Ft.: 1,881
Upper Level Sq. Ft.: 814
Bedrooms: 4
Bathrooms: 3½
Foundation: Basement
Materials List Available: Yes
Price Category: F

Images provided by designer/architect.

Upper Level Floor Plan

Copyright by designer/architect.

Plan #551101

Dimensions: 50' W x 40' D
Levels: 2
Heated Square Footage: 2,700
Main Level Sq. Ft.: 1,360
Upper Level Sq. Ft.: 1,340
Bedrooms: 4
Bathrooms: 2½
Foundation: Crawl space or walkout; slab or basement for fee
Material List Available: No
Price Category: F

Images provided by designer/architect.

Main Level Floor Plan

Upper Level Floor Plan

Copyright by designer/architect.

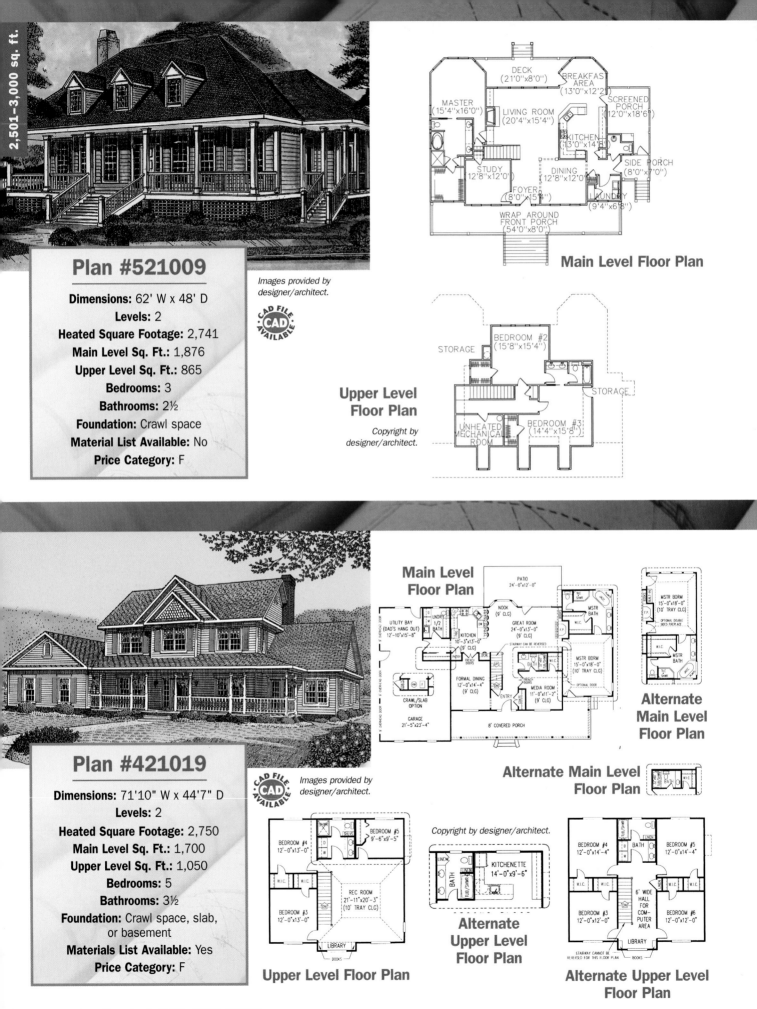

2,501–3,000 sq. ft.

Main Level Floor Plan

DECK (21'0"x8'0")
BREAKFAST AREA (13'0"x12'2")
MASTER (15'4"x16'0")
LIVING ROOM (20'4"x15'4")
SCREENED PORCH (12'0"x18'6")
KITCHEN (13'0"x14'8")
STUDY (12'8"x12'0")
DINING (12'8"x12'0")
SIDE PORCH (8'0"x7'0")
FOYER (8'0"x15'4")
LAUNDRY (9'4"x6'8")
WRAP AROUND FRONT PORCH (54'0"x8'0")

Upper Level Floor Plan

STORAGE
BEDROOM #2 (15'8"x15'4")
STORAGE
UNHEATED MECHANICAL ROOM
BEDROOM #3 (14'4"x15'8")

Copyright by designer/architect.

Plan #521009

Images provided by designer/architect.

CAD FILE CAD AVAILABLE

Dimensions: 62' W x 48' D
Levels: 2
Heated Square Footage: 2,741
Main Level Sq. Ft.: 1,876
Upper Level Sq. Ft.: 865
Bedrooms: 3
Bathrooms: 2½
Foundation: Crawl space
Material List Available: No
Price Category: F

Main Level Floor Plan

PATIO (24'-0"x12'-0")
NOOK (9' CLG)
UTILITY BAY (DAD'S HANG OUT) (12'-10"x15'-8")
LNDRY 1/2 BATH
KITCHEN 10'-3"x13'-0" (9' CLG)
GREAT ROOM 24'-0"x13'-0" (9' CLG)
MSTR BATH
W.I.C.
FORMAL DINING 12'-0"x14'-4" (9' CLG)
MSTR BDRM 15'-0"x18'-0" (10' TRAY CLG)
MEDIA ROOM 11'-0"x11'-2" (9' CLG)
CRAWL/SLAB OPTION
GARAGE 21'-5"x23'-4"
8' COVERED PORCH

Alternate Main Level Floor Plan

MSTR BDRM 15'-0"x18'-0" (10' TRAY CLG)
OPTIONAL DOUBLE SIDED FIREPLACE
W.I.C.
MSTR BATH

Alternate Main Level Floor Plan

Plan #421019

Images provided by designer/architect.

CAD FILE CAD AVAILABLE

Dimensions: 71'10" W x 44'7" D
Levels: 2
Heated Square Footage: 2,750
Main Level Sq. Ft.: 1,700
Upper Level Sq. Ft.: 1,050
Bedrooms: 5
Bathrooms: 3½
Foundation: Crawl space, slab, or basement
Materials List Available: Yes
Price Category: F

Upper Level Floor Plan

BEDROOM #4 (12'-0"x13'-0")
BEDROOM #5 (9'-6"x9'-5")
W.I.C.
W.I.C.
REC. ROOM 21'-11"x20'-3" (10' TRAY CLG)
BEDROOM #3 (12'-0"x13'-0")
LIBRARY
BOOKS

Alternate Upper Level Floor Plan

Copyright by designer/architect.

LINEN
BATH
KITCHENETTE 14'-0"x9'-6"

Alternate Upper Level Floor Plan

BEDROOM #4 12'-0"x14'-4"
BEDROOM #5 12'-0"x14'-4"
BATH
W.I.C.
W.I.C.
6' WIDE HALL FOR COMPUTER AREA
BEDROOM #3 12'-0"x12'-0"
BEDROOM #6 12'-0"x12'-0"
LIBRARY
STAIRWAY CANNOT BE REVERSED FOR THIS FLOOR PLAN
BOOKS

Plan #351153

Dimensions: 75'6" W x 70'10" D

Levels: 1

Heated Square Footage: 2,750

Bedrooms: 4

Bathrooms: 3½

Foundation: Crawl space, slab or basement

Materials List Available: Yes

Price Category: F

Images provided by designer/architect.

CAD FILE AVAILABLE

Bonus Area Floor Plan

Copyright by designer/architect.

Plan #221080

Dimensions: 67'8" W x 63' D

Levels: 2

Heated Square Footage: 2,772

Main Level Sq. Ft.: 1,902

Upper Level Sq. Ft.: 870

Bedrooms: 4

Bathrooms: 3½

Foundation: Basement

Material List Available: No

Price Category: F

Images provided by designer/architect.

CAD FILE AVAILABLE

Main Level Floor Plan

Upper Level Floor Plan

Copyright by designer/architect.

Plan #131029

Dimensions: 56'4" W x 46'6" D
Levels: 2
Heated Square Footage: 2,718
Main Level Sq. Ft.: 1,515
Upper Level Sq. Ft.: 1,203
Bedrooms: 4
Bathrooms: 2½
Foundation: Crawl space, slab, or basement
Materials List Available: Yes
Price Category: G

Images provided by designer/architect.

This home is ideal if you love the look of a country-style farmhouse.

Features:

- Foyer: Walk across the large wraparound porch that defines this home to enter this two-story foyer.

- Living Room: French doors from the foyer lead into this living room.

- Family Room: The whole family will love this room, with its vaulted ceiling, fireplace, and sliding glass doors that open to the wooden rear deck.

- Kitchen: A beautiful sit-down center island opens to the family room. There's also a breakfast nook with a lovely bay window.

- Master Suite: Luxury abounds with vaulted ceilings, walk-in closets, private bath with whirlpool tub, separate shower, and dual sinks.

- Loft: A special place with vaulted ceiling and view into the family room below.

This home, as shown in the photograph, may differ from the actual blueprints. For more detailed information, please check the floor plans carefully.

Main Level Floor Plan

Copyright by designer/architect.

Upper Level Floor Plan

Rear Elevation

Dining Room

Breakfast Area

Kitchen Island

Kitchen

Master Bathroom

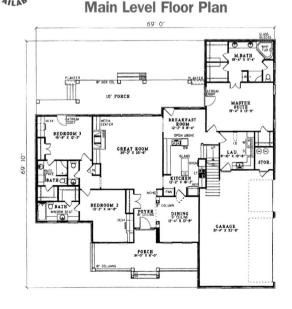

Plan #151018

Dimensions: 69' W x 69'10" D

Levels: 2

Heated Square Footage: 2,755

Main Level Sq. Ft.: 2,406

Upper Level Sq. Ft.: 349

Bedrooms: 3

Bathrooms: 4½

Foundation: Crawl space, slab, or basement

CompleteCost List Available: Yes

Price Category: F

Images provided by designer/architect.

Treasure the countless amenities that make this home ideal for a family and welcoming to guests.

Features:

• Great Room: A gas fireplace and built-in shelving beg for a warm, comfortable decorating scheme.

• Kitchen: An island counter here opens to the breakfast room, and a swinging door leads to the dining room with its formal entry columns.

• Laundry Room: You'll wonder how you ever kept the laundry organized without this room and its built-in ironing board and broom closet.

• Master Suite: Atrium doors to the porch are a highlight of the bedroom, with its two walk-in closets, a corner whirlpool tub with glass blocks, and a separate shower.

• Bedrooms: These large rooms will surely promote peaceful school-day mornings for the children because each room has both a private bath and a walk-in closet.

Main Level Floor Plan

Upper Level Floor Plan

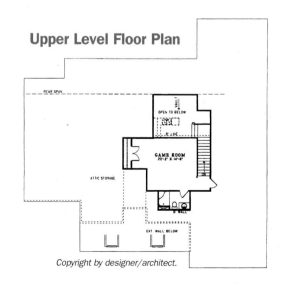

Copyright by designer/architect.

Plan #151015

Dimensions: 72'4" W x 48'4" D
Levels: 1.5
Heated Square Footage: 2,789
Main Level Sq. Ft.: 1,977
Upper Level Sq. Ft.: 812
Bedrooms: 4
Bathrooms: 3
Foundation: Crawl space, slab, or basement
CompleteCost List Available: Yes
Price Category: F

Images provided by designer/architect.

The spacious kitchen that opens to the breakfast room and the hearth room make this family home ideal for entertaining.

Features:

- Great Room: The fireplace will make a cozy winter focal point in this versatile space.
- Hearth Room: Enjoy the built-in entertainment center, built-in shelving, and fireplace here.
- Dining Room: A swing door leading to the kitchen is as attractive as it is practical.
- Study: A private bath and walk-in closet make this room an ideal spot for guests when needed.
- Kitchen: An island work area, a computer desk, and an eat-in bar add convenience and utility.
- Master Suite: Two vanities, two walk-in closets, a shower with a seat, and a whirlpool tub highlight this private space.

Upper Level Floor Plan

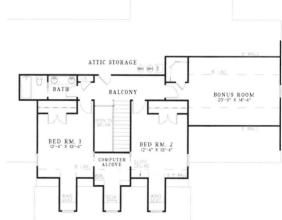

Main Level Floor Plan

Copyright by designer/architect.

Plan #161224

Dimensions: 87'4" W x 57'4" D
Levels: 1
Heated Square Footage: 2,796
Bedrooms: 2
Bathrooms: 2½
Foundation: Walkout
Materials List Available: Yes
Price Category: F

Images provided by designer/architect.

This single-level home places all of the spaces you need for comfortable living within easy reach.

Features:

- **Foyer:** This large foyer welcomes visitors and is centrally located to the main rooms of the home.

- **Great Room:** Walking straight through the foyer, you'll find this beautiful great room, complete with a corner fireplace.

- **Kitchen:** You'll love having company while preparing meals, as friends and family gather at the snack bar during get-togethers.

- **Master Suite:** This expansive master suite is complete with a corner tub, walk-in closet, and two separate vanities.

Alternate Front View

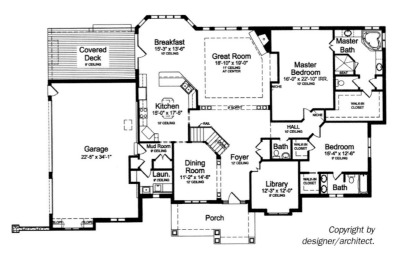

Copyright by designer/architect.

Plan #281032

Dimensions: 66' W x 49' D
Levels: 2
Square Footage: 2,904
Main Level Sq. Ft.: 1,494
Upper Level Sq. Ft.: 1,410
Bedrooms: 4
Bathrooms: 2½
Foundation: Basement
Material List Available: Yes
Price Category: F

Country style is alive and well in this attractive home.

Images provided by designer/architect.

Features:

- Front Porch: This front porch welcomes guests to your home. It's the perfect spot to sit and sip lemonade while visiting with friends or family.

- Family Room: Opening onto the rear porch, which comes in handy for enjoying the outdoors, this family room also features a fireplace for the times you would rather stay inside.

- Kitchen: This efficiently designed space features an L-shaped work area, pantry, and island with a raised eating bar. The room opens to the breakfast nook, giving meal times plenty of possibilities.

- Master Suite: Imagine a relaxing breakfast in bed in this luxurious master suite. It contains two large walk-in closets and a full master bath.

Rear Elevation

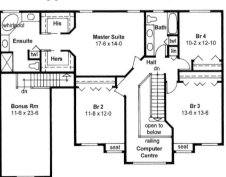

Main Level Floor Plan

Copyright by designer/architect.

Upper Level Floor Plan

Plan #371122

Dimensions: 88'2" W x 63'2½" D
Levels: 1
Heated Square Footage: 2,774
Bedrooms: 3
Bathrooms: 2½
Foundation: Crawl space, slab, or basement
Material List Available: No
Price Category: F

Images provided by designer/architect.

CAD FILE AVAILABLE

Bonus Area Floor Plan

Copyright by designer/architect.

Plan #151804

Dimensions: 82'6" W x 64'2" D
Levels: 1
Heated Square Footage: 2,806
Bedrooms: 4
Bathrooms: 2½
Foundation: Crawl space or slab
CompleteCost List Available: Yes
Price Category: F

Images provided by designer/architect.

CAD FILE AVAILABLE

Bonus Area Floor Plan

Copyright by designer/architect.

Main Level Floor Plan

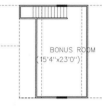

- REAR PORCH
- MASTER BEDROOM (18'4"x15'4")
- LIVING ROOM (18'8"x16'0")
- BRKFAST AREA (13'8"x9'0")
- SCREENED PORCH
- 2-CAR GARAGE (25'4x28'8")
- KITCHEN (13'8"x11'0")
- DINING ROOM (13'8"x12'8")
- FOYER
- FRONT PORCH

Upper Level Floor Plan

- BEDROOM #2 (11'4"x15'10")
- BEDROOM #3 (13'8"x12'2")
- BONUS ROOM (15'4"x23'0")
- STUDY PLAYROOM (13'8"x8'8")
- BEDROOM #4 (13'8"x12'8")

Copyright by designer/architect.

Plan #521006

Dimensions: 99'2" W x 47'5" D
Levels: 1.5
Heated Square Footage: 2,818
Main Level Sq. Ft.: 1,787
Upper Level Sq. Ft.: 1,031
Bedrooms: 4
Bathrooms: 3½
Foundation: Crawl space
Material List Available: No
Price Category: F

Images provided by designer/architect.

CAD FILE AVAILABLE

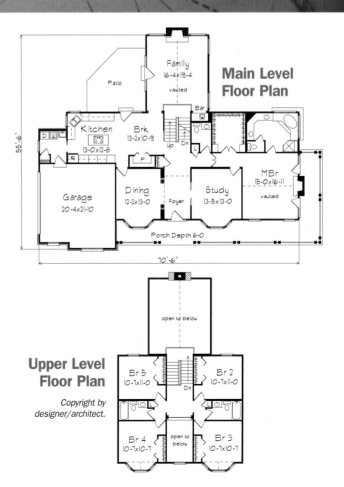

Main Level Floor Plan

- Family 16-4x19-4 vaulted
- Patio
- Bar
- Kitchen 13-0x12-8
- Brk 13-2x10-9
- Up Dn
- Garage 20-4x21-10
- Dining 12-2x13-0
- Foyer
- Study 13-5x13-0
- MBr 15-0x16-11 vaulted
- Porch Depth 6-0
- 55'-6"
- 70'-6"

Upper Level Floor Plan

- open to below
- Br 5 10-7x11-0
- Br 2 10-7x11-0
- Dn
- Br 4 10-7x10-7
- open to below
- Br 3 10-7x10-7

Copyright by designer/architect.

Plan #321054

Dimensions: 70'6" W x 55'6" D
Levels: 2
Heated Square Footage: 2,828
Main Level Sq. Ft.: 2,006
Upper Level Sq. Ft.: 822
Bedrooms: 5
Bathrooms: 3½
Foundation: Basement
Materials List Available: Yes
Price Category: F

Images provided by designer/architect.

CAD FILE AVAILABLE

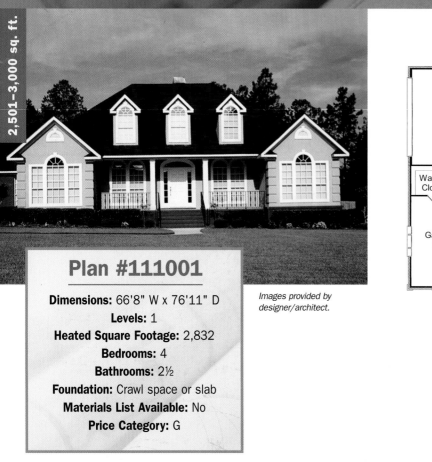

Plan #111001

Dimensions: 66'8" W x 76'11" D
Levels: 1
Heated Square Footage: 2,832
Bedrooms: 4
Bathrooms: 2½
Foundation: Crawl space or slab
Materials List Available: No
Price Category: G

Images provided by designer/architect.

Copyright by designer/architect.

Plan #151174

Dimensions: 57'4" W x 55'10" D
Levels: 2
Heated Square Footage: 2,815
Main Level Sq. Ft.: 2,142
Upper Level Sq. Ft.: 673
Bedrooms: 4
Bathrooms: 3
Foundation: Crawl space or slab; basement or walk out for fee
CompleteCost List Available: Yes
Price Category: F

Images provided by designer/architect.

CAD FILE AVAILABLE

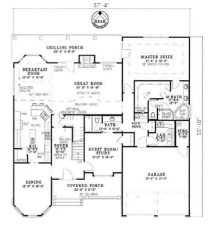

Main Level Floor Plan

Upper Level Floor Plan

Copyright by designer/architect.

Main Level Floor Plan

Images provided by designer/architect.

Rear View

Upper Level Floor Plan

Copyright by designer/architect.

Plan #461092

Dimensions: 81' W x 54' D
Levels: 2
Heated Square Footage: 2,844
Main Level Sq. Ft.: 2,128
Upper Level Sq. Ft.: 716
Bedrooms: 4
Bathrooms: 4
Foundation: Slab or basement; crawl space for fee
Material List Available: No
Price Category: F

Plan #441351

Dimensions: 35' W x 56' D
Levels: 2
Heated Square Footage: 2,859
Main Level Sq. Ft.: 1,491
Upper Level Sq. Ft.: 1,368
Bedrooms: 4
Bathrooms: 3½
Foundation: Crawl space
Materials List Available: Yes
Price Category: F

Images provided by designer/architect.

CAD FILE AVAILABLE

Main Level Floor Plan

Upper Level Floor Plan

Garage Floor Plan

Copyright by designer/architect.

Images provided by designer/architect.

Plan #291015

Dimensions: 88'6" W x 58'3" D

Levels: 1.5

Heated Square Footage: 2,901

Main Level Sq. Ft.: 2,078

Upper Level Sq. Ft.: 823

Bedrooms: 3

Bathrooms: 2½

Foundation: Basement

Materials List Available: No

Price Category: F

Upon entering this home, a cathedral-like timber-framed interior fills the eye.

Features:

- **Great Room:** This large gathering area's ceiling rises up two stories and is open to the kitchen. The beautiful fireplace is the focal point of this room.

- **Kitchen:** This island kitchen is open to the great room and the breakfast nook. Warm woods of all species enhance the great room and this space.

- **Master Suite:** This suite has a sloped ceiling and adjoins a luxurious master bath with twin walk-in closets that open to a sunroom with a private balcony.

- **Upper Level:** This upper level has an open lounge that leads to two bedrooms with vaulted ceilings and a generous second bath.

**Main Level
Floor Plan**

Copyright by designer/architect.

**Upper
Level
Floor
Plan**

Rear View

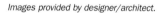
2,501-3,000 sq. ft.

Plan #101020

Dimensions: 55'8" W x 49'2" D

Levels: 2

Heated Square Footage: 2,972

Main Level Sq. Ft.: 1,986

Upper Level Sq. Ft.: 986

Bedrooms: 4

Bathrooms: 3½

Foundation: Basement, or walkout

Materials List Available: No

Price Category: F

Images provided by designer/architect.

CAD FILE AVAILABLE

This luxurious country home has an open-design main level that maximizes the use of space.

Features:

- Ceiling Height: 9 ft. unless otherwise noted.

- Foyer: Guests will be greeted by this grand two-story entry, with its graceful angled staircase.

- Dining Room: At nearly 12 ft. x 15 ft., this elegant dining room has plenty of room for large parties.

- Family Room: Everyone will be drawn to this 17-ft. x 19-ft. room, with its dramatic two-story ceiling and its handsome fireplace.

- Kitchen: This spacious kitchen is open to the family room and features a breakfast bar and built-in table in the cooktop island.

- Master Suite: This elegant retreat includes a bayed 18-ft.-5-in. x 14-ft.-9-in. bedroom and a beautiful corner his and her bath/closet arrangement.

- Secondary Bedrooms: Upstairs you'll find three spacious bathrooms, one with a private bath and two with access to a shared bath.

Main Level Floor Plan

Upper Level Floor Plan

Copyright by designer/architect.

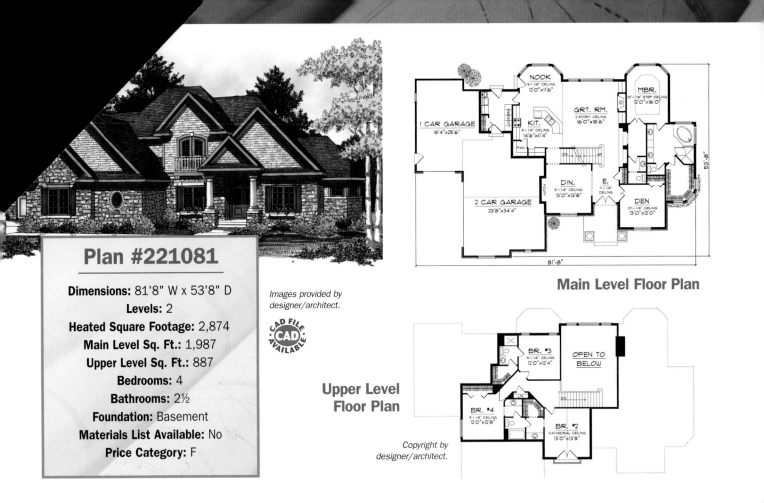

Plan #221081

Dimensions: 81'8" W x 53'8" D
Levels: 2
Heated Square Footage: 2,874
Main Level Sq. Ft.: 1,987
Upper Level Sq. Ft.: 887
Bedrooms: 4
Bathrooms: 2½
Foundation: Basement
Materials List Available: No
Price Category: F

Images provided by designer/architect.

CAD FILE AVAILABLE

Main Level Floor Plan

Upper Level Floor Plan

Copyright by designer/architect.

Plan #441011

Dimensions: 67' W x 46' D
Levels: 1
Heated Square Footage: 2,898
Main Level Sq. Ft.: 1,744
Basement Level Sq. Ft.: 1,154
Bedrooms: 3
Bathrooms: 2½
Foundation: Walkout basement
Materials List Available: Yes
Price Category: F

Images provided by designer/architect.

CAD FILE AVAILABLE

Rear Elevation

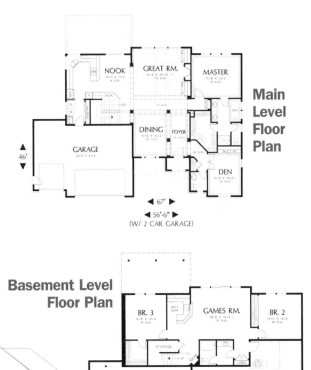

Main Level Floor Plan

Basement Level Floor Plan

Copyright by designer/architect.

Plan #521005

Dimensions: 62' W x 104'2" D
Levels: 1.5
Heated Square Footage: 2,932
Main Level Sq. Ft.: 2,026
Upper Level Sq. Ft.: 906
Bedrooms: 3
Bathrooms: 3½
Foundation: Crawl space
Materials List Available: No
Price Category: F

Images provided by designer/architect.

Main Level Floor Plan

Copyright by designer/architect.

Upper Level Floor Plan

Bonus Area Floor Plan

Plan #441350

Dimensions: 45' W x 54' D
Levels: 2
Heated Square Footage: 2,955
Main Level Sq. Ft.: 1,950
Upper Level Sq. Ft.: 1,005
Bedrooms: 3
Bathrooms: 2½
Foundation: Crawl space
Materials List Available: Yes
Price Category: F

Images provided by designer/architect.

This home, as shown in the illustration, may differ from the actual blueprints. For more detailed information, please check the floor plans carefully.

DETACHED GARAGE
LOCATION TO BE DETERMINED BY OWNER

Main Level Floor Plan

Copyright by designer/architect.

Upper Level Floor Plan

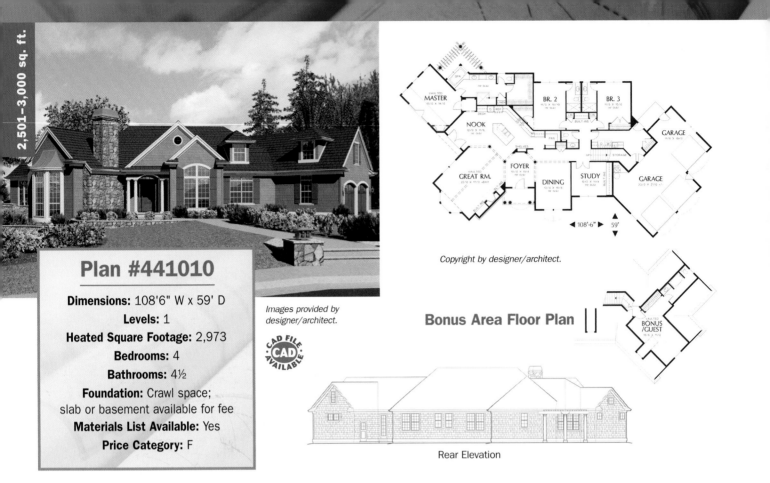

Plan #441010

Dimensions: 108'6" W x 59' D
Levels: 1
Heated Square Footage: 2,973
Bedrooms: 4
Bathrooms: 4½
Foundation: Crawl space;
slab or basement available for fee
Materials List Available: Yes
Price Category: F

Images provided by designer/architect.

CAD FILE AVAILABLE

Copyright by designer/architect.

Bonus Area Floor Plan

Rear Elevation

Plan #441313

Dimensions: 53' W x 77' D
Levels: 2
Heated Square Footage: 2,998
Main Level Sq. Ft.: 1,618
Upper Level Sq. Ft.: 1,380
Bedrooms: 4
Bathrooms: 2½
Foundation: Crawl space
Materials List Available: Yes
Price Category: F

Images provided by designer/architect.

CAD FILE AVAILABLE

**Main Level
Floor Plan**

**Upper Level
Floor Plan**

Copyright by designer/architect.

Upper Level Floor Plan

BEDROOM #3
13'-0"x15'-0"
(8' CLG)

BATH

BEDROOM #4
13'-0"x15'-0"
(8' CLG)

BONUS ROOM
23'-5"x18'-9"
(8' CLG)

BEDROOM #2
13'-0"x11'-0"
(8' CLG)

REC ROOM
24'-5"x13'-5"
(8' CLG)

VAULTED AREA

STORAGE

Main Level Floor Plan

Copyright by designer/architect.

MSTR BATH
(9' CLG)

W.I.C.

8' WIDE COVERED PORCH

MASTER BDRM
14'-0"x19'-4"
(10' TRAY CLG)

KITCHEN
16'-6"x14'-1"
(9' CLG)

LNDRY

GREAT ROOM
25'-5"x15'-0"
(9' CLG)

NOOK

SHOP/STORAGE
11'-10"x19'-3"

OFFICE/BDRM#5/
HOME SCHOOL
13'-0"x11'-1"
(9' CLG)

FORMAL DINING
13'-0"x13'-0"
(9' CLG)

PWDR

FOYER
(9' CLG)

GARAGE
24'-0"x24'-0"

8' WIDE COVERED PORCH

Optional Stair Location

FOYER
(9' CLG)

Plan #421028

Dimensions: 78' W x 61' D
Levels: 2
Heated Square Footage: 3,005
Main Level Sq. Ft.: 1,874
Upper Level Sq. Ft.: 1,131
Bedrooms: 5
Bathrooms: 2½
Foundation: Crawl space, slab or basement
Material List Available: Yes
Price Category: G

Images provided by designer/architect.

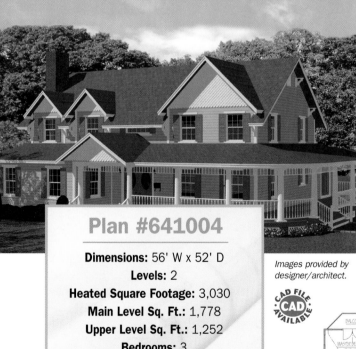

Main Level Floor Plan

Copyright by designer/architect.

DECK

DINING

LIVING ROOM

KITCHEN

DEN

LIBRARY

PORCH

Plan #641004

Dimensions: 56' W x 52' D
Levels: 2
Heated Square Footage: 3,030
Main Level Sq. Ft.: 1,778
Upper Level Sq. Ft.: 1,252
Bedrooms: 3
Bathrooms: 3½
Foundation: Basement; crawl space, slab or walkout for fee
Materials List Available: No
Price Category: G

Images provided by designer/architect.

CAD FILE AVAILABLE

Upper Level Floor Plan

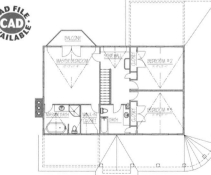

BALCONY

MASTER BEDROOM

BEDROOM #2

MASTER BATH

WALK-IN CLOSET

BATH

BEDROOM #3

Optional Basement Floor Plan

MUD ROOM

FAMILY ROOM

STORAGE

HALL

WORK ROOM

BATH

UTILITY ROOM

LAUNDRY

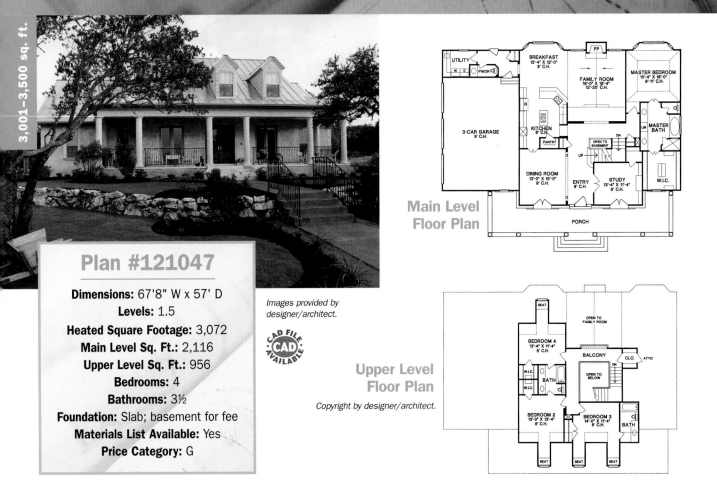

Main Level Floor Plan

Images provided by designer/architect.

Upper Level Floor Plan

Copyright by designer/architect.

Plan #121047

Dimensions: 67'8" W x 57' D
Levels: 1.5
Heated Square Footage: 3,072
Main Level Sq. Ft.: 2,116
Upper Level Sq. Ft.: 956
Bedrooms: 4
Bathrooms: 3½
Foundation: Slab; basement for fee
Materials List Available: Yes
Price Category: G

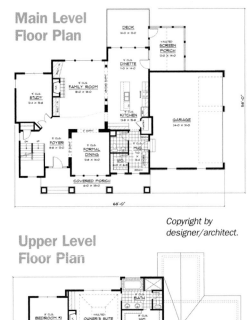

Plan #481125

Dimensions: 68' W x 52'6" D
Levels: 2
Heated Square Footage: 3,118
Main Level Sq. Ft.: 1,578
Upper Level Sq. Ft.: 1,540
Bedrooms: 4
Bathrooms: 3½
Foundation: Walkout
Materials List Available: No
Price Category: G

Images provided by designer/architect.

Main Level Floor Plan

Copyright by designer/architect.

Upper Level Floor Plan

Rear View

Main Level Floor Plan

Images provided by designer/architect.

Upper Level Floor Plan

Copyright by designer/architect.

Plan #641001

Dimensions: 61'6" W x 56' D
Levels: 2
Heated Square Footage: 3,034
Main Level Sq. Ft.: 1,323
Upper Level Sq. Ft.: 1,711
Bedrooms: 4
Bathrooms: 2½
Foundation: Basement or walkout; crawl space or slab for fee
Material List Available: No
Price Category: G

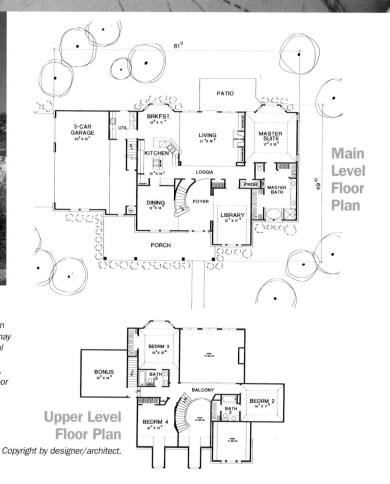

Main Level Floor Plan

Images provided by designer/architect.

This home, as shown in the photograph, may differ from the actual blueprints. For more detailed information, please check the floor plans carefully.

Upper Level Floor Plan

Copyright by designer/architect.

Plan #331004

Dimensions: 81' W x 49'10" D
Levels: 2
Heated Square Footage: 3,125
Main Level Sq. Ft.: 2,147
Upper Level Sq. Ft.: 978
Bedrooms: 4
Bathrooms: 3½
Foundation: Crawl space, slab, or basement
Materials List Available: No
Price Category: G

Main Level Floor Plan

Lower Level Floor Plan

Copyright by designer/architect.

Images provided by designer/architect.

Plan #441013

Dimensions: 69' W x 59' D
Levels: 2
Heated Square Footage: 3,317
Main Level Sq. Ft.: 2,657
Lower Level Sq. Ft.: 660
Bedrooms: 4
Bathrooms: 3½
Foundation: Slab
Materials List Available: Yes
Price Category: G

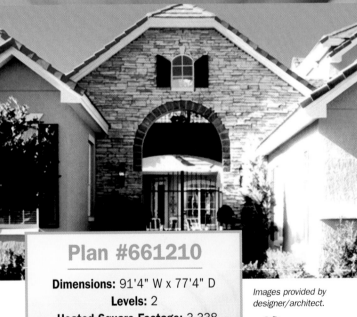

Main Level Floor Plan

Upper Level Floor Plan

Copyright by designer/architect.

Images provided by designer/architect.

Plan #661210

Dimensions: 91'4" W x 77'4" D
Levels: 2
Heated Square Footage: 3,338
Main Level Sq. Ft.: 2,854
Upper Level Sq. Ft.: 484
Bedrooms: 4
Bathrooms: 3½
Foundation: Slab
Material List Available: No
Price Category: G

Main Level Floor Plan

Copyright by designer/architect.

Plan #641007

Dimensions: 50' W x 50' D
Levels: 2
Heated Square Footage: 3,650
Main Level Sq. Ft.: 1,686
Upper Level Sq. Ft.: 1,964
Bedrooms: 4
Bathrooms: 3½
Foundation: Crawl space; slab, basement or walkout for fee
Materials List Available: No
Price Category: H

Images provided by designer/architect.

Upper Levels Floor Plans

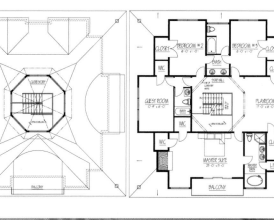

Plan #441012

Dimensions: 65' W x 55' D
Levels: 1
Square Footage: 3,682
Main Level Sq. Ft.: 2,192
Basement Level Sq. Ft.: 1,490
Bedrooms: 4
Bathrooms: 4
Foundation: Walkout
Materials List Available: No
Price Category: H

Images provided by designer/architect.

Basement Level Floor Plan

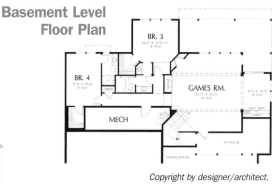

Rear Elevation

Copyright by designer/architect.

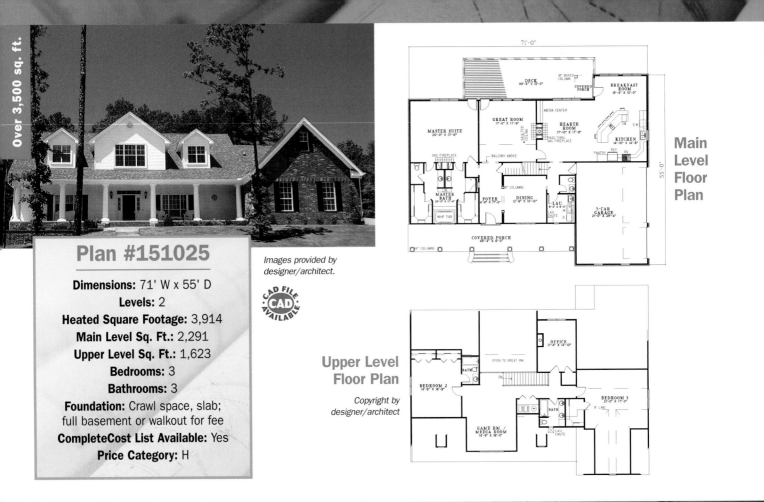

Main Level Floor Plan

Upper Level Floor Plan

Images provided by designer/architect.

Copyright by designer/architect

Plan #151025

Dimensions: 71' W x 55' D

Levels: 2

Heated Square Footage: 3,914

Main Level Sq. Ft.: 2,291

Upper Level Sq. Ft.: 1,623

Bedrooms: 3

Bathrooms: 3

Foundation: Crawl space, slab; full basement or walkout for fee

CompleteCost List Available: Yes

Price Category: H

Main Level Floor Plan

Upper Level Floor Plan

Images provided by designer/architect.

Copyright by designer/architect.

Plan #181301

Dimensions: 68' W x 64' D

Levels: 2

Heated Square Footage: 3,943

Main Level Sq. Ft.: 2,486

Upper Level Sq. Ft.: 1,457

Bedrooms: 4

Bathrooms: 3½

Foundation: Basement

Materials List Available: Yes

Price Category: H

Main Level Floor Plan

Lower Level Floor Plan

Copyright by designer/architect.

Plan #451124

Dimensions: 90' W x 52' D
Levels: 2
Heated Square Footage: 4,016
Main Level Sq. Ft.: 2,008
Lower Level Sq. Ft.: 2,088
Bedrooms: 4
Bathrooms: 3
Foundation: Walkout – insulated concrete form
Material List Available: No
Price Category: I

Images provided by designer/architect.

CAD FILE AVAILABLE

Main Level Floor Plan

Upper Level Floor Plan

Copyright by designer/architect.

Plan #481133

Dimensions: 98' W x 63'10" D
Levels: 2
Heated Square Footage: 4,171
Main Level Sq. Ft.: 1,701
Upper Level Sq. Ft.: 2,470
Bedrooms: 5
Bathrooms: 3½
Foundation: Walkout
Material List Available: No
Price Category: I

Images provided by designer/architect.

Plan #161061

Dimensions: 90' W x 69'10" D
Levels: 2
Heated Square Footage: 3,816
Main Level Sq. Ft.: 2,725
Upper Level Sq. Ft.: 1,091
Bedrooms: 4
Bathrooms: 3½
Foundation: Walkout basement
Materials List Available: No
Price Category: H

Images provided by designer/architect.

Luxurious amenities make living in this spacious home a true pleasure for the whole family.

Features:

- **Great Room:** A fireplace, flanking built-in shelves, a balcony above, and three lovely windows create a luxurious room that's always comfortable.

- **Hearth Room:** Another fireplace with surrounding built-ins and double doors to the outside deck (with its own fireplace) highlight this room.

- **Kitchen:** A butler's pantry, laundry room, and mudroom with a window seat and two walk-in closets complement this large kitchen.

- **Library:** Situated for privacy and quiet, this spacious room with a large window area may be reached from the master bedroom as well as the foyer.

- **Master Suite:** A sloped ceiling and windows on three walls create a lovely bedroom, and the huge walk-in closet, dressing room, and luxurious bath add up to total comfort.

Main Level Floor Plan

Upper Level Floor Plan

Copyright by designer/architect.

Plan #181251

Dimensions: 78' W x 64' D
Levels: 2
Heated Square Footage: 4,075
Main Level Sq. Ft.: 2,228
Upper Level Sq. Ft.: 1,847
Bedrooms: 4
Bathrooms: 3½
Foundation: Basement; crawl space or slab for fee
Materials List Available: Yes
Price Category: I

Images provided by designer/architect.

You'll love relaxing in the many indoor and outdoor areas this home provides.

CAD FILE AVAILABLE

Features:

- **Foyer:** Upon entering the home, this two-level foyer greets you and your guests.

- **Great Room:** Adjoining the kitchen through an eating bar, this great room is wonderful for casual gatherings or relaxing with your family.

- **Kitchen:** Centrally located, this kitchen makes moving food to the table easy and quick.

- **Master Suite:** Upstairs, this beautiful master suite includes a window-lined alcove, spacious walk-in closet, and a large bathroom with a tub and a dual-sink vanity.

Main Level Floor Plan

Upper Level Floor Plan

Copyright by designer/architect.

Plan #441031

Dimensions: 78'2" W x 68' D
Levels: 2
Heated Square Footage: 4,150
Main Level Sq. Ft.: 2,572
Upper Level Sq. Ft.: 1,578
Bedrooms: 4
Bathrooms: 4½
Foundation: Crawl space; slab or basement for fee
Materials List Available: Yes
Price Category: I

Images provided by designer/architect.

Graceful and gracious, this superb shingle design delights with handsome exterior elements. A whimsical turret, covered entry, upper-level balcony, and bay window all bring their charm to the facade.

Features:

- **Great Room:** The main level offers this commodious room, with its beamed ceiling, alcove, fireplace, and built-ins.

- **Kitchen:** Go up a few steps to the dining nook and this kitchen, and you'll find a baking center, walk-in pantry, and access to a covered side porch.

- **Formal Dining Room:** This formal room lies a few steps up from the foyer and sports a bay window and hutch space.

- **Guest Suite:** This suite, which is located at the end of the hall, features a private bathroom and walk-in closet.

- **Master Suite:** A fireplace flanked by built-ins warms this suite. Its bath contains a spa tub, compartmented toilet, and huge shower.

CAD FILE AVAILABLE

Main Level Floor Plan

Upper Level Floor Plan

Copyright by designer/architect.

Plan #541037

Dimensions: 93'10" W x 89'5" D
Levels: 1
Heated Square Footage: 4,219
Main Level Sq. Ft.: 2,500
Lower Level Sq. Ft.: 1,719
Bedrooms: 4
Bathrooms: 3
Foundation: Walkout; crawl space, slab, basement for fee
Material List Available: No
Price Category: I

Images provided by designer/architect.

You'll love making this cozy Craftsman-style house into your home.

CAD FILE AVAILABLE

Features:

- Entry: Enter through a porch into a stunning foyer with 10-ft.-high ceilings.

- Great Room: Vaulted ceilings and a quick exit to a covered deck make this great room ideal for entertaining guests indoors and out. A built-in bookshelf and elegant entertainment center are additive elements that make the room not only beautiful, but also practical.

- Study: The options are endless with this quaint room. Located on the end of the home for quiet and privacy, you can turn the room into a study and work from your house, or construct an inviting space for guests to feel at home.

- Master Suite: With vaulted ceilings and access to a private covered deck, this master bedroom is perhaps the most enticing space in the home. Equipped with a tub and spa, dual vanity sinks, and a walk-in closet, this suite is an amazing retreat for busy moms and dads.

Main Level Floor Plan

Lower Level Floor Plan

Copyright by designer/architect.

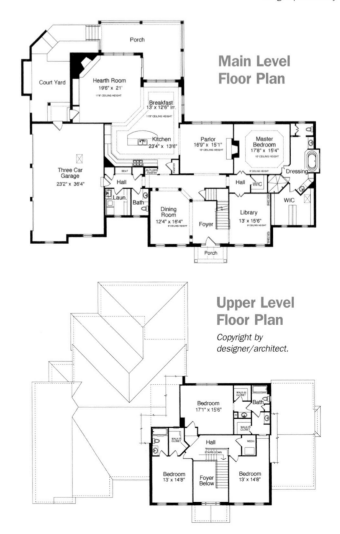

Images provided by designer/architect.

Plan #161213

Dimensions: 92'4" W x 75' D
Levels: 2
Heated Square Footage: 4,222
Main Level Sq. Ft.: 3,008
Upper Level Sq. Ft.: 1,214
Bedrooms: 4
Bathrooms: 3½
Foundation: Walkout; basement for fee
Materials List Available: Yes
Price Category: I

Large rooms, formal and informal spaces, and a variety of ceiling heights allow this house to function for all occasions.

Features:

- **Foyer:** Upon entering this foyer, your guests are greeted by the library, parlor, and dining room—an entrance that is sure to impress.

- **Kitchen:** This open kitchen features plenty of counter space and a center island.

- **Hearth Room:** Your guests and family will love relaxing in this beautiful hearth room, which connects to both the courtyard and porch outside.

- **Master Suite:** Located away from the main areas of the house, this master suite features a large bathroom with two walk-in closets, and a spacious bedroom area.

Main Level Floor Plan

Upper Level Floor Plan

Copyright by designer/architect.

Plan #151961

Dimensions: 112'2" W x 84'2" D

Levels: 2

Heated Square Footage: 4,378

Main Level Sq. Ft.: 2,666

Upper Level Sq. Ft.: 1,712

Bedrooms: 4

Bathrooms: 3½

Foundation: Crawl space or slab; basement or walk out for fee

CompleteCost List Available: Yes

Price Category: I

Images provided by designer/architect.

This expansive home's beautiful exterior will be a wonderful welcome home.

Features:

- **Great Room:** Located at the heart of the home, this great room is open to the second floor, making it airy and welcoming.

- **Kitchen:** This kitchen will be a joy when you are preparing meals. The room features plentiful counter space and an eating bar.

- **Outdoor living area:** At the rear of the home, a large grilling porch/outdoor living area is wonderful spot for entertaining or relaxing.

- **Master Suite:** With its own private access to the covered porch, this master suite features a whirlpool tub, large walk-in closet, and two separate vanities.

**Main Level
Floor Plan**

**Upper Level
Floor Plan**

Copyright by designer/architect.

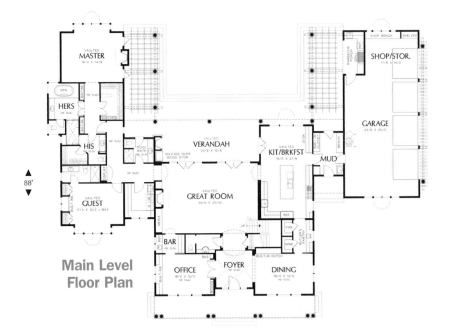

Plan #441275

Dimensions: 116' W x 88' D
Levels: 2
Heated Square Footage: 4,790
Main Level Sq. Ft.: 3,800
Upper Level Sq. Ft.: 990
Bedrooms: 4
Bathrooms: 6½
Foundation: Crawl space
Materials List Available: Yes
Price Category: I

Images provided by designer/architect.

**Upper Level
Floor Plan**

*Copyright by
designer/architect.*

This home features spacious outdoor living areas that are wonderful for relaxing with friends or family.

CAD FILE AVAILABLE

Features:

- **Porches:** At the front of the home is a covered porch that is perfect for greeting guests. At the rear is a verandah and large patio area that are perfect for entertaining.

- **Great Room:** Located at the heart of the home, this great room features access to the verandah and a large fireplace.

- **Kitchen/Breakfast Room:** This beautiful kitchen features plenty of workspace, a center island, and direct access to the verandah, which is perfect for dining outdoors.

- **Master Suite:** You'll love unwinding at the end of the day in this expansive master suite, which features a fireplace, direct access to the rear patio, and his and her bathrooms.

**Main Level
Floor Plan**

Plan #441015

Dimensions: 130'3" W x 79'3" D
Levels: 1
Heated Square Footage: 4,732
Main Level Sq. Ft.: 2,902
Lower Level Sq. Ft.: 1,830
Bedrooms: 4
Bathrooms: 3 full, 2 half
Foundation: Walkout basement
Materials List Available: Yes
Price Category: I

An artful use of stone was employed on the exterior of this rustic hillside home to complement other architectural elements, such as the angled, oversize four-car garage and the substantial roofline.

Features:

• **Great Room:** This massive vaulted room features a large stone fireplace at one end and a formal dining area at the other. A built-in media center and double doors separate the great room from a home office with its own hearth and built-ins.

• **Kitchen:** This kitchen features a walk-in pantry and snack counter and opens to a skylighted outdoor kitchen. Its appointments include a cooktop and a corner fireplace.

• **Home Theatre:** This space has a built-in viewing screen, a fireplace, and double terrace access.

• **Master Suite:** This private space is found at the other side of the home. Look closely for

expansive his and her walk-in closets, a spa tub, a skylighted double vanity area, and a corner fireplace in the salon.

• **Bedrooms:** Three family bedrooms are on the lower level; bedroom 4 has a private bathroom and walk-in closet.

• **Garage:** This large garage has room for four cars; don't miss the dog shower and grooming station just off the garage.

Images provided by designer/architect.

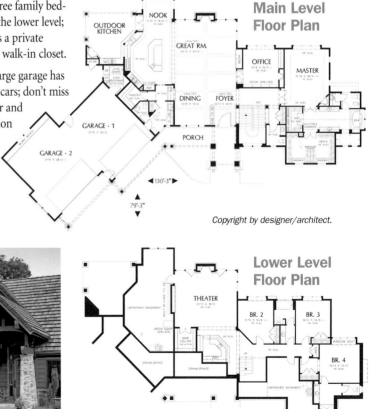

Main Level Floor Plan

Copyright by designer/architect.

Lower Level Floor Plan

Entry

Images provided by designer/architect.

Plan #441030

Dimensions: 117'6" W x 63'6" D
Levels: 2
Heated Square Footage: 5,180
Main Level Sq. Ft.: 3,030
Upper Level Sq. Ft.: 2,150
Bedrooms: 6
Bathrooms: 5
Foundation: Crawl space;
slab or basement available for fee
Materials List Available: No
Price Category: J

There's no doubt, this home plan is pure luxury. The plan incorporates a wealth of space on two levels, plus every amenity a family could desire.

CAD FILE AVAILABLE • CAD •

Features:

- **Great Room:** Defined by columns, this room with fireplace and built-in cabinet has an 11-ft.-high ceiling. There is access to the rear patio through French doors.

- **Kitchen:** Furnished with multiple work-stations, this kitchen can accommodate a cook and helpers. The island is equipped with a sink and dishwasher. The secondary sink occupies the half-wall facing the family room. The walk-in pantry beside the dining room supplements storage.

Rear View

- **Main Level:** The main level is host to rooms devoted to special interests-the office, complete with storage units and a French door to the front porch, and the crafts or hobby room, furnished with an L-shaped work surface.

- **Upper Level:** The upper level of the home accommodates three bedrooms, two bath rooms, the full-service laundry room, and the master suite, which is a dream come true. The master bedroom is divided into sitting and sleeping areas. French doors open it to a private deck. A two-sided fireplace warms both the sitting area and the master bath. The highlight of the spacious bath is the oval tub, which is tucked beneath a bay window.

Main Level Floor Plan

Upper Level Floor Plan

Copyright by designer/architect.

Let Us Help You
Plan Your Dream Home

Whether you've always dreamed of building your own home or you can't find the right house from among the dozens you've toured, our collection of Best-Selling Country & Farmhouse Home Plans can help you achieve the home of your dreams. You could have an architect create a one-of-a-kind home for you, but the design services alone could end up costing up to 15 percent of the cost of construction—a hefty premium for any building project. Isn't it a better idea to select from among the hundreds of unique designs shown in our collection for a fraction of the cost?

What Does Creative Homeowner Offer?

In this book, Creative Homeowner provides hundreds of home plans from North America's best architects and designers. Our designs are among the most popular available. By using this book or visiting our Web site, **ultimateplans.com,** you will be sure to find the house design best suited to you and your family. Our plan packages include detailed drawings to help you or your builder construct your dream house. **(See page 280.)**

Can I Make Changes to the Plans?

Creative Homeowner offers three ways to help you achieve a truly unique home design. Our customizing service allows for extensive changes to our designs—a custom home for thousands of dollars less. **(See page 281.)** We also provide reverse images of our plans, or we can give you and your builder the tools for making minor changes on your own. **(See page 284.)**

Can You Help Me Manage My Costs?

To help you stay within your budget, Creative Homeowner has teamed up with North America's leading estimating company to provide one of the most accurate, complete, and reliable building material take-offs in the industry, which will help you price out construction costs. **(See page 282.)** If that is too much detail for you, we can provide you with general construction costs based on your zip code. **(See page 284.)** If you don't want a take-off, you have the option of buying a materials list with many of our plans.

How Do I Begin the Building Process?

To get started building your dream home, fill out the order form on page 285, call our order department at **1-800-523-6789**, or visit our Web site, ultimateplans.com. If you plan on doing all or part of the work yourself, or want to keep tabs on your builder, we offer best-selling building and design books at **creativehomeowner.com.**

Our Plans Packages Offer:

"Square footage" refers to the total "heated square feet" of this plan. This number does not include the garage, porches, or unfinished areas. All of our home plans are the result of many hours of work by leading architects and professional designers. Most of our home plans include each of the following:

Frontal Sheet

This artist's rendering of the front of the house gives you an idea of how the house will look once it is completed and the property landscaped.

Detailed Floor Plans

These plans show the size and layout of the rooms. They also provide the locations of doors, windows, fireplaces, closets, stairs, and electrical outlets and switches.

Foundation Plan

A foundation plan gives the dimensions of basements, walk-out basements, crawl spaces, pier foundations, and slab construction. Each house design lists the type of foundation included. If the plan you choose does not have the foundation type you require, our customer service department can help you customize the plan to meet your needs.

Roof Plan

In addition to providing the pitch of the roof, these plans also show the locations of dormers, skylights, and other elements.

Exterior Elevations

These drawings show the front, rear, and sides of the house as if you were looking at it head on. Elevations also provide information about architectural features and finish materials.

Interior Elevations and Details

Interior elevations show specific details of such elements as fireplaces, kitchen and bathroom cabinets, built-ins, and other unique features of the design.

Cross Sections

These show the structure as if it were sliced to reveal construction requirements, such as insulation, flooring, and roofing details.

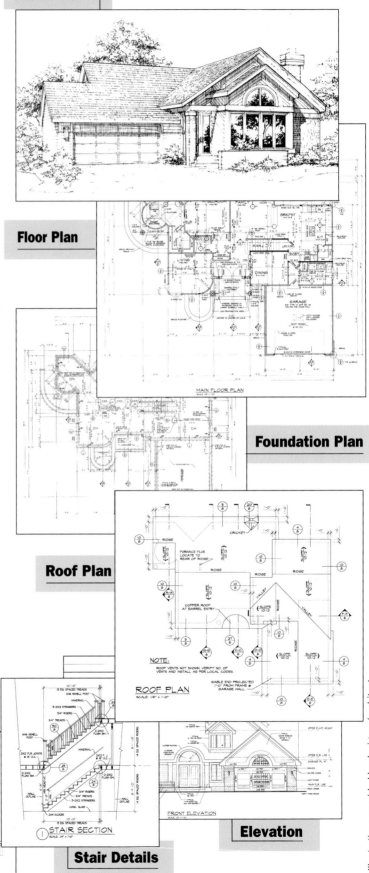

Frontal Sheet

Floor Plan

Foundation Plan

Roof Plan

Elevation

Stair Details

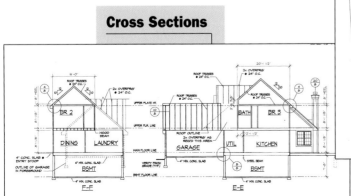

Cross Sections

Illustrations provided by designer/architect

Customize Your Plans in 4 Easy Steps

1 **Select the home plan** that most closely meets your needs. Purchase of a reproducible master, PDF files, or CAD files is necessary in order to make changes to a plan.

2 **Call** 1-800-523-6789 **to place your order.** Tell our sales representative you are interested in customizing your plan, and provide your contact information. Within a day or two you will be contacted (via phone or email) to provide a list or sketch of the changes requested to one of our plans. There is no consultation fee for this service.

3 **Within three business days** of receipt of your request, a detailed cost estimate will be provided to you.

4 **Once you approve the estimate,** you will purchase either the reproducible master, PDF files, or CAD files, and customization work will begin. During all phases of the project, you will receive progress prints by fax or email. On average, the project will be completed in two or three weeks. After completion of the work, modified plans will be shipped. You will receive one set of blueprints in addition to a reproducible master or CAD files, depending on which package you purchased.

Modification Pricing Guide

Categories	Average Cost For Modification
Add or remove living space	Quote required
Bathroom layout redesign	Starting at $150
Kitchen layout redesign	Starting at $120
Garage: add or remove	Starting at $600
Garage: front entry to side load or vice versa	Starting at $300
Foundation changes	Starting at $220
Exterior building materials change	Starting at $200
Exterior openings: add, move, or remove	$75 per opening
Roof line changes	Starting at $600
Ceiling height adjustments	Starting at $280
Fireplace: add or remove	Starting at $90
Screened porch: add	Starting at $300
Wall framing change from 2x4 to 2x6	Starting at $250
Bearing and/or exterior walls changes	Quote required
Non-bearing wall or room changes	$65 per room
Metric conversion of home plan	Starting at $495
Adjust plan for handicapped accessibility	Quote required
Adapt plans for local building code requirements	Quote required
Engineering stamping only	Quote required
Any other engineering services	Quote required
Interactive illustrations (choices of exterior materials)	Quote required

Note: Any home plan can be customized to accommodate your desired changes. The average prices above are provided only as examples of the most commonly requested changes, and are subject to change without notice. Prices for changes will vary according to the number of modifications requested, plan size, style, and method of design used by the original designer. To obtain a detailed cost estimate, please contact us.

Terms & Copyright

These home plans are protected under the terms of United States Copyright Law and may not be copied or reproduced in any way, by any means, unless you have purchased reproducible masters, which clearly indicate your right to copy or reproduce. We authorize the use of your chosen home plan as an aid in the construction of one single-family home only. You may not use this home plan to build a second or multiple dwellings without purchasing another blueprint or blueprints, or paying additional home plan fees.

Architectural Seals

Because of differences in building codes, some cities and states now require an architect or engineer licensed in that state to review and "seal" a blueprint, or officially approve it, prior to construction. Delaware, Nevada, New Jersey, New York, and some other states require that all plans for houses built in those states be redrawn by an architect licensed in the state in which the home will be built. We strongly advise you to consult with your local building official for information regarding architectural seals.

Before Customization

After

Turn your dream home into reality with

UltimateEstimate

When purchasing a home plan with Creative Homeowner, we recommend
that you order one of the most comprehensive materials lists in the industry.

1 What comes with an Ultimate Estimate?

Quote

- Basis of the entire estimate.

- Detailed list of all the framing materials needed to build your project, listed from the bottom up, in the order that each one will actually be used.

Comments

- Details pertinent information beyond the cost of materials.

- Includes any notes from our estimator.

Express List

- A version of the quote with space for SKU numbers listed for purchasing the items at your local lumberyard.

- Your local lumberyard can then price out the materials list.

Construction-Ready Framing Diagrams

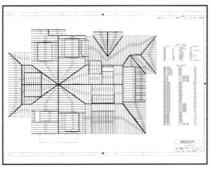

- Your "map" to exact roof and floor framing.

Millwork Report

- A complete count of the windows, doors, molding, and trim.

Man-Hour Report

- Calculates labor on a line-by-line basis for all items quoted and presented in man-hours.

2   Why an Ultimate Estimate?

Accurate. Professional estimators break down each individual item from the blueprints using advanced software, techniques, and equipment.

Timely. You will be able to start your home-building project quickly—knowing the exact framing materials you need and how to get them with Lowe's.

Detailed. Work with your local lumberyard associate to select the remaining products needed for your new home and get a final, accurate quote.

3   So how much does it cost?

Pricing is determined by the total square feet of the home plan—including living area, garages, decks, porches, finished basements, and finished attics.

Square Feet Range	UE Tier*	Price
Up to 5,000 total square feet	XB	$345.00
5,001 to 10,000 total square feet	XC	$545.00

*Please see the Plan Index to determine your plan's Ultimate Estimate Tier (UE Tier).
Note: All prices subject to change.

4   What else do I need to know?

Call our toll-free number (1-800-523-6789), or visit **ultimateplans.com** to order your Ultimate Estimate.

Turn your dream home into reality.

Decide What Type of Plan Package You Need

How many Plans Should You Order?

Standard 8-Set Package. We've found that our 8-set package is the best value for someone who is ready to start building. The 8-set package provides plans for you, your builder, the subcontractors, mortgage lender, and the building department.

Minimum 5-Set Package. If you are in the bidding process, you may want to order only five sets for the bidding round and reorder additional sets as needed.

1-Set Study Package. The 1-set package allows you to review your home plan in detail. The plan will be marked as a study print, and it is illegal to build a house from a study print alone. It is a violation of copyright law to reproduce a blueprint without permission.

Buying Additional Sets. If you require additional copies of blueprints for your home construction, you can order additional sets within 60 days of the original order date at a reduced price. The cost is $50.00 for each additional set. For more information, contact customer service.

Reproducible Masters

If you plan to make minor changes to one of our home plans, you can purchase reproducible masters. These plans are printed on bond or vellum paper that is easy to alter. They clearly indicate your right to modify, copy, or reproduce the plans. Reproducible masters allow an architect, designer, or builder to alter our plans to give you a customized home design. This package allows you to print as many copies of the modified plans as you need for the construction of one home.

PDF Files

PDF files are a complete set of home plans in electronic file format sent to you via email. These files cannot be altered electronically, once printed changes can be hand drawn. A PDF file gives you the license to modify the plans to fit your needs and build one home. Not available for all plans. Please contact our order department or visit our Web site to check the availability of PDF files for your plan.

CAD (Computer-Aided Design) Files

CAD files are the complete set of home plans in an electronic file format. Choose this option if there are multiple changes you wish made to the home plans and you have a local design professional able to make the changes. Not available for all plans. Please contact our order department or visit our Web site to check the availability of CAD files for your plan.

Mirror-Reverse Sets/Right-Reading Reverse

Plans can be printed in mirror-reverse—we can "flip" plans to create a site mirror image of the design. This is useful when the house would fit your or personal preferences if all the rooms were on the opposite side than shown. As the image is reversed, the lettering and dimensions will also be reversed, meaning they will read backwards. Therefore, when ordering mirror-reverse drawings, you must order at least one set of the original plan unreversed. A $50.00 fee per plan order will be charged for mirror-reverse (regardless of the number of mirror-reverse sets ordered). Some plans are available in right-reading reverse; this feature will show the plan in reverse, but the writing on the plan will be readable. A $150.00 fee per plan order will be charged for right-reading reverse (regardless of the number of right-reading reverse sets ordered). Please contact our order department or visit our Web site to check the availibility of this feature for your chosen plan.

Ultimate Estimate (See page 282).

Ultimate Estimate may take 2 to 3 weeks for delivery.

EZ Quote: Home Cost Estimator

EZ Quote is our response to a frequently asked question we hear from customers: "How much will the house cost me to build?" EZ Quote: Home Cost Estimator will enable you to obtain a calculated building cost to construct your home, based on labor rates and building material costs within your zip code area. This summary is useful for those who want to get an idea of the total construction costs before purchasing sets of home plans. It will also provide a level of comfort when you begin soliciting bids. The cost is $29.95 for the first EZ Quote and $19.95 for each additional one in the same order. Available only in the U.S. and Canada.

Materials List

Available for most of our plans, the Materials List provides you an invaluable resource in planning and estimating the cost of your home. Each Materials List outlines the quantity, dimensions, and type of materials needed to build your home (with the exception of mechanical systems). You will get faster, more-accurate bids from your contractors and building suppliers. A Materials List may only be ordered with the purchase of at least five sets of home plans.

CompleteCost Estimator

CompleteCost Estimator is a valuable tool for use in planning and constructing your new home. It provides more detail than a materials list and will act as a checklist for all items you will need to select or coordinate during your building process. CompleteCost Estimator is only available for certain plans (please see Plan Index) and may only be ordered with the purchase of at least five sets of home plans. The cost is $125.00 for CompleteCost Estimator.

Order Toll Free by Phone
1-800-523-6789
By Fax: 201-760-2431

Orders received 3PM ET, will be processed and shipped within two business days.

Order Online
www.ultimateplans.com

Mail Your Order
Creative Homeowner
Attn: Home Plans
24 Park Way
Upper Saddle River, NJ 07458

Canadian Customers
Order Toll Free 1-800-393-1883

Mail Your Order (Canada)
Creative Homeowner Canada
Attn: Home Plans
113-437 Martin St., Ste. 215
Penticton, BC V2A 5L1

Before You Order

Our Exchange Policy

Blueprints are nonrefundable. However, should you find that the plan you have purchased does not fit your needs, you may exchange that plan for another plan in our collection within 60 days from the date of your original order. The entire content of your original order must be returned before an exchange will be processed. You will be charged a processing fee of 20% of the amount of the original order, the cost difference between the new plan set and the original plan set (if applicable), and all related shipping costs for the new plans. Contact our order department for more information. Please note: reproducible masters may only be exchanged if the package is unopened. PDF files and CAD files cannot be exchanged and are nonrefundable.

Building Codes and Requirements

All plans offered for sale in this book and on our Web site (www.ultimateplans.com) are continually updated to meet the latest International Residential Code (IRC). Because building codes vary from area to area, some drawing modifications and/or the assistance of a professional designer or architect may be necessary to comply with your local codes or to accommodate specific building site conditions. We strongly advise you to consult with your local building official for information regarding codes governing your area.

Multiple Plan Discount

Purchase **3** different home plans in the **same order** and receive **5% off** the plan price.

Purchase **5** or more different home plans in the **same order** and receive **10% off** the plan price. (Please Note: study sets do not apply.)

Blueprint Price Schedule

Price Code	1 Set	5 Sets	8 Sets	Reproducible Masters or PDF Files	CAD	Materials List
A	$410	$470	$545	$660	$1,125	$85
B	$465	$540	$615	$740	$1,310	$85
C	$525	$620	$695	$820	$1,475	$85
D	$575	$670	$745	$870	$1,575	$95
E	$625	$730	$805	$925	$1,675	$95
F	$690	$790	$865	$990	$1,800	$95
G	$720	$820	$895	$1,020	$1,845	$95
H	$730	$830	$905	$1,045	$1,900	$95
I	$995	$1,095	$1,170	$1,290	$2,110	$105
J	$1,190	$1,290	$1,365	$1,490	$2,300	$105
K	$1,195	$1,295	$1,370	$1,495	$2,300	$105
L	$1,240	$1,335	$1,410	$1,535	$2,400	$105

Note: All prices subject to change

Ultimate Estimate Tier (UE Tier)

UE Tier*	Price
XB	$345
XC	$545

* Please see the Plan Index to determine your plan's Ultimate Estimate Tier (UE Tier).

Shipping & Handling

	1–4 Sets	5–7 Sets	8+ Sets or Reproducibles	CAD
US Regular (7–10 business days)	$18	$20	$25	$25
US Priority (3–5 business days)	$35	$40	$45	$45
US Express (1–2 business days)	$45	$60	$80	$50
Canada Express (3–4 business days)	$100	$100	$100	$100
Worldwide Express (3–5 business days)	** Quote Required **			

Note: All delivery times are from date the blueprint package is shipped (typically within 1–2 days of placing order).

Order Form Please send me the following:

Plan Number: _____ **Price Code:** _____ (See Plan Index.)

Indicate Foundation Type: (Select ONE. See plan page for availability.)
- ❏ Slab   ❏ Crawl space   ❏ Basement   ❏ Walk-out basement
- ❏ Optional Foundation for Fee _____ $_____
  (Please enter foundation here)

*Please call all our order department or visit our website for optional foundation fee

Basic Blueprint Package   Cost
- ❏ CAD Files $_____
- ❏ PDF Files $_____
- ❏ Reproducible Masters $_____
- ❏ 8-Set Plan Package $_____
- ❏ 5-Set Plan Package $_____
- ❏ 1-Set Study Package $_____
- ❏ Additional plan sets:
  __ sets at $50.00 per set $_____
- ❏ Print in mirror-reverse: $50.00 per order $_____
  *Please call all our order department or visit our website for availibility
- ❏ Print in right-reading reverse: $150.00 per order $_____
  *Please call all our order department or visit our website for availibility

Important Extras
- ❏ Ultimate Estimate (See Price Tier above.) $_____
- ❏ Materials List $_____
- ❏ CompleteCost Materials Report at $125.00 $_____
  Zip Code of Home/Building Site _____
- ❏ EZ Quote for Plan # _____ at $29.95 $_____
- ❏ Additional EZ Quotes for Plan #s _____
  at $19.95 each $_____
- **Shipping** (see chart above) $_____
- **SUBTOTAL** $_____
- **Sales Tax** (NJ residents only, add 7%) $_____
- **TOTAL** $_____

Order Toll Free: **1-800-523-6789**   By Fax: 201-760-2431
Creative Homeowner (Home Plans Order Dept.)
24 Park Way
Upper Saddle River, NJ 07458

Name _____
(Please print or type)

Street _____
(Please do not use a P.O. Box)

City _____ State _____

Country _____ Zip _____

Daytime telephone (____) _____

Fax (____) _____
(Required for reproducible orders)

E-Mail _____

Payment   ❏ Bank check/money order. No personal checks.
Make checks payable to Creative Homeowner

❏ VISA   ❏ MasterCard   ❏ AMERICAN EXPRESS Cards   ❏ DISCOVER

Credit card number _____

Expiration date (mm/yy) _____

Signature _____

Please check the appropriate box:
❏ Building home for myself   ❏ Building home for someone else

SOURCE CODE CA427

Index

For pricing, see page 285.

Plan #	Price Code	Page	Total Finished Sq. Ft.	Materials List	CompleteCost	UE Tier
101002	C	17	1296	N	N	XB
101014	D	68	2018	N	N	XB
101020	F	259	6038	N	N	XC
101022	D	138	4917	Y	N	XB
101022	D	139	4917	Y	N	XB
101032	E	162	2098	N	N	XB
101146	E	190	2296	N	N	XB
101147	B	9	953	N	N	XB
111001	G	256	4229	N	N	XB
111046	D	90	1768	N	N	XB
121006	C	82	2161	Y	N	XB
121012	B	15	1195	Y	N	XB
121016	E	230	2594	Y	N	XB
121028	F	229	4533	Y	N	XB
121035	B	33	2223	Y	N	XB
121047	G	264	5863	Y	N	XC
121064	D	106	3321	Y	N	XB
121083	F	245	5288	Y	N	XC
121121	C	25	1341	Y	N	XB
121123	E	177	2781	Y	N	XB
121153	D	128	2313	Y	N	XB
121153	D	129	2313	Y	N	XB
121160	D	168	3574	Y	N	XB
121164	E	196	3188	Y	N	XB
121176	D	164	2989	Y	N	XB
121190	E	176	2524	Y	N	XB
121192	C	70	3167	Y	N	XB
121199	B	45	2106	Y	N	XB
121208	E	228	4380	Y	N	XB
121331	G	83	2529	Y	N	XB
121482	C	79	2533	Y	N	XB
131002	D	84	3838	Y	N	XB
131003	C	48	3332	Y	N	XB
131003	C	49	3332	Y	N	XB
131004	C	14	2634	Y	N	XB
131013	C	41	1489	Y	N	XB
131016	E	117	4331	Y	N	XB
131017	C	39	3488	Y	N	XB
131027	F	226	5284	Y	N	XC
131027	F	227	5284	Y	N	XC
131029	G	248	4680	Y	N	XB
131029	G	249	4680	Y	N	XB
131030	F	210	4193	Y	N	XB
131030	F	211	4193	Y	N	XB
131034	C	11	2677	Y	N	XB
131035	E	114	4069	Y	N	XB
131041	D	77	3504	Y	N	XB
131043	E	120	4132	Y	N	XB
131046	F	173	4507	Y	N	XB
131047	D	98	5147	Y	N	XC
131047	D	99	5147	Y	N	XC
131051	F	203	4699	Y	N	XB
131075	C	60	1694	Y	N	XB
151014	F	241	5546	N	Y	XC
151015	F	251	5794	N	Y	XC
151016	C	91	3949	N	Y	XB
151018	F	250	2755	N	Y	XB
151025	H	268	4987	N	Y	XC
151027	E	193	3243	N	Y	XB
151028	E	176	2252	N	Y	XB
151035	B	44	1843	N	Y	XB
151045	E	175	3155	N	Y	XB
151076	D	165	2187	N	Y	XB
151089	E	122	5001	N	Y	XC
151089	E	123	5001	N	Y	XC
151105	D	148	5660	N	Y	XC
151113	D	167	6706	N	Y	XC
151133	D	146	2029	N	Y	XB
151171	D	163	2131	N	Y	XB
151172	F	204	5059	N	Y	XC
151174	F	256	2815	N	Y	XB
151176	E	208	2445	N	Y	XB
151177	E	209	2470	N	Y	XB
151181	E	206	3040	N	Y	XB
151196	C	96	1800	N	Y	XB
151204	E	201	4252	N	Y	XB
151237	E	212	3927	N	Y	XB
151408	C	61	2056	N	Y	XB
151411	B	42	2190	N	Y	XB
151412	B	34	1721	N	Y	XB
151413	B	30	1705	N	Y	XB
151445	E	190	3424	N	Y	XB
151490	D	110	2888	N	Y	XB
151529	B	38	2157	N	Y	XB
151537	F	231	4113	N	Y	XB
151542	D	124	4197	N	Y	XB
151742	D	113	2788	N	Y	XB
151743	E	207	3561	N	Y	XB
151804	F	254	5556	N	Y	XC
151961	I	275	6742	N	Y	XC
161014	C	81	4060	Y	N	XB
161024	C	76	3490	N	N	XB
161026	D	152	4593	N	N	XB
161026	D	153	4593	N	N	XB
161061	H	270	6474	N	N	XC
161079	B	46	3567	Y	N	XB
161109	D	163	2728	Y	N	XB
161115	E	178	4506	Y	N	XB
161121	D	103	1824	Y	N	XB
161162	B	26	1983	Y	N	XB
161164	C	91	2500	Y	N	XB
161182	E	225	3126	Y	N	XB
161213	I	274	8363	Y	N	XC
161224	F	252	6555	Y	N	XC
161249	E	174	5269	Y	N	XC
161263	D	101	3395	Y	N	XB
171001	B	22	1804	Y	N	XB
171002	B	42	1985	Y	N	XB
171006	C	71	2527	Y	N	XB
171007	C	78	2482	Y	N	XB
171009	C	90	2652	Y	N	XB
171011	D	149	2924	Y	N	XB
171015	D	156	3731	Y	N	XB
171017	E	225	3535	Y	N	XB
171023	C	75	3059	Y	N	XB
181021	B	13	2522	Y	N	XB
181032	D	103	2775	Y	N	XB
181034	F	244	5282	Y	N	XC
181035	D	162	4228	Y	N	XB
181053	E	200	4739	Y	N	XB
181067	B	23	1286	Y	N	XB
181074	D	87	3280	N	N	XB
181078	E	194	4050	Y	N	XB
181081	F	195	4472	Y	N	XB
181085	E	166	4438	Y	N	XB
181094	D	157	3786	Y	N	XB
181136	E	205	4213	Y	N	XB
181137	E	198	4228	Y	N	XB
181137	E	199	4228	Y	N	XB
181151	F	188	4328	Y	N	XB
181151	F	189	4328	Y	N	XB
181159	D	121	1992	Y	N	XB
181216	A	28	910	Y	N	XB
181217	C	65	2122	Y	N	XB
181219	B	26	1311	Y	N	XB
181223	B	37	1440	Y	N	XB
181226	B	43	1485	Y	N	XB
181227	B	21	1248	Y	N	XB
181243	E	172	4018	Y	N	XB
181251	I	271	5670	Y	N	XC
181256	E	174	4463	Y	N	XB
181262	B	19	1669	Y	N	XB
181301	H	268	4646	Y	N	XB
181307	D	145	3952	Y	N	XB
181345	B	12	2235	Y	N	XB
181714	B	20	1244	Y	N	XB
181724	D	101	2348	Y	N	XB
191003	C	94	2647	N	N	XB
191004	D	112	2851	Y	N	XB
191012	D	159	2123	N	N	XB
191024	C	81	1700	N	N	XB
191025	D	150	2052	N	N	XB
191026	D	151	2052	N	N	XB
191027	E	200	2354	N	N	XB
191028	F	244	5338	N	N	XC
191037	C	63	2562	N	N	XB
211016	B	18	1867	Y	N	XB
211024	B	35	2140	Y	N	XB
211030	C	69	2379	Y	N	XB
211036	D	93	2638	Y	N	XB
211048	D	144	3021	Y	N	XB
211062	F	240	3358	Y	N	XB
221032	D	105	4443	N	N	XB
221080	F	247	3588	N	N	XB
221081	F	260	4032	N	N	XB
241007	D	147	3277	N	N	XB
241017	E	206	2702	N	N	XB
241019	B	34	1397	N	N	XB
241041	C	70	2596	N	N	XB
251001	B	16	2040	Y	N	XB
251003	B	29	2032	Y	N	XB

UltimateEstimate

The fastest way to get started building your dream home

One of the most complete materials lists in the industry. Work with our order department to get you started today.

CRE∆TIVE
HOMEOWNER®

To learn more, go to page 282 or go to UltimatePlans.com and select Ultimate Estimate located under "Quick Links" for complete details on this program.

Copyright Notice

All home plans sold through this publication are protected by copyright. Reproduction of these home plans, either in whole or in part, including any form and/or preparation of derivative works thereof, for any reason without prior written permission is strictly prohibited. The purchase of a set of home plans in no way transfers any copyright or other ownership interest in it to the buyer except for a limited license to use that set of home plans for the construction of one, and only one, dwelling unit. The purchase of additional sets of the home plans at a reduced price from the original set or as a part of a multiple-set package does not convey to the buyer a license to construct more than one dwelling.

Similarly, the purchase of reproducible home plans (sepias, mylars, or bond) carries the same copyright protection as mentioned above. It is generally allowed to make up to a maximum of 10 copies for the construction of a single dwelling only. To use any plans more than once, and to avoid any copyright license infringement, it is necessary to contact the plan designer to receive a release and license for any extended use. Whereas a purchaser of reproducible plans is granted a license to make copies, it should be noted that because blueprints are copyrighted, making photocopies from them is illegal.

Copyright and licensing of home plans for construction exist to protect all parties. Copyright respects and supports the intellectual property of the original architect or designer. Copyright law has been reinforced over the past few years. Willful infringement could cause settlements for statutory damages to $150,000.00 plus attorney fees, damages, and loss of profits.